LIVES AND VOICES

A collection of
American Jewish memoirs

LIVES

and

VOICES

edited by

Stanley F. Chyet

The Jewish Publication Society of America
Philadelphia   5732 / 1972

For Jacob M. Chyet and Bess Singer Hyman

זכרונם לברכה

Acknowledgments

All the memoirs reproduced in this book have been taken from the files of the American Jewish Archives, where they are to be found either as originals or photoduplicates. They were deposited at the Archives by their donors with a view to ultimate publication. Except for Samuel Adler's, each of the memoirs was written in English. They have been slightly edited for spelling and punctuation, and headings have been added by the editor.

I am grateful to Professor Jacob Rader Marcus, Director of the American Jewish Archives, for enabling me to make use of all this material. He deserves my warm thanks for the gracious assistance I have had from him. *Lives and Voices* was his idea in the first place, and he helped me select the memoirs to be included. Indeed this volume is rightly to be regarded as a companion to his three-volume *Memoirs of American Jews, 1775–1865,* which The Jewish Publication Society of America issued in 1955.

Dr. Abraham I. Shinedling has put me in his debt by carefully proofreading the manuscript and compiling the index.

I owe Miss Fanny Sachs my thanks for her typing of the manuscript.

Miss Jeanette Weiss, Miss Sarah Grossman, Mrs. Ralph Zelcer, and Mrs. Rose Doty, all of the Archives staff, have offered me every encouragement. To say that their help has been indispensable is very much to understate the case.

S.F.C.

CONTENTS

Illustrations

. . . We turn our face again
So readily to life. . . .

Amy K. Blank

Introduction

History, Professor Gordon Childe has suggested, is essentially a record—admittedly "patchy and incomplete"—of human achievement. Few will readily quarrel with that definition, but we might go on to ask: What is the character, or what are the components, of that record? Is history the emergence of socioeconomic and political forces, trends, and tendencies in which individuals are of no or at most minimal consequence? Or is history the variegated creation of individuals, so that all forces and trends—all universals, really—are embodied in individuals or can be grasped only in relationship to individuals?

Either view offers its perplexities. If history is to be thought of only and strictly in terms of individuals, it becomes virtually unmanageable in any scientific or academic sense. What such a standpoint produces is an assortment of chronicles or romanticizations or mysticisms or psychologizings—but nothing that the modern temper would recognize as history. One begins and ends with Plutarch, who admits that it is his intention to "record, not history, but human destiny," or with Carlyle, who focuses on "the Heroic in human affairs" and thinks "all things that we see standing accomplished in the world . . . properly the outer material result, the practical realization and embodiment, of Thoughts that dwelt in the Great Men sent into the world." Or one is bound by Graetz's conviction that "history is not ruled by chance, but that a higher hand guides it, bringing to pass destined events by bloodshed and tears." All these are essentially romantic conceptions, impervious on the whole to an interest in social and economic factors. For such writers (and, as the names mentioned indicate, they can be very great writers), there is no history —there are only degrees of spiritualization.

On the other hand, if history is to be conceived of only and strictly in terms of forces, universals, sweeping change, it ceases to possess any human reference. It becomes something of a god in itself, to be worshiped or submitted to, but not studied or analyzed or participated in. What emerges from this view is less history than a sort of fatalism or messianism, or something mechanistic which can have no genuine meaning for us.

In the end, we require a combination of these two views. We need both the impersonal and the personal, both universals and particulars, both forces and men, both overarching change and the human spirit as it is manifest in the lives of individuals. We need both structural architects like Marx *and* humanists like Plutarch.

To be sure, human society is greater than any individual; but perhaps it is equally true that the individual is more interesting than society. Plutarch understood this; that is why he thought in terms of "revelation of character" and concentrated on "subjects which bear directly upon the spirit." One may tremble in reflecting on the fact that six million Jews (and how many millions of non-Jews?) were done to death by the Nazis. One may become indignant or give oneself to gestures of rage. But Anne Frank calls forth not so much trembling or indignation or rage as she does tears, pity in the highest sense, a feeling of loss—something inevitably closer to us and more palpable than the specter of six million dead. And yet to focus on Anne Frank to the exclusion of the six million would be to lose her significance, the tragedy she represents, just as to see only the six million without reference to Anne Frank would be to create a ritual, but to touch nothing human.

Modern historians are well advised to proceed with due skepticism, to reckon with the caveat of their profession. As Childe says, the record is "patchy and incomplete." History is inevitably a matter of *pars pro toto*—which is a great obstacle and even a great danger as historians seek to evaluate the experience of the past. The historian cannot know everything about the subject to which he addresses himself; he might omit something of decisive importance whose very existence he fails even to suspect. Not the least of the difficulties he encounters is the riddle of human personality. It is, after all, no simple matter to deal with human beings, human egos.

The question has been put: What is the character of history? Historians cannot avoid another question: What is personality? Is it in some way a process, a flowing on, so that the "river" is never twice the same? Does it exhibit unity —and how do we tell if it does? Is it a life-style, a philosophy of life, a sort of *modus spectandi?* What motivates personality —conflicts, needs, tensions, environment, heredity? Do we know enough to say? Can personality ever be represented except hypothetically? Personality has power and even mystique. What it never has is total clarity. It is always some-what fugitive. To speak of a man's personality is not to speak of facts; it is to formulate a hypothesis. Even if facts are known, is not the question of *pars pro toto* as applicable here as it is to assessments of historic change? Does a man know all the facts even about himself?

We can never be sure whether personality is, first and foremost, being and experience or whether it is, first and foremost, becoming and achieving. Perhaps the best we can say is that a personality would seem to function so as to transform itself slowly, painfully, into an instrument of ex-pression. What we can conclude—we historians in particu-lar—is that here are certain facts and a certain expressive-ness, and these all add up to one or another personality. And what is the value of such an observation? Does not its value lie in leading us to acquire for ourselves a sense of the richness of personality—and further, in leading us to relate that richness to ourselves, taking it into ourselves and il-luminating our own mysteries?

Hence this book, this assemblage of lives and voices. The historian will find here additional source material for his reconstruction of the American past; the general reader will discover how diverse individuals of Jewish origin saw and experienced America during the century between the mid-1800s and the mid-1900s. American life had never been simple, but those hundred years were, for the country as a whole and not least for its Jewish community, a time of dramatic change. As the period began America was a collec-tion of states with an undeveloped central government, an isolationist foreign policy, and a largely agrarian—partly slave-supported—laissez-faire economy; by the close of the period it had become a powerful federal union with a com-manding position on the international scene, a burgeoning industrial economy, and an accelerating "welfare state" social philosophy. In the mid-1800s, Protestant Anglo-Saxon nativism still dominated American society. A century later, the picture was considerably different: a religiously and ethnically pluralist structure had taken shape to challenge Anglo-Saxonism.

In 1850 there had been scarcely more than a handful of American Jews—mostly people of colonial Sephardic cultural heritage or, more commonly, of Central European immigrant background. In 1950, by contrast, American Jewry numbered something in excess of 5,000,000 persons and was predominantly East European in ancestry. Most nineteenth-century American Jews had been immigrants or the children of immigrants, but the mid-twentieth-century community was largely a native-born conglomerate that, unlike its forerunners of earlier generations, was given as much to professional as to commercial pursuits.

The Orthodoxy which, nominally at any rate, permeated mid-nineteenth-century American Jewish life had by 1950 been reduced to one of several spiritual options—Reform (itself bifurcated), Conservatism, Reconstructionism—and outright secularism (if not indifference to Jewish concerns). The mid-1800s had seen a scattering of Jewish settlements in America; the 1950s, however, knew increasingly the promise of a well-organized, rather muscular, unprecedentedly affluent, nationwide community. The Jews of 1850 had looked out on a world in which their brethren overseas were exposed virtually everywhere to social and political disabilities, but in which Europe—particularly beyond the Rhine—continued to occupy the center of the Jewish stage. A hundred years later European Jewry had all but vanished—"liquidated," to employ a twentieth-century euphemism—and the center of the Jewish stage was now shared by the free citizenries of the English-speaking lands and the infant prodigy known as Israel. All this is implicit, if not always or even frequently explicit, in the memoirs brought together here.

Wars and exploits do not appear in this book; at least they are not central to it. I cannot say with Carlyle: "We have undertaken to discourse here for a little on Great Men." With perhaps the exception of Samuel Adler, the lives and voices brought together in these pages are not those of "the modellers . . . of whatsoever the general mass of men contrived to do or to attain." Nor is it my intention —or within my competence—to offer a study in psychology or to develop a theory of personality. My goal is something else: to record the reactions of nine Jews, eight men and one woman, to American society. In one case, again that of Samuel Adler, even this is saying too much; what Adler's story reflects is the struggle he underwent in Germany before abandoning the Old World for the New. And there is another limitation to be noted. The portrayal undertaken in this book is drawn from a particular type of documentary source; the goal is to be approached from the standpoint of memoirs selected from the files of the American Jewish Archives in Cincinnati.

Most individuals leave behind them no memoirs. Those who do would seem to be possessed of especially vivid personalities, or at least to be more self-conscious than the generality of men. Their personalities represent a more aware, perhaps even more sophisticated, striving for utterance. They strive actively for insight into themselves and others; they are at pains to reveal themselves and the world in themselves. They have their reticences and their astigmatisms, too, of course—again, there is no escaping the shadow of *pars pro toto;* but whatever America is and whatever the Jews of America are, these nine memoirs, the lives and voices of this book, move toward a definition. "Here or nowhere is America."

LIVES AND VOICES

Samuel Adler

PRELUDE TO AMERICA

Born in the Rhenish town of Worms in 1809, Samuel, the son of Isak and Sarah Nickelsburg Adler, was no youngster when he came to America in 1857. After serving as rabbi of New York City's Emanu-El Congregation for seventeen years, he stepped aside for Gustav Gottheil, devoted himself to his studies, and died in New York in 1891. A social activist as well as a rabbinical scholar, Adler participated significantly in the Sturm und Drang *which shaped Reform Judaism both in Germany and in the United States. He deserves to be remembered for his efforts to free Jewish worship of what he took to be the "shocking lies," the "fustian and exaggeration" of medievalism. If he had anything to say about it, the service of the synagogue would be "clear, intelligible, instructive, and inspiring." He was an enviable man in that he never lacked for sympathizers.*

Yichus—*family lineage—counts for something in Jewish life, and Adler was enviable in that respect, too. His father had held a rabbinical post at Worms; one of his father's cousins, Nathan Adler (1741–1800), had presided over a famous Frankfurt am*

Main rabbinical academy; and another relative, Nathan Marcus Adler (1803–1890), became chief rabbi of the British Empire. One of Samuel Adler's sons, Felix (1851–1933), left the rabbinate in 1876 to establish the Ethical Culture movement and was celebrated as a leading figure on the American religious and educational scene.

Sometime before Adler's retirement from the Emanu-El pulpit in 1874, he wrote his autobiography. Family tradition has it that he was induced to do so by his daughter Sarah (later Mrs. Julius Goldman). The autobiography has been translated from the German and annotated by Sarah's daughter, Agnes, widow of Ashton Sanborn, of Cambridge, Massachusetts.

On December 3, 1809, at 9 A.M.—that is, the 25th of the month Kislev, in the year 5570 of the Jewish era, on the first evening of Hanukkah—I saw the light of this world. My father, of blessed memory, Isak Adler, inscribed my birthday in his *Mishnayot* [the collection of Jewish civil and religious law which forms the core of the Talmud] and indicated the year with the word *yishm'recho,* that is, "God watch over thee." And this word has been realized indeed through many inner and outer storms and dangers.

In the fall of 1815 I was sent to Hebrew school under a Rabbi Mordechai, who was also a Jewish butcher and did not stick to his teaching for ten minutes at a time. By the following spring I had not yet mastered the *alef bet* [the Hebrew alphabet]. My father took me away and from then on was my sole Hebrew teacher. In a few days I learned to read. Next followed translation of the Torah [Pentateuch], etc., and gradually the whole Bible. He did not find Rashi's commentary on the *Humash* [the Five Books of Moses, or Pentateuch] suitable for instruction; he was wont to say, "When you know *dikduk* [Hebrew grammar] and *Gemara*

[Talmud] you can then understand Rashi on your own, otherwise not." He placed great emphasis on grammar and was himself a distinguished grammarian, but he did not have the time to teach it at first hand. As soon as we—that is, my brother Jacob, older than I by a year and a half, and I—were capable of reading and understanding Hebrew, he gave us the grammar *Tsohar Ha-Tebah,* a textbook from which we had to instruct ourselves during the hour he took his afternoon rest.

It was his rule each Sabbath, according to talmudic precept, to recite out loud the week's Torah portion—the Hebrew text twice, the Aramaic translation once—verse by verse. We boys held the book open before us and were expected to follow the recitation silently but attentively, so that we became familiar not only with the Torah text but also with the Aramaic *Targum.** He instructed us in the Talmud for several hours daily in the following manner— he recited, translated, and elucidated each passage for us, and then each of us had to repeat it three times. A very useful practice in Talmud was also offered us. In Worms a Talmud society gathered daily after the evening prayer, and each day a different member in sequence had to expound a single page. As a result, a member not very well versed in the Talmud came to my father daily after the noon meal to prepare himself for the evening. My brother and I sat with the particular passage before us, listening in silent attention. At the society's session in the evening also we were allowed to attend as silent participants, and thus without much sweat and study we gradually and naturally became fairly familiar with the spirit, language, instructional

*Ancient translation or paraphrase of the Bible into the Aramaic vernacular; the most important is the translation of the Pentateuch.

material, and method of discussion of the Talmud.

Withal, the reading of the Bible was not to be neglected; daily our instruction began with it, and each of us had to present a chapter. The Bible and the Talmud were the sphere in which our intellects moved; everything else was excluded. So as not to be entirely helpless in secular life, I had some hours of private instruction in Hebrew cursive writing; and in order that I might also be able to employ German script, my father procured model writing copies with which we were to gain practice on our own. So that we might master the elements of arithmetic, we were given a primer in Jewish-German script. I had no impulse toward wider knowledge, nor was one stimulated in me. So my thirteenth year arrived and found me fairly well above the usual level for my age in Bible and Talmud comprehension, but in other knowledge still at a childish stage.

Ethrog and Lulav

On the second day after I reached bar mitzvah age [thirteen], my father fell ill with pneumonia and died eight days later. On his sick bed, he told our mother his last wishes. Her three sons should be continuously diligent in rabbinical studies; God would be helpful. My father died during the night between the 8th and 9th of Tebet—January 2, 1822. Early on the afternoon of the 9th, he was carried to his grave among a huge throng of people. The half day between his decease and burial was one of the most terrible of my life. We children felt terribly battered. Our mother grieved inconsolably. I, realizing that complete poverty was our heritage and that my mother was helpless, quietly determined to enlist all my strength to assist in our support. I thought, in my simplemindedness, that if I dragged firewood for people from the street to the storage bin, I could daily earn a few *kreutzer* [pennies]. But it did not come to that.

A few hours before the burial, a member of the Jewish community's governing body, the Vorstand, came to my mother and pacified her somewhat by telling her of the Vorstand's decision and promise that, until we children reached our majority, she would receive in weekly allotments one-half of my father's rabbinical salary of 300 florins —that is, 150 florins [about seventy-three dollars]—as a widow's pension. This aid was indeed given with all punctuality, and the money sufficed for the meager support of a mother with five children, simply because it had to suffice. But then, after scarcely a year and a half, a whole week passed without the appearance of the longed-for congregational servant with the three guilders; when my mother made inquiries, the word came that the money from now on had to be paid as a salary increase to the newly appointed rabbi, who incidentally had only one child and—unlike my father—also received free lodging. Nothing, therefore, remained for her. (The new rabbi had a brother-in-law in Worms who, with accomplices and additional helpers, had carried off this knavish trick.) It was a heavy blow. My older brother, Jacob, had already been away for a year attending the talmudic seminary at Frankfurt, so I, now being the eldest at home, in my ardor ran to the rabbi and poured out my heart in complaint and reproach. He stood shamefaced before a rebuking lad, shrugged his shoulders, and said he could do nothing.

Now was the time to pull ourselves together to escape hunger. In our little house, which we owned, a bedroom and sitting room were rented out for a trifle—our family restricted itself to two rooms. In the entryway a wooden partition was set up as a stall for a few pieces of hardware which mother took charge of in addition to her household duties, thus daily earning a few *groschen* [pennies]. The two girls, ten and eleven years old, were apprenticed, one to learn dressmaking, the other millinery. My younger brother, Abraham, continued the study of the Talmud, by himself, and I, now fourteen-and-a-half years old, went to the yeshiva in Frankfurt.

Naturally, I was not a student of the first order but could nevertheless keep pace with the majority in my studies. Oddly enough, an Alsatian *bachur* [unmarried yeshiva student], who was twice as old and as tall as I, gave me his good will and associated exclusively with me, prepared his Talmud studies in my company, and went about with me only, so that we were known among our fellow students by the nicknames of "Ethrog" and "Lulav" [the lemon-sized citron and long palm branch used together ritually during the Sukkot—Tabernacles—festival]. But this period did not last long. I had gone there in the spring; in the fall I had to return to our home. Wretched nourishment, massive nosebleeds, and frequent fever had brought me so low that it was not possible for me to remain. At home I recuperated completely and spent the winter industriously pursuing my Talmud studies. But I was impelled toward wider vistas and higher aims, and the following spring I went to Ingenheim, near Landau, where at that time a certain Rabbi Anschel Schoplich conducted a small yeshiva and had succeeded in obtaining in the neighborhood the reputation of being an outstanding Talmud scholar. But young though I was, I soon learned that this man was nothing but an ordinary rabbi, and one with repulsive habits to boot, who could not satisfy me. There was nothing for it but to return home. There could be no thought of leaving again.

Fortunately, an event occurred just at this time which made my residence at home more bearable and more advantageous for my struggles. The large yeshiva in Fuerth was discontinued by royal decree. The numerous *bachurim* were scattered in all the directions of the compass, and a few of them came to Worms in order to continue their talmudic education with Rabbi Jakob (Koppel) Bamberger, who had a reputation as a skilled *lamdan* [scholar]. The rabbi, fortunate in being the possessor of a small yeshiva of his own, discoursed daily, and I was happy to join aspiring colleagues and to advance my studies through the rabbi's daily lectures. In this way I acquired simultaneously a teacher, colleagues, and even pupils; for a few students who were not yet quite equal to the rabbi's dialectically involved lectures prepared and took follow-up exercises under me. In consequence some youths from Worms and the neighborhood developed a desire for higher Talmud studies. These became my pupils and paid me according to prevailing conditions.

How comforting it was for me not to have to eat the insufficient bread so painfully earned by my mother and sisters without some return—to know that I could contribute something to our support. My mother also glimpsed in this a gradual, even though small, beginning toward improvement of her circumstances. Her greater star of hope, however, was her older son, whose reputation as one of the most outstanding *bachurim* of the Frankfurt yeshiva had spread from Frankfurt to Worms. Yet how soon was this star of hope extinguished! Made ill through extreme exertion, he had to forgo his studies and come back to Worms; he succumbed the following winter to consumption. His burial did not want in tributes from many sides. Though only seventeen-and-a-half years old, he received at his grave the title of *Morenu* ("our teacher").

To our mother, bent with grief, this could give little consolation, but the blow roused me to more activity toward becoming a greater support to my mother. I began a trade in Hebrew books which brought in something, bought and sold *ethrogim* (citrons) and *lulavim* (palm branches) before the Sukkot festival, became a teacher in a benevolent society at which I lectured every Sabbath on the *Haftarah* [the prophetic passages read every week], and took on another source of income that turned out to be extremely sour for me. Some five to six weeks before Passover, they began grinding the meal for the matzot [unleavened bread]. To be certain that the Christian millers did nothing against kosher practice, two reliable persons had to be appointed, each of whom took turns keeping watch for a full twenty-four hours. I was favored as one of them. Each time my mother gave me a small package of bread and butter and ground coffee. With this I had to survive twenty-four hours. How often I envied the miller and his servants when at noon and eventide they sat before their full dishes! Most difficult, however, were the nights. I still shiver over my whole body when I think of it, how perhaps half a dozen times a night I forcibly had to rub the sleep out of my eyes and, dressed only in my thin little jacket, accompany the miller out into the cold mill. But I endured and was content as a result to have earned five or six florins.

My younger brother, Abraham (called Koppel), was more fortunate. He did not have to assist in supporting the family, was highly endowed with intelligence, and had a mind and ambition for extensive knowledge; he received private instruction in languages and general studies. He went to Karlsruhe to the yeshiva and from there to the lyceum, returning after two years and entering the second class of the gymnasium [high school] in Worms, where he completed his studies in orderly fashion. But his good luck spread its radiance over me. According to my whole inclination I might easily have remained imprisoned in talmudism, always a stranger in the modern world and never emerging from the darkness of the Middle Ages. He was my savior. Again and again he urged me to turn toward more general knowledge so that I might later attend a university and prepare myself to become a rabbi in tune with the times. I long refused, and my colleagues—the advanced *bachurim* who for their part wished to attend the university—supported me in my attitude. One man, they contended, must devote himself exclusively to Talmud study so that the others, when the occasion arose, could ask his advice about involved casuistic questions. Finally my brother prevailed. With reluctance I submitted and received from him instruction, inadequate enough, in Latin, German, and geography.

In the spring of 1831 I went, miserably prepared, to [the University of] Bonn, where at this time a number of competent young men were devoting themselves to Jewish theology. There I remained two and a half years, attending lectures on philosophy, philology, and history, but profiting little from all this, partly because, deeply embedded in Orthodoxy, I regarded these matters merely as a necessary evil. My heart and my zeal belonged to rabbinical literature, to which a part of the day and the larger share of the night were devoted. Another reason for my profiting little from the university was that, as a consequence of poverty, I was tormented by inadequate nourishment and insufficient clothing, in addition to many night vigils in a cold room. I sickened early in the winter of 1831, with violent vomiting of blood. This recurred periodically over many years. It did not come to a complete stop until the spring of 1843, thus distressingly intruding into my studies and especially crip-

pling me during my sojourn at Bonn. One advantage, however, this attack of illness did have for me; it brought me
to the attention of some benefactors who from then on
supported me every month with a small sum of money. At
their head was Jonas Cohn, a banker to whom I had been
recommended by old Eberstadt, of Worms; Cohn and his
sister Frau Seligmann even continued to send me financial
help semiannually while I was at [the University of]
Giessen.

A *"Freshly Baked"* Doktor

In the fall of 1833 my brother came to Bonn after complet-
ing the gymnasium. I moved to Giessen because I thought
it advisable for my future to attend the provincial university. Its reputation was far inferior to that of Bonn and
deservedly so, but what cared I, who took part in all this
only reluctantly anyway? But things turned out differently.
The Giessen professors whose lectures principally interested me were no researchers but they *were* teachers—and
extraordinarily valuable for my level of culture and future
education. My main teachers were Johann August Vullers
and Joseph Hillebrand. With the former I studied Arabic,
Syriac, and Persian in rapid succession, and was advanced
enough to receive from him recently published literary
works for reading before he even glanced at them. I even
wrote many little reviews which appeared in journals under
his name or anonymously. Hillebrand, however, under
whom I took almost all my disciplines in philosophy, was a
true angel of light for me. His lectures were so clear and
precise, so penetrating, that of necessity he aroused profound reflection in a serious listener.

And thus I gradually found myself involved in a fundamental transformation. What formerly seemed unquestionable began to waver. To penetrate to the first causes of truth now became the longing of my heart. Intellectual problems of the highest nature occupied my mind whenever and wherever I found myself alone. I could not attain complete satisfaction through the wrestling of the spirit, to be sure, yet it gave me satisfaction to realize that I was struggling for knowledge and that I felt myself liberated from the shackles of blind tradition. Abraham Geiger's periodical, *Wissenschaftliche Zeitschrift fuer Juedische Theologie,* which began appearing during my stay at Giessen, Samson Raphael Hirsch's twisted hyper-Orthodox brochures, Isaac Samuel Reggio's *Torah and Philosophy,* and similar writings equally gave me matter for thought and impulse to independent reflection. And so Giessen was the only university in which, although I did not live a student's existence, I pursued a happy life of study. Externally, too, my life was better, for by offering Hebrew instruction to Protestant theological students I obtained the means for a decent lodging, fuel, and miscellaneous necessities. To be sure, what I thus neglected in my own studies I had to retrieve in the late hours of the night, which was not beneficial to my health.

In the autumn of 1835 I felt I had wandered about enough in universities, and longed for home, but did not wish to return without my doctorate. This was partly because without one the prospect for an appointment was not good and partly because a bit of youthful vanity may have been involved. There was, however, a small obstacle—for me a mountain: money! To be sure, through friendly professors I had succeeded in getting permission to obtain the doctor's degree at half price, that is, for 150 florins— but then where was I to come by 150 florins? Most of the winter passed in private studies and exertions to raise the great sum. I gave more instruction, saved on myself and pinched pennies, while my poor sisters worked hard at home and saved, sending me what they had earned and put aside. Mid-February saw me in possession of 150 florins. By the end of the month I had received my doctorate, and at four o'clock on March 1, I said farewell to Giessen. I was one of the happiest men on earth.

On the trip home I stayed over several days in Frankfurt in order to renew my acquaintance with the old talmudic leaders there and with the scholars of secular learning. I also spent a few days in Darmstadt where, according to the custom, I had to present myself to the town councilor, Linde, chancellor of the university. Here in the Grand Ducal library, to which I was recommended by Professor Schaefer of Giessen, former court librarian, I looked up and borrowed for further study a number of the most magnificent Arabic and Persian works. On Purim [the Feast of Esther] I arrived in Worms. In the evening as I trod through the *Judengasse* and went to the synagogue, all eyes turned to the "freshly baked" *Doktor*. Without even having listened to me, they took it for granted that a *Doktor* must be a scholar and an orator, so after a few days a considerable number of the congregants got together and petitioned the Vorstand that at their expense—300 florins had been subscribed for the purpose—I should be allowed to preach every Sabbath. The Vorstand, which consisted of cultured young men or those who were friendly to culture and whose members themselves were among the subscribers, at once consented to the petition, and without further ado I began the practice of my calling.

It was a difficult beginning for me, but easier for the community. They were not used to anything better and regarded the imperfect as good value. It might have led me astray had I not recognized my own shortcomings and turned my strivings toward perfection. In the meantime, the community was satisfied. Everything proceeded without the slightest disturbance, without a whisper of dissatisfaction from any direction. The old rabbi was usually present during the sermon, and we associated with one another in the friendliest manner. In the spring of 1837, as the first year approached its close and the Vorstand had to prepare the estimate for the financial requirements of the following year and submit it to the district authorities for approval, they regarded it as appropriate for the community to take over the remuneration of the preacher, and included 300 florins a year for this purpose in the budget. Not a breath was raised against it. Then suddenly an abusive article declaring me totally incompetent and unworthy of the preacher's post appeared in the Grand Ducal newspaper of Darmstadt. Though the budget went only through the district council, it had to be declared valid by the Ministry. This was a thunderclap out of a clear sky. We soon discovered the author of the article. It was the Darmstadt rabbi, Dr. Benjamin Hirsch Auerbach, who had once enjoyed good treatment as a *yeshivah bachur* in my mother's house, but did not wish to see anyone on a par with himself. At that time Auerbach had, through a well-known confederate, the full ear of the Minister of Public Worship.

Dr. Auerbach, a pupil of the old rabbi of Worms, knew how to incite him into believing that the Vorstand and I planned to oust him from his post and leave him unemployed. Dr. Auerbach drove the rabbi into such fear and fury that he screamed on all sides for help and even ran to Frankfurt, to old Amschel von Rothschild, to supplicate his intervention against my appointment. Where a fire is stirred there are flames, and thus began the battling within the community itself. Super-Orthodox members of the Vor- stand (long since superseded) took the lead, and the rabble followed. The partisan battle raged and found outlets in petitions to the Ministry and in newspaper articles. Thus it went on all summer while I, naturally, was not allowed to preach without having gained consent. At last in the autumn the decision was made.

The Grand Ducal Ministry—thus read the rescript of the district councilor—had decided that nothing stood in the way of my continuing to preach for another year at private cost and *with the consent of the rabbi,* with the hope that in the meantime I would also succeed in winning over those in opposition. The Vorstand then called a meeting to which the rabbi and I were invited. After they had given both of us word of this decision, they called upon the rabbi to declare himself regarding his consent. The Vorstand thought it would be sufficient if the rabbi expressed his agreement once for all, but he demanded that I obtain it every week, adding: "Dr. Adler, after all, was my pupil, and I am his friend. All he needs to do is to submit his manu- script every Friday afternoon, and each time, without glanc- ing at it, I will write under it 'seen and approved.' " Natu- rally, no matter how great and marvelous the tolerance, this could not be agreed to.

Since we knew that the district councilor had been won over by the opposition and had frequently shown himself to be most presumptuous and arbitrary, we arranged for friends to investigate at the Ministry—and discovered that the words underlined in the district councilor's rescript were not to be found in the ministerial decree! We kept quiet but directed a request to the Ministry to cancel the proviso that required approval on the part of the rabbi. Imagine what a reprimand from higher quarters the district councilor must have received. Soon thereafter I received a summons from the councilor to appear Sunday morning in his home. I appeared. The man was wild, burning with fury. He thundered at me with abuse and threatened to use his power to prevent my ever obtaining a post in the Archduchy. I parried with the greatest calm and merely said in a quite cold-blooded manner: "Well, let us fight the battle through and see who remains the victor." That was water on the flames. He now took another tack, advising me to do nothing in the matter and begging me to win the Vorstand over to the same position. He promised to do everything for me if we kept quiet, guaranteeing that my appointment and the fixing of my salary would at once receive approval in the next budget. I promised silence, and he kept his word. So as not to be without activity and sustenance, I announced public lectures on Jewish history, which also required the consent of the district councilor. It followed at once. In the spring of 1838, when the Vorstand sent in the budget with the 300-florin post for me as preacher, agreement without objection or opposition ensued.

Now extensive activity began for me. The now-converted district councilor inquired whether I would agree, under an ordinance from him, to go twice a year into every rural Jewish community of his district to preach and inspect the religious schools, report the results to him, and make appropriate suggestions; I was to be reimbursed only for my travel expenses by the respective communities. I agreed with pleasure. It turned out to be a laborious undertaking. Few communities were pleased with the new ordinance. Naturally, the communities in which the worst conditions prevailed, and where the so-called teachers of the most deplorable kind trembled for their existence, were also the communities that stirred up antagonisms and did all in their power to have the ordinance repealed. When this failed, they made my stay with them quite disagreeable. But I was young and of good courage; I conducted myself with prudence and steadfast zeal and had the satisfaction, after continuing effort and labor, of directing better men onto the Vorstands and of seeing most of the religious schools freed from humdrum instructors and staffed with genuine teachers.

As a result, I could naturally operate more successfully in Worms also, where in any case there was more receptivity within the congregation; and the Vorstand went along with me. But even here it did not go without a struggle. Much effort was involved in gaining permission for me to give religious instruction to the Jewish pupils of the grammar school and gymnasium within the institutions themselves. What stimulated cooperation with other large communities and brought some success was our effort to abolish the shameful heritage from the French occupation which weighed heavily on the shoulders of the Jews of Rhine-Hesse, namely, the so-called moral patent, without which no one was admitted to a lawsuit, as well as the shocking form of the medievallike "Jewish oath."

In all matters of this kind the authorities were opposed to us. They appeared more favorable when it was a case of instituting improvements in Jewish life. Efforts in this direction had to be initiated very cautiously and circumspectly, and even so they did not succeed at first without powerful inner ferment. There were about a dozen *kohanim* ["priests," traditionally held to be descendants of the biblical Aaron] who sang the Priestly Blessing [Numbers 6:-24–26—"May the Lord bless you and keep you," etc.] on festival days with a dreadful wild confusion of screams. I sought and found means for them to meet before the festival and be trained to sing the blessing in chorus; those who did not appear at the rehearsal could not take part. A shriek of horror arose from the super-Orthodox. A revolution was threatened, but I put it through. Later, the former opponents were proud of their singing and certainly refused to be excluded.

There was a similar experience with another innovation in the interest of order which indeed penetrated more deeply and involved more difficulties. In the middle of the Worms synagogue there stood a truly stupendous structure, the Almemar, with the desk for the Torah-reading at its center; it took up just about half the synagogue space in length and breadth and almost touched the ceiling. No one behind the Almemar could hear the preacher, who stood in front of the Holy Ark. As soon as the sermon was to start, a mad rush from behind the Almemar to the front took place and in the reverse direction upon the close of the sermon. This could not be endured; the Almemar had to be removed and a place made for more seats and for accommodating the voice of the preacher.

Another great handicap was a special synagogue for the women that stood next to the one for the men, separated from it by a thick wall. The whole female sex was thus cut off from the essential benefits of public worship. Therefore this wall, too, had to fall. Heartrending indeed was the wailing of the super-Orthodox. Even here, in time, habit exercised its power, and after awhile all were reconciled. Thus it became easier to establish more decency and dignity in the service itself. A synagogue ordinance was drawn up and approved by the administrative authorities to remedy gross abuses, to ban the old prayers of vengeance, and to make a start at introducing the German language into public worship through the prayer for the regional government. Regulations aiming at order and dignity were also established for burials, which up to this time had taken place in wild and hideous disarray.

Heaven Had Spoken

What pleased me more, though, than these feeble beginnings at religious improvement was the privilege of establishing in my native town something enduring in the realm of welfare. Following the impulse of the heart inherited from my deceased father, who in his day established and superintended several benevolent societies, I succeeded in founding a women's society that worked effectively in many directions. Furthermore, for the already established societies—managed according to past usage, which not infrequently led to arbitrary actions and discord —I set up firm regulatory statutes.

During these rather extended activities I was, as far as outside life was concerned, very restricted. With my annual salary being only three hundred guilders, strict economy was necessary, and there could be no thought of supplementary earnings. Literally narrow, most excessively narrow, was the space in which I had to spend most of my time. A narrow room with a single little window was the only place in my mother's tiny house that could be put at my disposal; that was both my bedroom and study. Friends often urged me to rent a decent lodging, but I did not wish to move away from my mother and sisters. Sense and sensibility opposed it, and at no price did my mother wish to exchange the finest rented home for her own property. An apparent disaster, however, gave a fortunate turn to events. It was on a Sabbath afternoon, as I was returning to our home from the synagogue, that a friend confronted me with these words: "You're walking along so leisurely. Don't you know what has happened at home?" I: "What is it?" He: "Doelzchen [an old maid who lived in our house] developed smallpox during the night, and the police are at this very moment sealing up the house." Naturally, I hurried home in breathless haste and fortunately was allowed to enter for a minute to fetch several books. Then I sought out my family, who had already fled. Heaven had now spoken; the judgment was decreed. Even my mother never again wished to occupy such a house, infected by pestilential sickness; we had to rent elsewhere. I rented a splendid lodging with a magnificent garden that not only soon reconciled my mother to the change, but also placed me in a position to improve our finances, as I was able to take in several boarders who paid well.

Although all this did not suffice for me to establish an independent household, I nevertheless became engaged, in the summer of 1838, to my future wife, Henrietta, daughter of Rabbi Feibisch (Phoebus) Frankfurter in Friedberg, with whom I had previously become acquainted. I risked the move (1) because more lodgers were in the offing, and (2) because my gray-haired future father-in-law hopefully contemplated relinquishing his post and obtaining it for me. Both considerations proved empty hopes. The number of lodgers failed to increase, and my father-in-law's plan met with serious difficulties. Thus years passed without change of circumstance or prospects. Then it happened, while I was spending a few days late in the summer of 1841 at Frankfurt in the home of I. S. Adler, my father-in-law's brother-in-law, that a special messenger arrived with the news that the Friedberg rabbi had suddenly succumbed. I rushed there without delay in order to deliver the funeral oration for my venerated father-in-law and to comfort, to the best of my abilities, my dejected bride. The blow hit her terribly hard, and she was sickly for some time thereafter.

A drop of balm for her deep sorrow was the thought that now, without doubt, I would soon be appointed her father's successor in the rabbinical office. In fact, all indications were favorable. The Vorstand of the Friedberg community, together with the authorities of several nearby rural communities, immediately petitioned the Ministry to give me the vacant post. The city and district magistracies did their part to support the petition strongly. A favorable decision seemed beyond doubt; we waited every day with full assurance for the ratification. Like a thunderclap came the ministerial decree: the vacant post of rabbi should not be filled again. Why not? A silly question; highly placed ministers need offer no reasons. But we knew well the reason. Through superior influence the rabbi of Giessen had succeeded in convincing the court in Darmstadt that the deceased archduke had once promised him in an audience that the Friedberg rabbinical office, when vacant, would be united with his own and that he would become rabbi of all of Upper Hesse.

Now only a small speck of hope, a very feeble one, remained. There was talk of establishing a district rabbinical office in Alzey. The Vorstand of the chief community of Alzey, which would have to pay by far the largest part of the salary and consequently also had the leading voice, had, to be sure, set its eyes on me and had petitioned for me to the Ministry. But a mighty mountain blocked the way. The above-mentioned individual [the Giessen rabbi], the factotum of the Minister of Public Worship, had an incompetent son who was studying theology; Dr. Auerbach, also previously mentioned, was his teacher. Naturally, he was the minister's designated appointee for the post. In fact, he sent the candidate to Alzey with a confidential letter to the district councilor himself requesting that he do all in his power to influence the community favorably toward the candidate. At the request and with the support of the district councilor, the Giessen rabbi's son was allowed to deliver a trial sermon. If the congregation had originally been disinclined toward him, they were now horrified that the authorities should attempt to impose such a man on them. Fearing a bold stroke from above, the community took a daring step; they sent a deputation to the Minister of Public Worship threatening revolution and declaring that the synagogue and the pulpit were their property, that they would let no one set foot there without their approval.

However greatly the fine gentleman was taken aback and however harsh the words he let slip, he was nonetheless impressed. After a few weeks the Grand Ducal decree appointing me district rabbi for Alzey came. In Alzey, the community rejoiced. In Worms, the news spread alarm. The Vorstand immediately convened to deliberate on how I might be retained, and thereupon sent me their written decision to increase my stipend to 500 guilder annually if I would contract to stay with them for ten years. So far did liberality go at that time in Worms. Nonetheless, it was well meant and had perhaps been intended only as a token of loyalty in anticipation of my expected refusal. On the last day of Sukkot, I gave my farewell address in Worms and that evening received a big farewell dinner, as well as an honorarium from the congregation. The next day, October 2, 1842, I moved into my new residence.

A Cry of Horror

Herewith began a new epoch, a new life and struggle. Life indeed became brighter and more hopeful, but the struggle more laborious. No spade had ever broken up for cultivation the spiritual ground I was to work. The so-called worship service was as undisciplined and repulsive as in the most demoralized village communities, and there was no trace of religious instruction of the young. I had to undertake the task from the beginning. It was alleviated somewhat by the fact that the Vorstand was with me in mind and purpose, although the whole work, the remedies and putting them into practice, the written communications with the secular authorities (including those which were conducted in the name of the Vorstand) devolved exclusively on me.

The first goal we attempted was the orderly religious instruction of schoolchildren—within, moreover, both the public and private schools. In the private schools it went over without much trouble, but greater difficulty was encountered with the public schools. Our application for instruction in the elementary schools, which went to the city school authorities, consisting of the mayor and the Protestant and Catholic pastors, was turned down without explanation. Later, the liberal mayor took it into his own hands to grant us permission and it remained unopposed. It is of interest that the very same Catholic priest who reported to the school authorities on our request, and was responsible for their refusal, was deluded by the [separatist] "German-Catholic" humbug a year and a half later. Moreover, he allowed himself to be taken in for material motives, as was well known, and accepted the post of pastor for the "German-Catholic" parish in Alzey. When a public place for his religious instruction was denied him, he begged me to lend him my designated place for one hour. For instruction in the secondary schools, which were under the jurisdiction of the district school administration, we Jews had to struggle longer but in the end were all the more victorious, in that

Jewish religious teaching was then declared compulsory, on a par with the two Christian confessions, and was given an equal place and voice in all conferences concerning schools as a whole.

On February 21, 1843, I brought home my bride. The wedding was held in Frankfurt at her uncle's. On the 22nd, I returned with her to Alzey. The following two months were spent in joyful activity under inner and outer conditions of unmolested happiness and peace. But whoever wishes to work for enlightenment among mankind must not count on continuous peace. Throughout the winter I had not attempted the slightest alteration in religious life, as I wished to familiarize myself with the community and to make my way carefully, being aware of the total lack of enlightened standards among the majority of its members.

At length I took the bold step of announcing from the pulpit on the Sabbath before the Passover that even from the most Orthodox point of view it is not forbidden to eat leguminous vegetables at the Passover. This aroused a cry of horror among the ignorant majority, and the report spread like wildfire through the whole region, igniting the fanaticism of the rabbis, the pious, and the bigoted to the point where they regarded it as their holy duty to alienate the confidence of my congregation and the neighboring communities, to declare me ignorant and unworthy, and to incite and maintain a venomous baiting. To be sure, I had not anticipated such a degree of demoralization nor deemed it possible, but I calculated that the whole manifestation had been artificially created and must soon disappear. I paid no further attention to it. Only to the rabbi in Mainz, whom I knew as an ordinarily peace-loving individual but one who had allowed himself to be dragged into the chase, did I write a passionate letter, armored with all talmudic and rabbinical weapons. That silenced him, and soon the unholy fire was quenched.

Not long thereafter the outbreak of a second storm was threatened, but it passed over quickly without any considerable harm. At Shavuot, the Pentecost festival, I conducted the confirmation of the qualified children, both boys and girls, of the religious school. That was enough to start the flow of bile in some of the bigoted. But worse was yet to come. Some days previously the Vorstand had removed, at my request, the rampart from the part of the gallery where the women sat, to give these segregated souls a view of the preacher and facilitate their participation in the complete service. This so enraged the overpious that a few of them, the wealthiest among them, even had the cheek to abuse me in the synagogue with vulgar invective. But they remained in the minority. Even the unenlightened majority of the congregation approved of this innovation, and the whole furious outbreak by the bigots had no further consequence —except that they, three in number, no longer attended the synagogue, and whenever their spokesman met me on the street, he spat in front of me to the accompaniment of abusive language.

The years 1844 to 1846, in which the rabbinical conventions took place at Braunschweig, Frankfurt am Main, and Breslau, conventions in which I was an active participant, were for me years of joyful activity. The one in Braunschweig was of a preparatory nature and had no practical results. On the other hand, in view of existing conditions the two following ones cut fairly deeply into the practices of public religious worship. The most striking reform resolutions were omission of all outdated [messianic and particularistic] views and hopes in prayers, establishment of triennial cycles of Torah readings instead of the completion of the readings in a single year, and complete abolition of the second-day celebration of holidays. Only a very few rabbis were in a position to introduce the reforms. The communities opposed them. By this time I was so well entrenched in the confidence of my community that, through instruction from the pulpit and discussion of the topics in private circles, I was able to win over my congregation for all these reforms. Only abolishing the second-day holiday caused some difficulty and evoked some excitement; but through constant sermons and personal example, I gradually put it through and during the whole controversy remained personally unassailed.

But this peaceable existence was not to continue in all respects. A mighty tempest broke loose—the arrival of the year 1848, in which thrones were shaken, revolution broke out in all social strata, and even my own existence was seriously threatened. I was full of enthusiasm for the radiant dawn of liberty and did not conceal it in the pulpit or in private circles. This created enemies among the public and undercover reactionaries, who openly and secretly agitated against me in newspaper articles and by denouncing me to the government. It seemed a marvel that I happily escaped all the missiles. But financially I suffered under it very much. All administration was out of control. The rural communities withdrew their contributions to the rabbi's stipend, as did the philanthropic Belmont Fund [originally established in 1790 by the children of Isaac Simon Belmont to defray communal expenses]. Three of the richest of the congregants withdrew from the congregation, while others sought all kinds of excuses for not paying. Suffice it to say that for a whole year I could not draw any salary. On top of that, to increase my dilemma, a dear relative in Frankfurt urgently besought me to help him out of his financial straits with my small means, a debt which he would certainly repay in a few weeks. But the weeks dragged out into a very long time before he was in a position to repay the sum gradually, without interest of course, in small installments. It was a difficult period. But I remained steadfast in conviction, expression, and efficacy until the clouds parted and life became normal again.

Hardly was this period of pressure overcome when suddenly a heavy new cloud rose up, threatening disaster and bringing serious misfortune to the family. My brother, Abraham (Koppel), who after my departure from Worms had received there the post of preacher and second rabbi and had worked with great zeal for the reform of Judaism, had also participated very energetically during the stormy year of 1848 in the efforts to alter political conditions. The revolution was suppressed. Those heavily involved were imprisoned or took flight, but others who had worked for change only in speech or writing were, it seemed, to remain unmolested. At this juncture, on the eve of the Day of Atonement, just as I was on the point of entering the synagogue, I received word that my brother that very afternoon (with what refinement the time was chosen) had been picked up by the police in his study and taken to the iron dungeon in Mainz. How I felt and how I carried on the Yom Kippur services, at which I nonetheless functioned as usual, one may well imagine.

Before dawn the next morning I took off for Mainz, where with great effort I obtained permission to see my brother. From there I went to Darmstadt to exert my influence in his behalf, and so it went all winter from here to there, sometimes also to Worms, to brace poor Rachel, Koppel's wife, without completely neglecting my calling in

Alzey. In the meantime, as a result of all this heavy suffering, Rachel became dangerously ill, a fact which could not be totally concealed from my imprisoned brother. Toward spring she was on the verge of death, and it was essential to make the greatest effort to gain permission for her husband to see her once again. At last we succeeded in freeing him on bail. Not long thereafter he was acquitted by the tribunal but deprived of his post by the government. He thereupon founded a school for girls, in which his now-recovered and thoroughly competent Rachel zealously cooperated.

The sunshine of well-being seemed again to break out on the horizon, but it was only a brief radiance. The illnesses which my brother had suffered in prison, associated with the torments over his wife's sicknesses, affected his nervous system, so that he himself fell ill and continued in poor health until released by death in the winter of 1856. When I think back to this sad period with all its particulars and how throughout this time I was kept in a constant state of tension, grinding anxiety, and continuous work, I am astonished that I overcame it all without damage to myself. I would never have ascribed so much elasticity and physical strength to myself.

The Rule of God in This World

Just as every misfortune is followed by a salutary consequence, so even this tragic family destiny indirectly had a favorable influence on my position and future. For I was called in the spring of 1854, on the recommendation of Abraham Geiger, to the Jewish community of Lemberg [present-day Lwów], Galicia, as rabbi and preacher of its temple. I first stipulated that I was to travel to Lemberg at communal expense to look over conditions. They agreed. I traveled there, remained three weeks, preached several times, and not only found conditions satisfactory and enticing, but was enthusiastic over the large sphere of activity and the universal attention and friendliness of people toward me. I accepted the post on contract, stipulating as the only condition my wife's agreement. She did not look with a friendly eye on migration to Poland, but willingly gave in when she realized my enthusiasm for the position.

Another difficulty had yet to be removed. The rabbinical post had to be approved, or rather decreed, by the Austrian emperor. This, in the eyes of the communal Vorstand, was a very minor difficulty, since the highest city and provincial authorities—who had attended one of my sermons—agreed to give their support. But the affair took another course. As soon as the Ministry in Vienna had received the request of the Vorstand for consent to my appointment, they directed an inquiry to the Grand Ducal Ministry of Hesse as to my political opinions. The reply was to the effect that, although no political offense on my part was known of, nevertheless everyone regarded me as an outspoken and zealous democrat. Moderately enough, the Austrian Ministry thereafter ordained that I should receive the post provisionally for one year; if I did not fall into any political error during this time, I was to be permanently appointed. The Vorstand urged me to regard this danger as fanciful and to accept, but I insisted that I could not come until Vienna decreed an unconditional, definite appointment. Thereupon the Vorstand took an energetic step; they dispatched a commission of competent individuals to Vienna to negotiate directly in the affair. They stayed there in the last months of summer, and their waiting and working were crowned with success.

In the course of this summer, however, there was a change in our family life which was of importance for me. My seventy-six-year-old mother, as a result of my brother's illness, could no longer enjoy the required rest and care in his home. I had to take her with me to Alzey. But how would it be if I moved to Lemberg? Surely, I said to myself, I cannot transplant my mother in her old age to an entirely alien world. This gave me little anxiety; Lemberg was in my eyes a lost cause anyway. But when, in the fall of 1854, a thick letter arrived from the Lemberg Vorstand full of rejoicing and exclamations of joy stating the imperial decree for my definitive appointment had arrived, it was like a thunderclap that made every nerve in my body tremble. I stood there between two powerful conflicting duties: on the one hand, my pledged word to Lemberg, added to the great sacrifices they had made for my appointment; on the other, the sacred filial duty toward my mother. This dilemma burned for a time like a fire within me. Little by little I succeeded in weighing the situation from all sides with deliberation and came to this decision: I must refuse, for Lemberg would not be orphaned; there were other rabbis. Were I to go there, however, whether I dragged my mother with me or left her behind in a miserable situation, her life might be in danger, and I could not function happily with such a weight on my conscience. With a bleeding heart and weeping, I wrote the letter of refusal to Lemberg. It was the most difficult, the most distressing document I ever inscribed.

What followed thereafter is extraordinary. Many may call it coincidence, I call it the rule of God in this world. My mother was in my home for over two years, silently grieving over her invalid son and awaiting in devout resignation release from her suffering through death. On the day before Yom Kippur, 1856, we laid her to rest in her grave. As difficult for me as that of some two years before [when his brother, Koppel, had been arrested] was this Yom Kippur, with its heavy responsibilities. At its close I returned exhausted to my home—to find a letter from New York with the announcement that a missive from the Board of Temple Emanu-El was already on the way, containing a call to become rabbi of the congregation. Thus, because of my mother, I had to relinquish the post at Lemberg, but one day after her burial I was surprised by the news that I was about to get a call to New York. And this compensation of New York for Lemberg, America for Galicia, is in every respect more than satisfactory. The bitter times which I endured because of my brother contributed indirectly to the fact that I now rejoice in this appointment in a free America, to one of the most liberal of congregations, for which I cannot be sufficiently thankful.

When the call actually came from the New York board, my wife was enthusiastic and urged immediate acceptance, and I needed only a few days of deliberation to accept the post. My Alzey community was reluctant to see me leave but in good conscience could offer no objections. I myself could leave this community only with a heavy heart, a community to which I gave birth, which I educated and fashioned into one that was widely respected. Yet it had to be done both out of consideration for my family, to provide them with a better future, and not less to gain for myself a more extended field of action. It was a satisfaction to realize that I had accomplished numerous worthwhile things in Alzey and that my name would long survive there

From *Leslie's Illustrated Newspaper*

Interior of Temple Emanu–El, New York City

in honored and affectionate remembrance. On the 21st of February, 1857 (our wedding anniversary), I gave my farewell address, and on the next morning (Washington's birthday), I left Alzey accompanied by the good wishes of the whole community.

Nathan H. Cohen

CON BRIO

In the mid-1800s when Nathan H. Cohen was born, there were perhaps 50,000 Jews in the United States. By 1920, when he recorded his reminiscences, the country's Jewish population had grown to 3,000,000—only one index to the changes Cohen saw in a long, active, and quite public life.

Interestingly enough, in writing his memoir Cohen took little notice of the Jewish experience in America. He offers the reader scarcely any glimpse at all into Jewish affairs. It is, for the most part, to exuberant recollections of "Anglo-Saxon" mid-America that he adverts in these pages. Even so, Cohen was not detached from Jewish involvements, and the people he felt closest to seem to have been Jews—notably his fellow ben b'rith *Albert Eisner, whose death in December 1926 deprived Cohen of a lifelong friend. Two years later, on December 28, 1928, Cohen himself died in Hollywood, California, where he and his wife were spending the winter. The B'nai B'rith Grand Prairie Lodge No. 281 of Champaign, Illinois, which he had joined nearly fifty years before, in 1879, set aside a page in its minute book "to perpetuate the memory of a good and upright man."*

Cohen, his memoir makes clear, was deeply interested in music —so much so, indeed, that at one point he contemplated a musical career for himself. Circumstances led him to abandon such a plan in favor of the business interests which he carried on in Urbana, Illinois, for some thirty-five years until his retirement in 1912. His son, Sol B. Cohen, however, picking up where Nathan had left off, was to become a distinguished violinist and composer.

❦

I was born in Philadelphia, they tell me, in 1850 or 1851. My parents had no record that I have ever had an opportunity to see. Well, a year or so makes no difference, so I cannot hold a grudge against them, as my brothers and sisters were so numerous and came so often that it was a difficult task to remember dates. I am one of eleven of my father's second marriage. He had ten with his first wife. He was a great student of the Bible and believed it was his sacred duty to "be fruitful and multiply." He was a grand man, devoted to his family and doing all in his power to provide for them. He was a highly cultured man, an artist by profession, painting miniatures, when he lived in England. He came to America in 1834, I believe, on account of the illness of his first wife. He found painting not a very profitable occupation in this country, and he abandoned it a short time after his first wife passed on. About five years later, he went back to England and married my mother, then returned to America with her and settled in New York. They were blessed with six sons and five daughters.

My mother was a good, gentle-hearted woman who gave up everything to bring up her family with the modest income she had to contend with. Her family was one of the finest Portuguese extraction. She spent the early years of her life in Lisbon and the Azores, and could speak the language fluently. Judith Barent Cohen, the wife of the great Jewish philanthropist Moses Montefiore, was a relative. My mother's family was connected with the old Spanish Jews who were driven out of Spain to Morocco. One of her aunts was stolen by the Moors and was never heard of after.

My parents went from New York to Philadelphia, leaving there about 1854 for Cincinnati. Railroad transportation was then in its infancy, and most of the traveling was done by canal or stage[coach]. It took days instead of hours to get to any destination of considerable distance. We went to Harrisburg, Pennsylvania, by canal boat, then to Pittsburgh, and from there to Cincinnati by boat. I have no remembrance of anything important transpiring during the trip, as I was only three years old (the baby of the family at that time).

On our arrival at Cincinnati, the family located on Pearl Street. My father started a lead-pencil factory, that being the occupation of his father in England. There was no such factory in America, but it was difficult to get equipment, and he had to make them by hand, which was a slow process. Even so, he managed to make a good livelihood for the family. Things went on for several years without anything worthy of note as far as I was concerned. I started to school at six years of age.

When I was ten, the [Civil] war broke out, and great excitement prevailed throughout the land. Cincinnati being one of the principal points for transportation of troops to the South, one could hear drums and fifes night and day, soldiers coming in from all parts of the state. The market house was used for feeding thousands of soldiers. Women of every age and nationality were in readiness at their stations helping to feed the weary soldiers as they came in. My brother Moses and I—he could play the fife, and I the drum

Cincinnati

From *Rambles in the Path of the Steam Horse*, by Eli Bowen (1855)

—played at the recruiting office after school, and we did make some noise and got recruits. My brother Isaac was at Indianapolis at the time, at a large demonstration in favor of the war at which Sam Bernstein, who later became my uncle, being my wife's uncle, made an eloquent patriotic appeal for all young men to enlist. Isaac enlisted, joined the 100th Indiana, and served his time honorably in the great conflict.

I was still at school, but when school was out I was anxious to help the cause and told my mother I thought I could make some money by selling pies to the soldiers. She made some for me, but I am unable to tell of what material they were made. Suffice it to say none of my customers ordered a second pie, there being no dentist near enough for them to take the chance. I went over the pontoon bridge every day and was challenged by the guards, who wanted the password, and I didn't have it. After I showed them my pies, they laughed and let me go on. I sold out every trip, and I think my mother improved on the pies or lots of the soldiers had better teeth. I turned all my money in, which came very acceptably at the time, as all business was at a standstill and money was scarce everywhere.

Well, school was out, and I had nothing to do but watch soldiers come in and out. I had a hankering to make a little money. The pie deal got me started. One of my schoolmates was a fresh lad by the name of Jack. His father and mother were English Jews and none of the choicest, but moneymakers. One morning I saw him with a basket of matches in the market house. He was yelling his wares at the top of his voice. He called me and wanted to know why I didn't sell matches. I told him at once I would if I had the chance. After he had disposed of his stock, we went home and he made a proposition that he and I go up the river on the *Magnolia* to Ripley, Ohio, and take a big basket of matches and work our way up. All I would have to invest was a few dollars, and if we sold out, we could have at least ten dollars apiece. After long consultation with my parents, they reluctantly consented to let me go. We were to be gone three days, unless we sold out. After an affectionate farewell of the family and with urgent requests to take care of myself, Jack and I started for the river to board the *Magnolia*. I think we had one dollar between us, and our stock of matches.

We sneaked on with our basket and got behind a lot of trunks on the deck. One of the deckhands saw us and asked us where we were going. We told him Ripley. Then he asked us if we wanted something to eat. We had had our dinner but replied in the affirmative, whereupon he brought us coffee, dried apples, bread, and something else, I forget what. After an hour or so, nearing New Richmond, Ohio, the mate caught sight of us and came up with a very sour face. He asked us where we were going and if we had paid our fare. We answered no. He said we had nerve, and he was going to put us off at New Richmond. I spoke up and asked him if we could work our way to Ripley. Then he asked what we wanted to do at Ripley. "Sell matches," I replied. "Well, boys, if you are that anxious to make money, I'll let you ride, but I want you both to put off that pile of empty peach boxes at Augusta." So we got out of our hiding place, made ourselves comfortable, and viewed the scenery on both sides of the Ohio, which looked beautiful to us. Boats passing often added to our excitement. At last we reached Augusta. The deckhands unloaded the heavy freight and then yelled: "Boys, get busy with those boxes." We started in, one box at a time down the gangplank between the men, until we had them all on the Kentucky side of the river. After that, we were deck passengers and mixed with the deckhands at perfect ease.

In a few hours we were in sight of Ripley. It was almost dark when we landed. We bid our companions good-bye, took our basket, and walked up the levee until we reached a small German hotel. A little old corpulent German woman was behind the bar, for every grocery and tavern in those days had a bar attached to it. She had a good-natured face and a sympathetic voice. She addressed us and wanted to know if we had had supper. I told her we would like to eat and sleep if it was cheap enough. She asked what we were selling. I told her that it was vacation in our school and we lived in Cincinnati; we thought we could make a little money selling matches, and our parents were satisfied for us to be away from home for a few days. She looked at us smilingly and said, "You can eat and sleep, and you don't need money. I need matches." The bargain was struck immediately. It took very little time to wash in the tin basin, and in a few moments we were at the table. I hesitated at the ham, but my appetite got the better of my religion, and I cleaned up. It didn't make any difference to Jack. He was a Jew without religion and would eat anything in sight. After supper we walked out to see the boats ply up and down. There was one in sight all the time. Nearly all travel was by water as railroad transportation was limited.

We retired to a small but comfortable room and slept in a feather bed. We were up early, and after greetings by the landlady and her husband, we ate a good breakfast and paid the good woman our bill in matches. We started out and agreed the first to sell out was to help the other. I beat Jack, and as I was cleaned out by ten o'clock, I sold part of his. The first house I came to, the lady came to the door and asked what I wanted. I told her my business. She smiled and

asked me to come in, which I did. They were eating breakfast and asked me if I had had mine. I told them I had. They
questioned me about myself, and when I told them it was
vacation and I wanted to make a little money, they were
very kind and made me eat again. They bought more
matches than they could use in a year, and seemed pleased
and told me if I ever came again to be sure and come to
their house.

I met Jack at the hotel, not a match left, and we could
have sold double the amount. We went down to the wharf
and waited for a boat going down. Several passed, and we
waited probably four hours before one landed. I know we
got on, but forget any of the circumstances connected with
the return trip. All I know is we arrived in Cincinnati on the
morning of the third day. My parents were delighted to see
me back. I emptied my pockets which were filled with
[paper] "shin plasters" (money was called by that name in
those days). Denominations were 5, 10, 25, and 50 cents,
no silver in sight. I think I was between eight and ten dollars
to the good. I was about thirteen years old at this time.

Keep the Change

I had another associate who used to meet me at the
Plum Street Temple every Saturday morning. We always
went to temple, rain or shine. This boy's name was Simmonds. His older brother was treasurer of Pike's Opera
House, the most magnificent theater in the country. One
Saturday afternoon I met my friend by appointment in front
of the opera house. He promised to take me in to hear the
opera. The Famous Grand Opera Company had a six weeks'
engagement there. Some of the greatest singers of the day
were connected with that company. Opera on a grand scale

Courtesy of the American Jewish Archives, Hebrew Union College–
Jewish Institute of Religion, Cincinnati

Isaac M. Wise (Plum Street) Temple, Cincinnati (1888);
also shown, Robinson's Opera House, Unitarian Church

was new in Cincinnati. Maurice Grau was the only impresario of importance in the country. Then later Max Marezek came with a wonderful company.

Simmonds met me at the appointed time. He called on his brother, who passed us both in. The sight was dazzling. My first time in Pike's! A beautiful large chandelier in the center with a thousand jets burning looked like fairyland to my inexperienced eyes. In a few moments the large orchestra opened, the curtain rose to the first act of Bellini's *Norma,* with Pasquale Brignoli, tenor, Susini, bass, Mme. Loreni, soprano, and Mme. Marinsi, contralto, four of the greatest artists of the time. I got the fever right there and then after the opera.

We were just going out when Simmonds, the treasurer, asked my friend, his brother, if he could get a boy to parade a goat around the streets, as they were to produce Giacomo Meyerbeer's *Dinorah* the following Monday and the animal was one of the cast. It wore a red coat covered with trimmings of gold and the word DINORAH in conspicuous letters on each side of the cloth.

Simmonds asked me if I wanted the job, and I immediately replied yes. I thought that doing this might lead to my further connection with the opera. The property man told me in which streets to exploit the goat, and to come to the box office for my pay when the job was finished. I started down Fourth Street with the goat, and it was a terrible job to keep it on the sidewalks. Crowds of boys followed me and threw stones at it. No matter—I went on. The goat got unruly at times, but I put in two hours of it with the sweat pouring down my face. I finally reached the stage door and turned it over to the property man, and went to the box office for my pay, which was, I believe, twenty-five cents. I asked the man if he had anything more for me to do. He

Pike's Opera House

Interior of Pike's Opera House

said, "Do you think you could sell opera books and librettos?" I replied I could. He told me to be at the opera house on Monday night.

This did not interfere with my school work. I was eager to get into the game and could scarcely wait for Monday night. I was there an hour before the time. There was one man in charge of the boys. I told him Mr. Simmonds had sent me. The opera was *Dinorah*. He gave me twenty-five librettos and said I could have five cents for each book I sold at twenty-five cents but not to charge any more. He gave me my section of the dress circle.

I started in at 7:30 and sold out. I got twenty-five more and sold them before the curtain rose. A great many of the people gave me tips. One officer had two ladies in one of the boxes. He bought two and gave me a two-dollar bill. I was feeling in my pocket for the change rather slowly when one of the ladies said: "Keep the change." I bowed and thanked her. That occurred several times during the season, and I would make as much as six or eight dollars a night.

After the opera I would go home and empty my pockets of the scrip, to the surprise of the family. Once in awhile I would go into a restaurant before going home, for an oyster stew or a sandwich, but most of the money would go where it could be used to better advantage. I got used to the work and had my regular customers. I heard all the fine old operas and the best singers; among some I remember were Brignoli, Susini, Amodico, Stefani, Karl Formes, Joseph Herman, Lotti Masalini, Morrelli, Ettore Barili (who was Adelina Patti's teacher), [Filippo?] Coletti, Theo. Habelmann, Mme. Loreno, Angelini Cordici, Anna Caroline de La Grange, Mme. Maurice Strakosch, Morensi, the best contralto of the time, and several more I cannot recall to mind, all great artists. The operas given were *Norma, La*

Sonnambula, I Puritani, Un Ballo in Maschera, Don Juan, Il Trovatore, Martha, Robert le Diable, Sicilian Vespers, Don Pasquale, Faust, Dinorah, Ernani, Lucrezia Borgia, La Juive, Der Freischütz, and *Alessandro Stradella.*

After a few weeks in the service, I was often called behind the stage. After the second act, there were no books sold, so my time was my own. One very hot night I was sent for. I found the famous bass, Karl Formes, was extremely thirsty. He was singing Marcel in *The Huguenots.* He wanted someone to get him a jug of cold beer. I was directed to his room. "Boy," he said, "take this pitcher, go up to Fidler's saloon (about one block away) and have it filled with beer, and come back as quick as you can." He gave me a two-dollar bill. I made a beeline for my destination and returned in a few minutes with the jug filled. He took it from my hand hurriedly. In a short time the jug was half finished. I handed him the change, and he said to never mind, it was worth it. Then he passed it to one of the ladies. The jug was emptied before the bell rang for the third act. He was one of the greatest basses that ever lived and an excellent actor. I met him in California years later when I was studying with Mulder. He still had a wonderful voice, especially his lower tones, but was not always sure of his pitch. However, he made a great hit there.

After the opera season I was lost, as my six weeks' experience gave me a taste for the profession in some form or other. I knew I had a voice, but I was too young and it had not yet undergone the change. I left school, and my parents were anxious for me to learn a trade. We had an old friend who visited us occasionally, by the name of Len Benjamin. He was a cigar maker and suggested I learn the trade. I was satisfied, and my father made arrangements with Mr. William Renau, who kept a cigar store on Third

Street. I was to remain three years, the first year at $1.25 a week, the second $2, and the third I don't remember, as I never served my time out. I started stripping tobacco and in a few months was at the bench making cigars that were salable. Before my first year was up, I was making two hundred cigars a day, all for $1.25 a week and no thanks.

I had a job part of the time evenings at Wood's Theater selling bouquets and renting opera glasses. I made quite a little at that and gave it all to the family. I would occasionally carry one of the actors' baskets from the hotel to the theater. The stars would change their wardrobes for each play and had a basket made for the purpose of carrying their clothes. Among the actors whom I remember were John E. Owens and Joseph Proctor. The great ones that I heard were Joseph Jefferson, J. Wilkes Booth, Edwin Booth, Maggie Mitchell, June Coombes, Barney Williams, Emma Waller, Charlotte Cushman, J. S. Clark, John Ellsler, E. L. Davenport, J. H. Hackett, J. S. Chanfran, J. S. Coldook [*sic*—Charles Walter Couldock?], Mrs. G. H. Gilbert, Laura Keene, E. H. Sothern the elder, Lawrence Barrett, John Adams, Lotta Crabtree, and Effie Ellsler. All these celebrated artists played engagements at Wood's Theater during the season.

A star played from one to two weeks' engagement, changing bills almost every night with the exception of a few. Maggie Mitchell played "Fanchon" in *The Cricket* for two weeks. Couldock played *Chimney Corner* a week. Billy Florence played *Colleen Bawn* a week, but most of the other stars played a different bill every night. The poor actor had to study all the time, and stock companies were poorly paid. These good old-timers worked hard, rehearsed every day, and studied new parts two or three times a week on a very small salary. Admission was from fifteen to fifty cents. I still remember the names of these old players who are long since forgotten with the exception of a very few. Most of them were middle-aged at that time.

I Did Not Worry

When the season closed, I had nothing to think about but my trade. I was working steady and improving. I made up my mind to ask for a raise, so I spoke up to Mr. Renau, my boss, and told him I was making two hundred cigars a day, and even if I had agreed to work for $1.25 a week, he ought to give me more. He said a contract was a contract and would do nothing. I expected it, so when I went home I told my father that I was going to quit and leave Cincinnati and go where Mr. Renau could not find me. My father did not think it the right thing to do, but I insisted and would not go back. My brother Isaac was in Indianapolis with the Mosslers, who at that time were in the clothing business. They were relatives, and I decided to go there. My parents knew I would be looked after, so I packed my grip, which was extremely light, and started on my journey.

My father paid my fare and gave me one dollar. He knew Isaac would see that I had all I wanted until I could help myself. Isaac met me at the train and took me to the Mosslers. They seemed glad to see me. Rachel was a good, generous soul and wanted me to remain with them. I told her I would until I got a job, as I would rather be on my own hook. The day after my arrival I walked down Washington Street, looking for cigar stores. I found one in a little while on Pennsylvania Street, walked in, and asked for the boss. A large man behind the counter informed me he was the proprietor and asked me what I wanted. I replied: "A job." He said he did not need a stripper. I told him I was a cigar maker. He laughed and asked me where I had served my time. I told him my story and all about my apprenticeship. He said: "I need a man, and if you can do the work, boy, all right. Go back in the shop and let me see what you can do."

So in a few minutes I had my jacket off and was at the bench. The men laughed and thought me a joke, but after I made the first cigar, they looked at each other and said no more. Andy Sharp, the boss, said I could go to work at once and was glad to get me. The following Monday I went to work at eleven dollars per thousand. My work was satisfactory, and I made twelve dollars the first week. I could have made more, but I did not want to make the men jealous. I sent all my money home except what I needed for board and clothes. I boarded next door to the shop at Mrs. Reed's. They treated me well, the only objection being that the food was not kosher, which worried my parents.

The first letter from home informed me my old boss was out looking for me and offering inducements if I would come back. There being 115 miles between us, I did not worry. I got along fine for several months and became very proficient at my work. My brothers, Michael and Mandel, lived in Chicago. I was anxious to see more of the world and so left for Chicago. Arriving there, I stopped at the Massasort House, opposite the Old Illinois Central Depot, which was then at the foot of Randolph Street.

In the morning I paid my bill and started to walk to the North Side to take the streetcar for Michael's house, which was at 500 North Wells Street. While walking over the bridge, strange to say, I met Michael, who hailed me, and after the usual greetings we took the streetcar for his home. I met all his family, and in a few days I was ready to look for work. I had no trouble in finding employment. The first job I had was at Falk's, where I worked about four weeks and changed again. I was then living at brother Mandel's on Division Street.

A few months later my parents moved to Chicago. This was sometime during 1866, and I was about sixteen years old. They located at 281 Division Street, a few blocks from Mandel's. In a few weeks they were settled, and I then boarded at home. Business became stagnant in the city, and I had an opportunity to get work in Peoria. Two cigar makers who worked with me persuaded me to go with them. My parents would have preferred that I remain at home, but as they did not object seriously, I went down to Peoria.

We arrived there at 7 A.M. and went to see Mr. Burton, the man who advertised for cigar makers. He was a little Polish Jew and had stolen a Scotch name. I asked him who the proprietor was. He said: "Dat's me," with a Yiddish accent. I then said that we had come in answer to his advertisement for men and were ready to go to work; we had just arrived from Chicago. "You are good cigar makers?" he remarked. "You will be able to judge that when you see our work," we replied. We started in that day. I found a boardinghouse at $3.50 a week, board and lodging. Everything was put on the table at once, and everyone grabbed. At the same time there was plenty of food, such as it was—but no napkins or finger bowls. I had had very little experience with boardinghouses and imagined this was a fair sample for the price and the class of boarders, who were mostly laborers.

We slept two in a bed, and there were two beds in a room. The ventilation was very bad and the bugs galore. I stuck it out for a week and then tried another, which was somewhat better and cleaner. We came down one morning to work and to our surprise were out of a job. If I remember correctly, the revenue collector had Burton for trying to sell cigars packed in old boxes, which was against the law. He said he was in trouble and we had to go.

Most of my last week's money I had sent home, but I had a few dollars after paying my board. A young man from Montreal, who had worked with me, by the name of Sam Kochinthal, had about five dollars and wanted to divide. I told him it would be better for us to go to La Salle or Ottawa, Illinois, and try to get a job. We took the train for La Salle in the afternoon. We had our satchels and went to a boardinghouse. The lady assigned us to a room on the third floor. We washed and then went out to look for work, but in vain. We had our supper and went to bed.

Our money was almost gone. I thought of a scheme. The bed in our room was one of those old-fashioned trundle beds with a rope bottom. In about two hours we had enough rope to let our satchels down in the back yard. I went downstairs and waited for my friend to let the satchels down. As no one was up, I took the satchels and made my escape to the canal. He followed me, and we walked about a mile before we caught up with a canal boat. At the locks they let us on, and we went as far as Ottawa, arriving there at four in the afternoon.

We walked to the business section of the city. Seeing a wooden Indian in front of a cigar store, we went in and applied for work. The proprietor was a small Hebrew by the name of Meyer, who was very good-natured. He gave us a job at once, which relieved our anxiety. He invited us home to supper. We cleaned up and felt very comfortable. We had located a good hotel and spent Sunday looking about the town. We went to work Monday. I remained in Ottawa about six weeks, going back to Chicago for the holidays. We found the name of the woman in La Salle whom we had deserted without paying for our room and sent her seventy-five cents apiece. I was glad to be at home again and to see the folks, and they were glad to see me too. I related my experiences. My friend Sam went back to Montreal, and I have heard from him only once since that time.

I started to work in Chicago for Ben Oppenheimer, then a young man. This was the beginning of a lifelong friendship with this noble fellow. In all my years of experience, I have never met a nobler man. Thoughtful, kind, he would go any length to serve one whom he liked. He has proved this on many occasions, especially at one time when I was confronted with a strike in my own factory years later. I did not remain with him long, as he moved to St. Joseph, Missouri. I went to Kankakee and worked for Weinreb and Alpiner. I remained there about three months. My sister Dinah lived there at the time.

I went back to Chicago and was employed by Levi Solomon, who gave me charge of the business. My brother Sol learned his trade there at this time. Mr. Solomon insisted on my living with his family, and so I accepted his proposition, but I paid a regular amount to him each week. This lasted about six months. I had no idea I was old enough to go in business for myself. Mr. Solomon encouraged me, so did Mr. Rothschild, his brother-in-law, who came to his house each week. He was in the wholesale tobacco business and an excellent man. I told him of my plans and he said: "Go ahead! I'll give you all the tobacco you want on credit, and you can pay when you are able." He advised me to go to South Bend the following week. I went, but could not find a location except one-half of a clothing store owned by the Kahn Brothers. We made arrangements about the rent, and in a week or so I was comfortably located in South Bend, working all the time. My goods were easy to sell, and as I had no room for any more men, I thought I would sell out my retail store and get some room upstairs and manufacture cigars for the trade.

The Marble Pillar

While looking for a location I met a man on the street who told me they had just received word that Chicago was on fire. The news soon spread, and every hour it got worse. By evening one could plainly see the reflection at South Bend, a distance of eighty-five miles. I was anxious about my family and in the morning started for Chicago. The sight on entering the city was beyond description. Railroad tracks bent like rainbows, ruins, ruins for miles was all one could see. I went to the West Side and called on some of my old friends to find what they knew of my family. There was no trace of them for three days. At last I found them. They had slept on the prairie the night of the fire and had lost everything with the exception of some relics my mother carried with her. My father had passed away in March of the same year, 1871. The fire was in October.

The family was separated for some time. I insisted on them coming to South Bend and living with me until Chicago was partially rebuilt; so they came, and I rented a comfortable house. They lived there about three months, but had a hankering for Chicago and had to get back home. So they left and got located somewhere on the North Side.

I remained a few months longer and then sold out. I was doing well enough, but thought Chicago would be better after the fire. Mr. Solomon owned a place on West Randolph Street. I went to him for advice and he told me

Chicago in flames

From *Harper's Weekly*; courtesy of the Free Library of Philadelphia he wanted to go into the railroad ticket-scalping business and would sell his place to me. We came to terms, and the following week I was in business for myself. Business was good, as so many people had burnt out on the North and South Sides. The West Side was overpopulated, and all retail business flourished. I had a good friend and customer who came to my place every day. He was a prominent lawyer, Ennis by name. He would remain for hours of an evening talking. He told me of a building one of his clients was putting up ten doors from Hooley's Theater on Randolph Street; it was going to be occupied by a Mr. Michaelson as a sample room (that was a genteel name for a saloon), and he would rent the front part for a cigar stand. He thought he could get it for me. That part of the city was being built up rapidly, and the proposition looked good. In a few weeks we had the matter settled, and I took a year's lease. It was a beautiful place called the "Marble Pillar." Business started up immense in the sample room. All the patrons of Hooley's would come in to quench their thirst between acts, and cigarettes were in demand, so I got my share of trade.

As the place was a sort of rendezvous for the professional people, I became acquainted with the actors. They all smoked and drank, and Hooley became a good friend. Bartley Campbell, the playwright, was another. At that time there was a famous bass singer by the name of Frank Lombard. He had a national reputation as a campaign singer and was a piano tuner by profession. He also frequented the "Marble Pillar." One day he was feeling good and asked me whether I sang. I said yes. I was singing in the temple on the North Side at that time. "Do you know 'Lombard Watch'?" "Yes," said I. "Well, let's try it!" I hesitated at first, but a bunch of actors, Mr. Hooley included, and all feeling good, told me to go ahead. John Dillen, the celebrated actor, was another in the party. So we started. We sang the two verses, and they were all surprised. Frank Lombard took me by the hand and said: "Young fellow, you've got them all beat on 'Lombard Watch.' " I felt quite proud at such a compliment from so famous a bass. He was a brother of the celebrated Jules Lombard of the Italian opera. He would come over every day or so and we would sing.

John Dillen took a liking to me and wanted me to take the part of the baron in the farce *Jennie Lind* at his benefit. I gladly accepted. Phyllis Glover took the part of Jennie Lind. She was a soubrette and a wonderful singer for an actress. They gave me several rehearsals until I was perfect in the part and ready to go on. My folks came to Hooley's the night of the performance to hear me. I made up my mind I would do my best. The house was packed, as John Dillen was a great favorite with everyone. I got a fine ovation from my friends. Phyllis Glover, John Dillen, and Hooley complimented me and said my voice was fresh and clear and I acted like an old-timer. A few weeks later a gentleman named Sharp who used to frequent the "Marble Pillar" and who was stage manager at McVicker's asked me if I thought I could learn a small Shakespearean part that required singing. I told him I could. They were to produce *As You Like It* with Adelaide Neilson, the great English star, as Rosalind, and wanted someone with a voice to play Amiens. No one in the stock company was available, so I got the chance, knowing Sharp. James O'Neil, a very young man and a handsome fellow, was Orlando. I studied my part and was ready at the rehearsal. It ran for a week. Sharp was well pleased, and I was complimented for my singing by the star and company.

My lease on the cigar store had almost expired, and the proprietor refused me a new one on any terms, as he thought I was making a little money. I tried my best to induce him to give me another year, but to no purpose. He wanted to have it himself. At the expiration of the lease, I invoiced, and he paid me for my stock on hand. I looked around for several weeks, but not finding anything suitable I made up my mind to go to California. I had three sisters living in San Francisco at that time, Sarah, Caroline, and Millie. I was anxious to see them. I had a trade and a voice, and I could use either or both in a pinch to make a living. So I made all arrangements for leaving.

A Form Arrayed in Beauty Rare

My brother Moses, of blessed memory—a better-hearted fellow never lived—went with me to the depot to see me off. It was a very interesting trip over the Union Pacific, which had been only a few years in operation. Beyond Omaha, the country was a vast wilderness, only here and there a town. One could see antelope occasionally at a distance; Indians all the way from Grand Island, Nebraska, to the Rockies. There was an Indian uprising at Rawlins, Wyoming, at the time I speak of, and several people were massacred near there, but the Indians never attacked a train. All kinds of rumors were afloat concerning this disturbance. You could see thousands of cattle all along from the Platte to Cheyenne, Wyoming, and then the Great Desert until you reached Ogden, Utah. It was refreshing to view the beautiful scenery for about one hundred miles through Echo and Webber canyons. After we passed the Great Salt Lake, there was only desert for one thousand miles until we reached Reno, then beauty all the way

Over the Rockies

through the Sierras and Coast Range. It was all very surprising to me, as I had never seen anything so magnificent, and it was all new to me.

We arrived at Oakland on time. My sisters Sarah and Millie met me, and we took the regular boat to San Francisco and were at Sarah's house by evening. A great meal was prepared for my reception, and the whole family congregated to hear all the news from home. I was kept busy until midnight, and they had me sing. Lillie Mish, Sarah's daughter, who was quite an artist and talented, accompanied me. They seemed to think I could sing a little. In a few days I looked around to see what was best for me to do. Sarah asked me if I would like to go in the millinery business. They had a wholesale business and could use me. I was not sure I would like it and did not accept the offer, as I had other plans. I saw a few cigar makers and was offered a good job at Gordon and Burk's. I did not want to depend on my relatives, so I concluded to go to work for a while and save money to get vocal instruction.

I had a chance to sing at a temperance meeting at Dashaway Hall. Lillie played my accompaniment and I sang "If Thou Could'st Know." I was encored and complimented by the master of ceremonies, who begged me to come and sing again. All the cigar makers who worked with me came out and applauded to a finish. On the following Monday morning they celebrated my success in the next-door saloon and told me I was a fool to make cigars with such a voice. They were a good lot.

I called on a vocal teacher named Morley, an Italian opera singer who was stranded in 'Frisco. He had been singing on and off when he was needed. He had a fine voice and knew how to teach. He began at the beginning with me and encouraged me very much. He said I possessed a genuine lyric tenor and had a great future if I would be careful and work hard. His price was three dollars a lesson, but he gave me mine for two dollars. I got along fine with him, but he did not let me sing in public. I needed money and was offered an engagement with a local prima donna by the name of Fannie Marston. She had a wonderful voice, not highly cultivated, but she pleased the people. So I gave Morley notice that I was going to leave town and would come to him on my return. Then I signed up with the Marston Company and rehearsed several duets with Miss Marston.

We opened in Vallejo. I made a hit from the start. My songs seemed to take, and my duets were encored everywhere. I made the tour with her and was successful everywhere but at Sacramento. The critic there did not like me. A singer himself, he said I had a good voice but did not know how to sing and some other things that I cannot remember at present. I never forgot that notice, as I had thought I was making a hit, for I was encored and got my share of applause. Every other paper gave me a fine notice whenever we appeared. We went back to San Francisco, and that ended my engagement with the Marston Company. The manager thanked me and told me to be in readiness, as they would need me the following season.

I remained in the city and went back to my trade for a while, as things were dull. I lived with my sister Millie and had a fine home. In a short time I secured an engagement in the [Jewish] temple and sang every Friday night and Saturday morning. I got along all right and liked the work. I had several other minor engagements that made me a little money.

I happened to sing at the Bush Street Opera House for some benefit, I don't know what. Richard Mulder, director of the Mulder-Fabbri Opera Company and a celebrated vocal instructor, heard me and asked who I was. Later I was introduced to him, and he asked me to call at his house. "You have a voice," he said. I went at the time appointed. He asked all about me and said he could make an artist of me. I told him I did not object. He tried my voice and called Mme. Fabbri to hear me. She smiled and spoke to him in German, part of which I understood. The substance was that I would do for the part of Tamino in *The Magic Flute.* Their pupils were to produce it, but they had no tenor. I found out I was right. He promised to give me lessons free if I would sing the part, and I assented.

In a few days we went to work in earnest. He gave me a lesson almost every day. I began studying the part. I was never a good reader and had to work hard. I was fortunate in being acquainted with a young lady, a niece of my brother-in-law's, who was an excellent pianist. She gave me an hour or two a day, and I finally got the part committed to memory and was ready for rehearsals. I was still working at my trade and making enough to keep me. We began rehearsals, and Mulder was surprised that I knew all the music.

The balance of the cast was excellent; all young, fresh voices. The "Pamina" was Miss Ivy Wandesford, a handsome blond with a beautiful, light soprano voice, well trained. She was perfectly fitted for the part in looks and acting. We rehearsed the duet and trio until we satisfied our director. The "Sarastro" was Cornelius Makin, a printer by trade. He possessed a wonderful voice, powerful and of excellent quality. He was a large man, dignified and well adapted for the stately role of "Sarastro." Mme. Babcock was the Queen of the Night, a part originally sung by Ilma De Murska in London, England. Mozart wrote the part for his sister-in-law, who possessed a remarkably high soprano. Several times it reaches high F, which must be sung staccato. Mme. Babcock was adequate for the task. Her voice was sweet, and she sang with great ease.

The other parts were all exceptionally good, and the chorus of sixty was fine. The orchestra numbered sixty also. The stage settings and decorations were elegant. Nothing was left for the management to do that was not accomplished to make the event a success. The musical world was anxiously waiting to hear the first production by amateurs of this famous opera. Mulder-Fabbri's reputation was of the highest among the Californians. They knew he would not put anything on unless it was acceptable.

After continuous rehearsing for six weeks, the date was set, and the box sheets opened. The house for both nights was sold out. The musical people from far and near were anxious to hear Mozart's celebrated opera. Well, the event was at hand. I had a friend make me up for the part of the Egyptian prince. I weighed about 135 pounds, wore my black mustache, and looked the part.

After the overture the curtain rose, and I rushed on and sang my first recitative: "Oh, aid me! Oh, aid me! For great is the danger; with a huge serpent after me." When three of the fairies came to my aid, after their trio, they presented me with the picture of Pamina with instructions where to find her. Then came my test, the first great air, "A form arrayed in beauty rare." I felt confident in a moment or so and sang with ease. I received a splendid ovation, and Mulder shouted "Bravo" from the orchestra. When I came off from my first scene, Mme. Fabbri and the company shook me by the hand and said I was splendid. My heart swelled, and as I had more to do I felt confidence.

Well, to make it short, the opera was a grand success.

Every one of the cast surprised the audience. The press was lavish with its praise. I received some very fine notices from *The Chronicle, Call, Journal, Golden Era,* and the German papers. The opera was repeated with the same success. My sister and family were proud of my success. Every cigar maker in San Francisco attended, and I celebrated with them later on. Mulder had me study other operas, among them *Lucrezia Borgia.*

The Driver Was a Character

The season was closed, and I appeared in only three or four concerts after this. Ilma De Murska, the famous prima donna, and company came from the East to give a series of concerts in California. Her company consisted of Gaetano Braga, the celebrated violoncellist; Emil Sauret, violinist; and his wife, Mme. Carreno Sauret, pianist. They had a wonderful success and were to go to Australia after the California engagement, but some difficulty arose between the manager, Mr. De Vivo, and Sauret and his wife. So the company split up, De Murska and company going to Australia, the Saurets remaining on the Coast.

They intended to tour the state. I was recommended as tenor by Oscar Weil, a prominent violinist of San Francisco. He called on me and asked me if I would like an engagement for two months to tour the Coast. I had nothing to do at the time, and after arrangements were made regarding salary, he made an appointment with me to meet Carreno at the Occidental Hotel. I was there at the appointed time and in a few minutes was introduced to the famous pianist. She was a beautiful woman, very modest and charming. She asked me whether I had brought anything with me to sing. I replied in the affirmative and produced my old standby, "If Thou Could'st Know," and "M'appari." She played for me and smiled when I finished. I had a nice voice, she said, and she would be glad to have me with her company. I was to make all my arrangements with Oscar Weil. They engaged a prima donna named Mme. Valerga, an Italian and a singer of note. She had a wonderful light soprano and sang coloratura parts to perfection. She was not blessed with beauty, but one forgot that when she sang. The accompanist was a very clever musician, a German by the name of Shad. We had a week or so of rehearsal prior to our departure. We were to open in Los Angeles. The only way to get there was by ocean, the railroad being only half completed.

I made all my arrangements, bid the family good-bye and met the party at the wharf. We boarded the boat, an old type; it was not large, but looked comfortable. After a lot of farewells with the rest of the company and their friends, tears and flowers, handkerchiefs waving until the craft was out of sight, in a little while we were steaming through the Golden Gate. The sea was rather rough, and most of the company retired to their cabins. I managed to keep my dinner to myself and amused myself looking at the wide expanse of water, seagulls flying about seeking for anything that might be cast on the water. It was all new to me, my first experience on the ocean. I sat alone watching the waves as they dashed against the bow of the boat. I remained outside on deck and smoked for hours. There was quite a sea on, and very few passengers were to be seen on deck. I went down to the stateroom, remained awhile, but was not satisfied to be confined when there was so much to be seen. We were not out of sight of land at any time.

Supper was announced. I was not very hungry, but I thought I would go through the form of eating. Mr. Shad was there, but the rest of the artists were confined to their rooms. I did not see any of them until the next day, when it was time to disembark at San Pedro, where we took a train for Los Angeles. In an hour or so we were at Los Angeles. It looked like a quaint, old Spanish town; low buildings of ancient architecture reminded one of a foreign city. Still, there was a great deal of bustle and business. The old Angelus Church was on the principal street, and several old houses were walled in with gardens at the back that were not visible. We were located at the Pico House, the best hotel at that time. I had a very comfortable room, and the rest of the company were nicely situated. That evening I met Carreno and Sauret, and we had a pleasant talk. About 10 P.M., we ate a lunch with some fine Bass ale. I found Carreno very interesting and talkative. She told me she had been seasick on the boat and excused herself for not being seen during the trip.

We were to open the following night at the Turner Hall. There was a good sprinkling of high-class Germans who were musical in Los Angeles, and the house was pretty nearly sold out. We were all anxious for the first night and were fortunate in having a good piano. We rehearsed in the morning, and all went well. I practiced my duets with Mme. Valerga, and we worked very well together. We opened the concert with "Back to Our Mountains," from *Trovatore*, and were encored. We then sang "Say Once Again," from *Don Pasquale.* Carreno and Sauret seemed very much pleased. Then the great hit was Sauret. The audience went wild. He responded to ten encores. Carreno had the same success. She played marvelously. Valerga also made a splendid impression. The audience warmed up, and my solo and duets went fine and were encored. Sauret then played his Wieniawski Faust and was recalled at least four times. After the concert we were entertained by the musical people, and the expression of all was that the entertainment was the most artistic and enjoyable event of the season. We gave three more concerts in Los Angeles and were called on to play an engagement at Anaheim, a German settlement and a wine-growing center. We found a delightful, very appreciative audience. They treated us royally after the concert.

We then returned to Los Angeles, giving one more concert. The last Sunday we were there Sauret wanted to take a trip to the ocean, so he engaged a carriage and started out for the day. Our destination was Santa Monica, about sixteen miles, a beautiful ride. The weather was delightful, scenery superb, and one could see mountains at a distance on all sides. The foliage was at its best with radiant coloration that enchanted the eye. We reached the seaside in about three hours, remained there all day, and returned in the evening.

We had several other engagements in southern California. Our next stop was at San Luis Obispo. Bright and early on the following Monday morning, the stage was to leave our hotel. There were only two other passengers besides our company. I got into conversation with the driver, and the thrilling tales he related were amusing. We began to climb up the mountains with six horses going ahead, and one would have thought we would go over the embankment every minute. I never witnessed such scenery. In a few hours we were in the clouds. We could see them beneath us as they rose above us. I cannot describe the grandeur. We were on the side of the mountain on a narrow ledge barely wide enough for the coach, the horses going at a rapid gait. I was afraid to look down as it must have been two thousand feet. The driver laughed and said about five years ago a stage had gone down right up there ahead of us and all had dropped to the bottom. They never knew what happened. I was not feeling very comfortable about that time. When we reached the summit, the road was much wider on the descent. This driver was a character, but he knew his business. We changed horses at the foot of the mountain and ate dinner.

We arrived at San Luis Obispo in the evening, and the concert was not till the next day. The town was not billed very well, so I took the job in my hands and got acquainted with several prominent citizens who helped to get a good attendance. To our surprise the house was filled to capacity. Carreno told me I would make a good manager. The concert was, as usual, a great success. The audience applauded all the numbers to the limit.

Next morning we took the stage to Santa Barbara. It was a wonderful experience. Carreno took a place on top of the stage, and the driver sat between us. We told minstrel jokes and sang "Nigger songs," to the amusement of the driver. She was full of fun and enjoyed being on top of the stage. We would watch the ground squirrels run in front of the stage—there were thousands of them, the ground was covered with these pests for miles, especially on the low ground. After stopping two or three times to change horses and eat, we neared Santa Barbara. The road part of the way was along the coast and gave a most beautiful view of the high rocks with the waves washing against them. The road was close, and we had a fine view of the ocean. The sun sinking as we moved along and the reflection on the sky and water made a beautiful picture. It was dark when we reached Santa Barbara. We drove to the hotel and were assigned to our rooms. I cleaned up, went to the bar, and partook of a glass of native wine. Sauret and the accompanist joined me. After dinner I took in the town, a beautiful little place. We gave our concert the next evening with our usual success, Sauret and Carreno getting a wonderful ovation with every number. The vocal numbers were also well received, and we responded to several encores. We had the usual reception after the concert and left Santa Barbara the next day. We made a host of friends there and were earnestly requested to come again.

Our next stop was Ventura, a splendid ride partly along the coast. Nothing unusual occurred between Santa Barbara and Ventura; only Carreno and I rode as usual on the outside seat and sang for the driver, who had a grin on his face and said he wished he had us every trip. Of course we felt flattered. At last we arrived at Ventura. Our concert was to take place the next evening. There was a nice little opera house, and it was pretty nearly sold out before we arrived, as concerts of that character with such great artists as Sauret and Carreno very rarely came to places of that size.

We opened as usual with our duets and retired to our dressing rooms, when all of a sudden I heard a crash. The curtain was down. There came a tirade in French. The beautiful Carreno looked like a demon; her eyes bulged and the adjectives in French rolled out in lightning fashion, all hurled at the meek little Sauret. All excited, the other artists came up wondering what had caused the explosion when, behold, on the stage floor lay the remnants of a $10,000 Stradivarius. In a short time all was serene. The cause was this: They had been playing a duet for piano and violin, one of the principal numbers on the program. Sauret insisted on beating time with his foot during the performance. When it was over, she remarked to him that she was artist enough to play in time without his assistance. His French temper got the best of him, and he smashed that famous violin on the stage floor, leaving the precious pieces of a wonderful instrument made two hundred years before scattered about in every direction, in a strange land, thousands of miles from the home of its creation. After the concert, we were taken to the hotel in a conveyance. Carreno seemed much distressed and retired to her room. I saw them the next morning at breakfast. They did not speak to each other, and I had to be the go-between. We left the same day for Santa Cruz and played several towns—Watsonville, Gilray, San Jose. The two stars became reconciled, and the performances went on as usual. We did not play to such good houses in the above-mentioned places as we did in the others.

I Don't Know the Name of That Song

After six weeks we returned to San Francisco. While in 'Frisco, I was offered an engagement in the Bush Street Opera House, to begin a month later. I informed Carreno of the offer and asked her if they needed my services any longer. She replied they would like me to go with them to Virginia City, Nevada, for a week's engagement and after that their season would terminate. That just suited me, as I would be back in time to open at the Bush Street Opera House. We made arrangements for the trip but had no soprano. Valerga could not go. Carreno had a good voice but did not use it professionally. She agreed, however, to sing the duets with me, and I was surprised she had not made more use of her voice. I found out later that it was her intention to appear in opera on her return to Europe. I could not understand that, as she was considered the most brilliant woman pianist in the country. We were short of a prima donna, so I was pleased to have her sing with me, as I knew she would make good.

We started out Monday morning and after an all-day

and all-night trip arrived at Carson City, changed cars, and went up the long incline about five thousand feet up until we reached Virginia City, the famous mining center, a quaint, picturesque city with irregular streets, some almost perpendicular grades which were difficult to ascend. Every other building was a saloon or concert hall. All the riff-raff from all over the continent seemed to be in this ephemeral city. Gambling houses were licensed. Every saloon and hotel had a faro game or a roulette wheel with no restrictions. These resorts were open night and day, and very little attention was paid when a shot was heard. Scarcely a day passed without something of this sort happening. Thousands of miners were working night and day. The Consolidated Virginia, Ophir, Big Bonanza, California Imperial, Gould and Curry, and several other large mines were located here, and millions in bullion were taken out of these mines every month.

We located at the principal hotel, which was excellent for a place so far from civilization. The office was on one side, and the roulette wheel and faro bank on the other. People were lined up to these games night and day. Everyone played and thought nothing of it. I looked on and saw the stack of twenty-dollar gold pieces the first night I was there. I had a little money with me and bought ten dollars' worth of chips—which lasted me about five minutes. I wanted revenge, so I went to Sauret's room and borrowed twenty dollars more. This was about 11 P.M. I struck a bit of luck and won about $175. I went to bed feeling rich, but could not sleep. I tossed about in bed and imagined I had quit too soon, so I got up, dressed, and returned to the game. This was about 3 A.M. I bought a stack of chips, then another, and at 5:30 I was broke. A man who was playing next to me at the wheel asked me to breakfast. They are good, rough sort of fellows and will always help out when you are broke. I had enough for that day and was sorry I hadn't remained in bed.

Piper's Opera House was a large, rough building with a good, large stage. We had some trouble getting a good piano, and I remember it cost twenty dollars to move it. The house was sold out for both nights. It was remarkable there were so many music-loving people in a place so remote. I changed my song the first night and sang "The Cruiskeen Lawn." I never sang before a more appreciative audience. Carreno did remarkably in our duets. She herself felt proud of her efforts. We were encored and repeated the "Allegro." My song made a big hit, and I sang a funny one for encore and was recalled. Sauret was encored time after time. He seemed to be at his best. The audience was warm, and that made the difference to us all. We had a great many callers after the concert at the hotel, and the press gave us some excellent notices.

After Sauret and Carreno had retired, I thought I would go over to a German saloon called the "Friedrich Burgher." I had been there the same day for lunch. I sat down at a table and ordered a sandwich and a glass of beer. While I was eating, a large man with a red face and a slouch hat came up to me and said: "Say, didn't I hear you sing tonight at the theater?" I said: "Yes, if you were there, perhaps you did." "Well," he said, "I don't know the name of that song you sang, but I liked it. I would like to hear it again." I remarked that I did not sing in saloons. "Well," said he, "you will sing it in this one, and right now!" When I protested he pulled out a six-shooter. I said: "Never mind that, I'll sing," and started "The Cruiskeen Lawn," without trying the pitch. I never sang it with so much emotion before in my life. When I finished, he said: "Good. Everyone take a drink with me." And the place was full. He said he had meant no harm, only wanted to hear the song again. The barkeeper said I did the right thing, as the man had a bad reputation in Virginia City; he got anything he wanted, but was not a bad fellow at that. I did not stay long after that as I was afraid the fellow might take a notion that he wanted more singing.

We gave our second concert with the same success, then left there for Carson City, where we had a splendid house. This ended my experience with these celebrated artists. Carreno was a charming woman, always in good humor. She had a great love for her first teacher, Louis Moreau Gottschalk, and would often play his "Last Hope" for an encore. She spoke Spanish, French, and German, as well as English, and was familiar with other tongues; and she did not always talk shop. They were bound for New York, and I for 'Frisco. With a few farewell greetings, I thanked them for the great pleasure and experience they had given me. I boarded my train for San Francisco the following day and on my arrival was fondly greeted by my sister Millie and her family.

A few days later I reported to the Bush Opera House. The company, organized with James A. Herne as manager, was to open with a musical extravaganza entitled *The Fair One with Golden Locks.* The cast was Marion Singer, William Crane, Thomas Whiffen, Mrs. Thomas Whiffen, [David?] Kennedy, David Belasco, and myself. There were several vaudeville acts introduced and a large chorus. Belasco and I had our dressing room together, and we became great friends. He always showed a genius for dramatic details and effects. His parents lived in 'Frisco, and many a pleasant evening I spent at his home after the performance. Mr. Edward Ellis, then drama critic for *The Chronicle,* was one of our party. Dave's father was a fine whistler, and he gave us a few selections whenever we assembled at his home.

Herne saw there was something more than ordinary in Belasco, and they frequently got together for the purpose of writing plays. I found out Belasco's ability when one Sunday he invited me to go with him as he was to direct an amateur company for a play to be given by some club. He displayed wonderful ability, and I was astonished to see how easy it was for him to make these inexperienced people act. (I am not surprised but pleased to know that he has become the foremost playwright of modern times and has acquired an immense fortune. But with all this marvelous success he is the same David Belasco he was in the old days. I felt grateful and proud on receiving his photo and letter a few months ago [in 1920]. He remembered the olden times and assured me he was anxious to see me and would be happy to talk about the bygone days whenever I came to New York, which I hope to do soon.)

William Crane made a hit with the Californians. He had come out with Hooley's stock company to play *The Two Orphans.* The company returned east, but Crane remained to play at the Bush Street Opera House. A funny incident occurred one night. Crane, Marion Singer, and I were singing the trio from *Attila,* when all at once we heard a hiss. We were astonished and looked at one another, but kept on singing. It got worse, and the audience looked at one another to see who was doing the hissing. We retired from the stage disgusted when, to our surprise, the stage manager told us the gas pipe had burst and the gas was escaping. Crane said he thought the trio was doing fine until the hissing began—then he hadn't known what to think!

We played several other light burlesques and comic operas during the season. Herne proved to be a very efficient stage manager and a splendid actor. His first wife was Lucille Western, a gifted actress who starred several years in Ellen Wood's *East Lynne.* His second marriage was to her sister, Helen Western, an actress of a different type. *Jack Sheppard* and *The French Spy* are two pieces of her repertoire, I remember. Herne separated from Belasco later on and starred all through the East in a play of his own, *Shore Acres,* which made him a fortune.

The Ghost Did Not Walk

Our season closed, and I made up my mind to go east and see my people, as I had spent about two years in California and had had varied experiences, from grand opera to minstrels. Things were very quiet everywhere in the profession, and it was difficult to get any engagement that was profitable. I had a little money, and my brother Lewis wanted to go east also; so we made the necessary arrangements, bought second-class tickets, bade all the folks goodbye, and wended our way eastward.

After we left Reno, trouble began. Snowbound for three days, we bought out everything the stores had near there and with great difficulty kept from freezing. There was no sleeper or dining car on this train, and we divided our rations with one another and made the best of it. Finally a snowplow and engine came along and pulled us out. We were off again, but no headway did we make for hours. At last we reached the summit, and then it was not difficult to descend, as the track was clear. We were about twelve days on the trip without much comfort, but with lots of experience. My brother Lewis sang all the way and made no complaint. We arrived at Chicago in the afternoon and immediately went to see my mother and sisters, who were delighted to see us both. In a few days it seemed natural to be back, and I was ready for work at anything where I could make a living. There was nothing doing in the theater profession then, so I got a job at my old trade and worked for several weeks.

One day I met Hooley on the street. I hailed him and he seemed pleased to see me. He asked what I was doing. I replied that I was working at my trade. He said he was organizing a minstrel company and would engage me if I desired. I went to his office, met his manager, and was engaged as ballad singer and to act in any of the farces I was cast in. It was one of the strongest companies ever organized in the West. Hooley never did anything by halves. A week's rehearsal and everything was ready for the opening at the Olympic Theater on Clark Street. For several weeks business was excellent, but it dwindled down as the weather got warmer. The management concluded to go to other large cities and make week stands. We opened in Cincinnati and played to good business for a week. My brother Morton resided there. I called on him and asked him and his family to the show. After the performance, he invited several of us to his home. We sang and drank his wine and beer until three in the morning. He had all the relations there and felt honored to have the "Nigger" singers—as they were called —there entertaining them.

We left for Louisville and played to bad business. The weather was hot and people would rather be on the streets. The Providence Baseball Club was playing there at the time and were stopping at the same hotel. We found them a jolly lot of fellows. They were champions that season. They were to be at St. Louis at the same time as we were, our dates being the same. After the show, we got together in one of the beer gardens and spent hours singing together. One night a very wealthy distiller asked us to go to his house to serenade his family. He seemed to be the right sort, as he hired a few carriages. Most of our double quartette were there, and we piled in and in a few minutes were at his splendid mansion. It stood back about one hundred feet from the walk. We quietly got in front of the porch and began singing "How Can I Bear to Leave Thee?" The night was very quiet, without a breeze, and I never heard the song sound so well. Our voices were very clear as we had been in the beer garden several hours. This was about 1 A.M. In a few minutes some lights appeared through the windows, then the door opened, and we were invited in. After introductions, refreshments were brought, and we sang, ate, and drank until 4 A.M. The host sent us back to our hotel in carriages, and we did not get up in the morning for rehearsal.

We left Louisville for Evansville, played one night and matinee, then Indianapolis and Milwaukee, where business was bad. The ghost did not walk for several weeks. That means in theatrical language—no payday. Hooley was an honest man, and all his players loved him, so we made up our minds to go the limit with him. So on to St. Louis. We arrived there and were taken to the Laclede Hotel, where we met our ballplayers again. The weather was intensely hot, and the Olympic had no ventilation to speak of. The dressing rooms were close, and there was nothing but a back alley to get any air from. The burnt cork rolled down our faces while [we were] on the stage for the first part. The company that had no equal was playing to seventy-five or a hundred dollars a night. Reason: the heat. Hooley had to disband, leaving the company with six weeks' salary coming. Thank heaven I was not paid for if I had been, I probably would have continued in the profession. Completely out of funds, I was compelled to wear my "first part" pants on the street. I became disgusted with that kind of life and made up my mind to abandon it.

So it was in July 1878 I finally left the profession, playing my last engagement with the famous Hooley Minstrels. The company included such celebrated stars as John Hart, Billy Rice, E. M. Hall, Ed Kane, Little Mac, Primrose West, and Johnson Bruno, the finest ballad singers of that time.

I decided to look for employment in the cigar trade in some small place. I happened to be acquainted with Sam Eppstein, who owned a cigar factory in Champaign, Illinois. I wrote him from Chicago, and in a few weeks I received an answer that he would be glad to employ me at once, which I did. This event proved to be the turning point of my career. The new associations were more congenial to me by far, and in a short time I became acquainted with many of the prominent families through my singing, which I was only doing for my own pleasure. My voice seemed to make an impression on those who heard me, and my services were in demand, as there were very few singers in that town who had had any professional experience.

Engaged for the Campaign

One of my early experiences which I call to mind was trying out my voice in a barroom to ascertain if it would answer as well as money for a glass of beer. I had made the acquaintance of Albert Eisner, a young Hungarian who was employed as salesman at Eichberg's dry goods store, a genial fellow with a light heart and nearly always a flat pocketbook except on payday, at the end of the month. He was always ready for a practical joke. In later years, he was to make a great success in life, to rear a charming family, and to become a foremost citizen of Champaign. I am proud of my lifelong friendship with him.

One sultry night in July, when all places of business except saloons were closed, I met my new acquaintance at the corner. He hailed me and asked if I would like a glass of beer. I immediately replied in the affirmative. We started for Hempel's, at that time the well-known rendezvous on Market Street. The proprietor was a genial good-hearted German of about 300 pounds' weight. He was popularly known as "The Baron." My friend Albert, on taking an inventory of his resources, found they did not quite reach the price of two beers. I looked amazed and told him I was in the same condition. It became hotter every minute, and the perspiration was flowing profusely down our faces. It was too late, however, to weaken. I looked at the door, then at the corpulent host, and told my friend I was going to try singing for the drinks. In we went and called for two glasses of beer.

"Fine hot evening," remarked the host, and handed out two foaming glasses of "Schlitz's best." At that I started singing "Take a Letter to My Mother," and never sang it with more feeling in my life. At the second verse, the tears began to flow down the "Baron's" face, and at the end of the last verse, he was crying and asked in a very sympathetic tone: "Gentlemen, what will you have to drink?" We both cried in unison: "Two more beers!" I sang the song once more during the evening at his request, for he said it made him think of his old mother way off in Germany, and insisted on us being his guests all evening.

During this period, Hempel's was a sort of meeting place for businessmen and politicians. If you wanted a friendly chat with anyone, it was always Hempel's after 8

P.M. In those days a "thirst parlor" of this character was considered quite reputable, and no one was thought less of for frequenting an orderly saloon. At that time, moreover, it was considered quite proper to get political dope at Hempel's. When a presidential campaign was on in those good old-fashioned Republican times, the Glee Club torchlight processions were at the height of their glory. All those talented along oratorical lines did their bit toward bringing about a victory for the party. When Joe Cannon was the candidate for Congress from this district, he chanced to hear me sing at a local meeting and told the committee he thought that kind of singing would make Republican votes and that I should be engaged at once for the campaign. So I was fortunate enough to find three other voices that were just the quality for outdoor singing. Tom Borden, then agent for the American Express Company and also the director of the Presbyterian choir, had a large voice of good quality and became my second tenor. John McPherson, leader of the band and an all-round musician with a powerful baritone, was first bass. Robert Blum, a tuner, was the only other available bass, but he was a Democrat and objected to singing Republican campaign songs. After a great deal of persuasion, he consented to try it out, and after a week or so of singing, you couldn't have driven him out with a cannon. In six weeks he had become the strongest Republican in the bunch, and once he said to me that he was sorry he had ever voted the Democratic ticket.

Early in the campaign, Mr. Lake, chairman of the County Central Committee of Macon County, wired our chairman to send the Glee Club to Decatur for a great mass meeting at the Wigwam. It was to be the banner meeting of the campaign, and the main speaker was to be Benjamin Harrison, then United States senator from Indiana. The place was packed, even the stage. The meeting was called to order by the chairman and he told the audience he took great pleasure in introducing the famous Champaign County Glee Club, the best in the state and one which never failed to make Republican votes.

We opened with "A Thousand Years, My Own Columbia," responding to an encore with "Marching through Georgia," after which we took our seats. Then the chairman arose to introduce Benjamin Harrison, who was taking off his gloves preparatory to addressing the audience. However, the audience kept shouting and clamoring for music —"Glee Club!" To the evident disgust of the senator, we were obliged to sing again, and I gave them "Old Shady." The applause was terrific, and it was at least five minutes before the dignified statesman started to take off his gloves again and finally got the attention of the audience, which he held for two hours. We closed the meeting with several songs and decided by the demonstration we had received that we had made quite a hit. The senator refrained from complimenting us, however. I think he was annoyed at our reception.

We sang through the campaign until the November election, during which time we were associated with some of the most distinguished speakers of the nation, including James G. Blaine, John A. Logan, Ben Butterworth, Joe Cannon, Governor Dick Oglesby, and others. I remember the few meetings we had with John Logan. I admired his personality exceedingly, and he was very appreciative. He would tell the audience that the inspiration in the singing was enough to make any man consent to Republicanism. On one occasion after the meeting, he had me come to his hotel and sing "The Sword of Bunker Hill," which he was very fond of. A grand man was "Black Jack" Logan. Another grand old statesman, the pride of Illinois for years, governor for two terms and also United States senator, was Richard Oglesby. He was blunt, outspoken, and never apologized for any of his utterances. He had a wonderful influence over men; he could say what he wanted, and no one took offense.

I remember one incident which should be recorded, even though it is not in harmony with conditions of the present day. Governor Oglesby was billed to speak at Bement. The Glee Club met him there about noon, and the speech was to take place at 1:30. I was in the parlor of the hotel, and the governor called me, asking if I knew where he could get a drink. I told him we were looking for the same thing, but I found the town was dry. He said: "By God, I've got to have a drink before I speak." I assured him I would see what could be done and tried ten drugstores without result. I almost gave up, when I saw a G. A. R. man with a touch of crimson on his nose and said to myself: "Here's my chance." I approached him, greeted him, and asked if he was going to hear "Old Dick" in the afternoon. "Old Dick! You bet your life! I was under him the best part of the [Civil] war and I love every bone in his body," he quickly answered. I said then that the governor had to speak in the afternoon and was feeling badly and had sent me out to see if I could get him a little stimulant. I had tried all the drugstores, but with no result, and it would be a crime to go back empty-handed. He gave me one look, then said: "You don't have to. Anything I have Old Dick can have. Come with me to my home." I walked a few blocks with him. He offered me his hospitality which I did not refuse and filled a pint bottle and said: "Take this to Comrade Oglesby and tell him Comrade (I forget his name) is delighted to be of service to his old commander." When I got back to the hotel, the governor was delighted with the pint and also with the message from the old soldier. He thanked me for my part in the performance. The meeting went on at the scheduled time, and the governor was at his best. After the meeting the Glee Club entertained while the governor held the usual reception. We drove to Monticello for the evening meeting and then returned to the Twin Cities [Champaign-Urbana].

Rehearsals with Miss Bernstein

I was still working at my trade when not singing. My acquaintances were growing numerous as we appeared in almost every town and schoolhouse in the district. Almost every farmer had heard us at one time or another. And whenever any of them met me they would say: "Nat, when are you going to sing out our way again?" I did not know what way they meant, but told them, sometime before the campaign was ended. One very funny incident occurred while we were traveling with Joe Cannon. But before telling it, I want to say that, of all the men with whom I came in contact the many years of my political life, I never knew one that was equal to Uncle Joe—as they called him. He was absolutely in a class by himself. No one could touch the heart of an audience as he could; kindhearted and generous, he could be approached by anyone. He would pat little children on the head and pick them up. It was natural with him and not done to create an impression. His knowledge of the issues of the day was much greater than that of any other of his colleagues. His constituents loved him and wanted no other man to represent them.

Now to go on with the story. We were traveling in a carriage from Monticello to Bement, and Cannon had just made a three-hour speech on tariff. This was in October. I had heard it since July and knew it as well as he did, so I said: "Joe, you know you left out part of that tariff plank this afternoon." He turned around and looked me in the face and said: "You go to hell and get some new songs!" The laugh was on me.

I remember one evening, many years after. It was Saturday night before election. He always made the last speech at the Soldiers' Home in Danville. He telephoned me asking if I could come over to sing for his last meeting. I told him I would be glad to do so and went over on the car with my son Julius, who was to accompany me. We arrived at Mr. Cannon's home about 6 P.M. He was alone with only the servant in the house. A dinner of bacon and eggs was quickly prepared, and during the meal he told me he could have had the nomination for president without any effort on his part if he had consented to allow the duty to be taken off pulp. Every metropolitan newspaper in the United States would have supported him, but he refused as he was then chairman of the Appropriations Committee and was an absolute protectionist. He refused the highest gift the American people could give for the sake of principle.

After the election of James A. Garfield, I settled down to business, kept on making cigars and singing when the opportunity presented itself. I was now fully satisfied that I would not return to the stage and was anxious to know what the future had in store for me. My friends requested me to give a concert. I thought the matter over and, convinced that it might be well to awaken an interest in a better class of music than is usually given at a country concert, I made all the arrangements and got my performers together. I found I was sadly in need of a soprano with whom I could sing my favorite duet in Italian. I had sung this several times on the Coast with Mme. Valerga and other artists of note at that time. Some of my friends told me of a young girl by the name of Addie Bernstein who had a beautiful voice; they thought that with only a little rehearsal she would fill the bill. I was acquainted with her father and so asked his consent to allow her to take part in my concert, which he readily gave.

My arrangements were now completed. My rehearsals with Miss Bernstein—who, by the way, has been my wife for forty years—were a success. Her voice was clear and of splendid quality and, moreover, she possessed keen musical intelligence. She mastered the difficult duet in a few rehearsals. We probably had more rehearsals than necessary, as something more than Addie's voice attracted me to the Bernstein home. I volunteered to give her vocal instruction, and her progress was rapid. Certain members of the family maintained that the lessons I was giving were noiseless—which I thought a very cruel remark. I blushed a little at the assertion and did not deny there might be ground for it.

Our concert was extensively advertised, and Barrett Hall was selected for the event in the winter of 1878. The night of the concert was at hand, the hall was packed. Each number was greeted with clamorous applause. The fourth number was the long looked for duet by Nat Cohen and Miss Bernstein. We received a magnificent ovation and were compelled to repeat the whole duet. Miss Bernstein's voice astonished the audience with its purity and strength. After the concert, congratulations came from every direction, and one old lady was heard to remark: "I'll bet that makes a match." The receipts were more than I had anticipated, and I was thankful to the good people of Champaign for their splendid appreciation of my humble efforts.

I kept up my work making cigars and worked overtime to get a start. I had made up my mind to settle down and see what could be done with energy and perseverance. Mose Epstein owned a cigar store in Urbana. He was tired of it and wanted something more lucrative. He was not a practical man and depended on his brother for supplies. They made me an offer—I think about eight hundred dollars (it was worth about four hundred dollars), but I wanted to go into business for myself. So we bargained, they giving me one year to pay with interest—I think I had three hundred dollars to spare. I was in the habit of sending money to my parents each week and was grateful for being able to do so. I started out and went to work. The first thing on my mind was to get out of debt and be under obligations to no one. So I worked from five o'clock in the morning until eleven at night and stripped my tobacco after that. I was never in bed until midnight. My task was five hundred cigars each day. Sunday I packed them and Saturday afternoon sold them. My first real customer was Bill Maxwell. Of course the Griggs House took all they could use, as I was living there. Business picked up, and I was compelled to hire a man. I felt so encouraged and my goods met with such success that I kept on putting on men until I had a good-sized factory. I was out of debt and at liberty to buy what I chose. It was easy for me to sell goods in the country for everyone knew me. Most of them had heard me sing during the campaign and were glad to patronize me.

I thought life was not worth living singlehanded. Success meant nothing without someone to share it; so I opened a correspondence with the little girl whom I had sung the duet with. The family had left Champaign a year or so prior, and I thought it about time for her to begin singing lessons again. After continued correspondence, I was encouraged to make the trip to her home in Napoleon, Ohio. I was received very cordially, and after the usual understanding we were engaged and had a happy time with them all. We were married a year later and had a splendid old-fashioned wedding with plenty of eatables and wine. We made our escape on the Wabash, arriving at our home in Urbana on May 21, 1880, at three in the morning.

My business continued to improve, and my place of business became headquarters for the engineers of the then I.B. and W.R.R. All trains stopped in Urbana and changed engines. The engineers were a splendid lot of men, and many a pleasant hour I spent with them when they came in from their runs. I want to relate a little incident to show what kind of hearts these men had. I was in Monticello on business and had a telephone call in which I was informed that my wife had given birth to my second son, Julius. I took the Wabash to Mansfield and just made the connection with the Big Four going east. I lived about one-half mile from the station, and it was raining torrents when we reached Urbana. I asked the engineer if he could slow up when he passed my house and told him the circumstances. He said he would try, and when we reached the spot, the train came to a full stop. I jumped off, and the conductor congratulated me on the new arrival. I always felt under everlasting obligation to these noble fellows who took the responsibility of stopping a mail train out of pure friendship.

No One Came to Work

Politics were commencing to loom up, and I received orders from the County Committee to get my Glee Club together. After rehearsing for several weeks, we were ready for business. Among the prominent speakers that were selected to preach Republicanism was Milt Mathews, one of the finest orators in the state who afterwards became state senator. He had run for Congress against Joe Cannon, but the organization wanted Joe and Milt failed to get the nomination. But he still went on with his silvery tongue, preaching the gospel of the Republican party, as though he never aspired for congressional honors. He could hold his audience better than any speaker in the district, and almost all his speeches were extemporaneous. He was never at a loss for a word. He was state's attorney for two terms and finally landed the state senatorship. There is no telling where he would have stopped had he been blessed with good health. He passed away when he was a little over forty-six years old. His death was a sad blow to this community. He was my neighbor and a dear friend, and did more to help the Republican party in this district than anyone I know of. My Glee Club and I kept on working for the Republican cause until the election. Benjamin Harrison was elected president [in 1888], and the country settled down to its normal condition.

I gave my entire time thereafter to my Urbana business and pushed the Bouquet cigar to about 100,000 a year. I had no one representing me. I did all the work myself on the road most of the time. I had an ambition to own my own factory, so I purchased the lot my present building is on from Mrs. W. H. Smith, who was living here at that time. She was the wife of the original promoter and owner of the I.B. and W., who made his headquarters and home in Urbana. I gave the contract for the building to Martin Kancher. Had three storerooms on the first floor and a second story which I occupied with my factory.

Things went on smoothly until a few agitators working in the factory began to make trouble. As a pretext they

Republican National Convention, 1888

informed the men that I had too many apprentices for the amount of men employed. According to the union bylaws, one apprentice was allowed for every five men. I had six apprentices and twenty-eight men. I had no room for more or would have employed them, and they knew it. All these agitators wanted was trouble. A committee called on me on Saturday afternoon and told me I must employ two more men or let one of the boys go. I told them there was no more room in the factory; it was crowded in its present condition. That was nothing to them, and unless I did one thing or the other, they would strike. I saw how I was being imposed upon. The men who had been with me for years did not want to go. I told them I could not let one of the boys go, as I had promised to teach them the trade.

At four o'clock the committee came in and told me the shop was on strike. I had already prepared tobacco for the coming week which would spoil if not used in a short time but that made no difference to them. Those agitators wanted trouble and came to work for that purpose, so they all went. I thought the old men would return, but they were frightened, as they had been threatened with expulsion from the union. A week passed, but no one came to work. I had orders for thousands of cigars from all parts of the country. I advertised in the Chicago papers for men. Several came, but they were run out of town in a few days by the strikers. I was boycotted. The men went to other unions and told the men not to use my cigars or buy anything of merchants that did, so I was up against it, but made up my mind I would close indefinitely before I would yield.

In about six months I had a few men to work and had a lot of goods made in other factories. I had a dear friend in Chicago who had been very near to our family in years past. He owned a large factory in that city. His name was

Ben Oppenheimer, and if there ever was a prince, he was one. He undertook to manufacture all my brands there, which was a great accommodation. He had a union shop, and union men could not refuse to smoke my cigars. A committee from Urbana went to Chicago and informed the union there that the Oppenheimer shop was furnishing a strike factory in my town with goods. A committee of the Chicago union called on Oppenheimer and informed him that it was against their bylaws for a union shop to sell goods to a factory where the union had a strike on. He dismissed the committee in a hurry and told them he would make goods for whom he pleased and was prepared to stand the consequences. They saw he meant business. In a few months most of my old men returned to work, and my "Bouquet" flourished as of old. It was considered one of the leading brands in central Illinois. The strike was costly and uncalled for, but I weathered through it with the help of my dear old friend Oppenheimer.

About this time, in 1896, everything was ripe for a great political campaign. The Republican party was prepared to contest hard for supremacy. Though the Democrats were in power with Cleveland as president and the Solid South and administration backing him, dissatisfaction was rife in all other parts of the country. Business was panicky, money tight, and labor scarce. There was a general feeling of depression everywhere. The North led in an effort to bring about a decided change in the affairs of the nation. The Democratic Convention in Chicago, after several days' session, nominated William Jennings Bryan, the silver-tongued orator of the Platte, to the surprise of everyone. Prominent among Bryan's followers was William H. Harvey, known as "Coin" Harvey [for his bimetallist tract,

Coin's Financial School, published in 1894]. I had the pleasure of meeting him in Urbana.

At the Republican Convention, William McKinley, then governor of Ohio, was nominated. The whole party was elated at the choice and felt that the right man had been selected to lead the Republican party to victory and to restore once more the confidence of the people. I got busy and rehearsed my Glee Club for the sixteenth year, the eighth campaign. We rehearsed the old songs and learned several new ones which were adapted to the political issues of the day.

Frank Robeson was chairman of the County Central Committee. He had the assistance of Pat Richards, one of the squarest politicians I have ever met, a man of good judgment and a friend who could be depended upon; but the brains of the organization was Judge Francis M. Wright. Nothing was put over without his sanction. His knowledge of the game was supreme. Meetings were thick and fast. The Glee Club was kept busy day and night as there were meetings in different parts of the county, and many speakers were expounding Republican doctrine to thousands of listeners. John Tanner was elected governor. McKinley was elected president by an overwhelming majority. Without much difficulty, the Republican party had swept the country. The people were tired of Democratic mismanagement, and the reaction was tremendous. By degrees business became settled and confidence spread throughout the land. At the inauguration of Governor John Tanner, I sang "Illinois." I think it was the first time I sang that famous song in public, and I made use of it afterwards at different state conventions and other public affairs wherever I was asked to sing.

A Member of the Fish Commission

After all the state officers were installed, I went to Springfield and called on the new state auditor, my friend James H. McCullough, a one-armed war veteran. I received a cordial reception, and Jim asked me if he could do anything for me. I thought a moment and replied in the affirmative. "Well, Nat, what do you want?" "Jim," I said, "you know I've always been a fish crank and give the study of fish a great deal of my leisure time. I should like to be a member of the Fish Commission. The board consists of three members without compensation except for actual expenses. It's a splendid work and to my liking. I would take great interest and give considerable time to the work, as my business is sufficiently established to justify my leaving it. So if you can help me land it, it would please me very much." "Well, Nat, I'll see the governor and see what can be done." I left for home, got busy with my friends, asking them to write to Governor Tanner to endorse my application for fish commissioner. In a few weeks I had things going. There were several applications for this office from all over the state. The river people wanted a man who lived on the river, and two of the candidates had a strong following and were turning heaven and earth to reach the goal. McCullough informed me of this and told me he was doing all he could. He urged me to get as busy as I could and get the Champaign County Committee to endorse me. I went to the chairman and found to my surprise they had someone else for another state job, whom they wanted appointed. Naturally, I could not expect any backing from that source. I thought it very ungrateful of them. After singing for years for the love of the Republican cause, I was not able to get the endorsement from the County Central Committee. I aired my grievance to my old friend Pat Richards. He said:

"You could not depend on the committee. See Judge Wright before it is too late. I just got word from Springfield that there was a large delegation going to see Judge Wright as soon as possible."

The judge was holding court at Monticello. I took the first train in the morning, called on the judge, and told him my trouble. I knew he had a murder trial that would take at least two days more, but he asked me to come to the courthouse at eleven o'clock. This was Thursday. I arrived at the time expected, and the judge had me come up and sit next to him. The courthouse was packed. After three or four witnesses were examined, the judge called the sheriff and, to the surprise of the attorneys and the vast throng, had the sheriff adjourn the court until the following Monday. He called me into the anteroom and said: "I am not going to let those fellows over home get the best of you if I can. I am going over to Springfield on the one o'clock train and see the governor." I was surprised a judge would adjourn court in the middle of an important murder trial to do a friend a favor, but such a man was Frank Wright. His friendship was golden. He never forsook a friend. He remembered any little kindness done him, never asked favors for himself, but always granted them to others, if within his power. To sum this noble character up—you could go to sleep under his wing and know you would wake again.

Judge Wright arrived at Springfield that afternoon and called at once on Governor Tanner. The governor was an old-time friend and asked him in an offhand way: "Frank, what can I do for you?" The judge then said: "John, do you remember some time ago you came to Urbana? You were candidate for state treasurer and called on me. Doc Thompson and I were going in the courthouse. At that time we controlled the politics of Champaign County. You asked me if it would be possible to have Champaign County instruct its delegates for you. It would be a great help, as Champaign County was one of the first on the list alphabetically, and it would give you prestige. I told you then that we intended to go uninstructed to the convention, as we always did. You pleaded that you were an old soldier and so was I. So after consultation with Doc Thompson we concluded to have Champaign County instruct for you. You told me then that if ever I wanted a favor and it was within your power to grant it, you would." "Well, Frank, what do you want?" "Well, Governor, I will call the whole deal square if you will appoint Nat Cohen on the Fish Commission. I just adjourned an unfinished murder case at Monticello to get that job for him." The governor took out his little red book and wrote something, then said: "Frank, your man is appointed. You are just in time, as the delegation will be here tomorrow with a strong pull for a man from Havana." He went on to say: "Tell Cohen not to mention it for a few days." He told the judge he was glad he could pay his debt so easily; he had met Cohen once, and if he could fish as good as he could sing, he would make good. The dear old judge has since passed on—blessed be his memory. He was one in a million!

A week later I received a wire from Springfield to come at once and receive my commission. This was March 18, 1897. I went at once to Springfield upon receipt of the telegram and proceeded to the governor's office, where I received my commission and was introduced to my colleagues, one of whom was S. P. Bartlett, of Quincy, the founder of the Illinois Fish Commission, the U. S. branch of this service. It was fortunate for the new commission to have a man of his experience connected with the board. He was familiar with the work and the governor had him in mind all the time. I felt very grateful to be connected with one who was so well qualified. It made things look brighter, and I knew with a little time the new commission would be quite a valuable acquisition to the new administration. The other member of the board was August Lenke, Chicago coal merchant. A splendid man without any knowledge of the responsibilities that were to be imposed upon him, Lenke was merely a political appointee of Henry Herty, a great friend of the governor. Lenke had helped Herty put things over for the governor, and in gratitude Herty had him appointed on the Fish Commission. He told us all he knew of fish was to eat them. We told him it was not necessary to know anything about the work, as we would do it and he would receive credit with us. He felt better, then said: "Go ahead, boys, and whatever you do, count me in."

I was elected president of the board, and the event was celebrated by a big banquet in Chicago, with Lenke as host. Col. Bartlett and I were to do the work, so we lost no time securing a steamboat, the *Lotus,* a splendid little craft that could accommodate twenty-four people comfortably. The purpose of the boat was to collect fishes from the overflows of the Illinois and Mississippi rivers and distribute them in the depleted rivers and lakes in the state from July until November. A special crew was engaged for this work. When the waters receded sufficiently from the Illinois and Mississippi, the depressions on the land adjacent were filled with fish that could not escape. Our work was to collect these fish for distribution; otherwise they would have perished from heat or climatic conditions. After being collected from these overflows, they would be taken on the boat and placed in receptacles for their safekeeping: tanks with an air aerating device which would keep the fish alive for several days. Our receiving station was at Havana, Illinois, where the fish were taken and assorted. City water was used at a low temperature, which was particularly adapted to "harden" the fish, and transportation distribution would begin in August. Fish would be sent by messengers all over the state upon application to the commission by those who wished them. In this way a great many private ponds were started. Our main work was to place fish in public waters, and we were able to restore the depleted waters, which in a few years I found gave excellent results. The press and public acknowledged this, and I left the board in high repute with the administration.

Boys, This Is Glorious

The *Lotus* was used in the closed season for the enforcement of the law. The social events on the *Lotus* were numerous and varied. Governors, congressmen, senators—in fact, most of the prominent men of Illinois—were entertained on this goodly craft. We entertained the judges of the Supreme Court and their families every June when court adjourned. They remained with us a week and forgot their dignity and acted like a lot of boys. They fished, played games, sang, and never overlooked anything that would amuse them.

I remember the first trip with the judges. It was a stag party and Judges Wright and Harker of the Appellate Court were with us on this trip. We expected our supplies at Meredosia. We left Havana about noon and found that we had nothing in the drinking line but malt marrow. We were to get the other refreshments at Meredosia. We arrived there, but to the disappointment of the court nothing was there. Judge Phillips, a splendid type of manhood who made a record in the Civil War for bravery and was one of the brightest legal minds in the state, said to me: "Commodore, I have got to have a drink. This malt marrow will do for the other judges and children, but not for me." Meredosia was dry at the time, as saloons had been voted out a year before. I knew a few of the old-timers, and the crew was well acquainted with the ex-saloonkeepers; so I told the judge I would see what I could do. I went uptown about 10 P.M. and knocked at the door of an ex-saloon-keeper. He answered, asked my business, but recognized me. I told him Captain Williams was very sick with the cramps and was in danger—he must have some whiskey. He said the town was dry, but Williams was a friend of his, and if I would be mum he would let me have a quart. I told him not to fear; so he went in the cellar and brought up a quart of Hunter and one of Taylor and asked which I wanted. I said I'd take both and let Williams decide. I gave him a five and blessed him, and made a beeline for the boat. The judge and several others were on the watch and saw my arms were not empty. They greeted me as if I were a hero. The malt marrow was discarded, and in a short time sociability was at its height and stories and reminiscences were related until midnight. I was grateful I had the honor of entertaining such a distinguished party.

River trips were numerous during the season. When orders came from headquarters that some party would like a few days on the boat, we were always ready to receive them at Havana. Governor Tanner—a better man and a better governor never lived—wired he wanted the boat for a few days. He wanted to get away from all business and worry and shoot a few ducks. We made preparations and had everything shipshape to receive the governor. We had a conveyance at the station and escorted him to the boat. He looked around and was delighted. He said: "Boys, this is glorious." After we started, we had supper, then sat on deck until dark, and the governor suggested a little game of poker to pass the time. We played penny ante and the governor said he enjoyed it more than a big game. About ten o'clock he was ready to retire, and we showed him to his room. He undressed and, opening his grip, pulled out a pair of pajamas and held them up and said: "Boys, when I lived down in Clay County in my boyhood days I did not have these things. I went to bed in the same shirt I wore all day; but times have changed and I suppose I'll have to wear these. Good night, boys, I am having a good rest and am glad I came." We came back to Havana with the governor in a few days. We fished and hunted and were away from official business and office seekers. He wanted a rest, and we let him have it. He said on leaving that he had never had a more enjoyable visit or a better rest, thanked Col. Bartlett and me, and left on the morning train for Springfield.

Through all of Governor Tanner's administration, we never had any difficulty in getting whatever legislation was necessary in promoting our work. He understood and left everything connected with this department in our charge. I regret I cannot say as much for one of the other governors whom I served under some years later, but in the four years of Charles Deneen's administration we formed a fine organization—our wardens became efficient, the law was being enforced, fewer violations each year were recorded. We regretted that Tanner refused to make the race for governor for a second term. Politics were on in earnest. A vigorous campaign ensued, and the convention at Peoria nominated Richard Yates after a struggle, William Lorimer turning the Chicago delegation in his favor. Most of the other counties wanted to get on the bandwagon, and so Yates was nominated. He was elected in November. In

January he appointed Col. Bartlett and myself, and our names were sent to the Senate for confirmation. William Garst was the third man on our board, a splendid man, a son-in-law of D. Crane, of Chicago. He knew nothing about fish but accepted purely as an honorary position. He entertained us on several occasions at the Union League Club. This poor, unfortunate man lost two children in the Iroquois Theater fire [in 1903]. We wrote a letter of condolence, but never saw much of him after that except when we needed his signature.

We had the boat renovated during the winter. In the spring we invited the governor and his family to take a trip with us on the boat. He thanked us for the invitation and said he would let us know in a few days when he would be able to take a trip. He wired Col. Bartlett to meet him and his party at Meredosia the following Monday. We had all the arrangements made to give the governor and his family a week on the river. The trees bore their spring coat of leaves, and the foliage on both sides of the river was beautiful and refreshing to the eye. We met the party at the station at the appointed time, and escorted them to the boat, the *Illinois.* We took them to St. Louis, remained there a day, then returned to the Illinois River. After four days of a fine spring outing, this party left for Springfield.

Governor Yates was a candidate to succeed himself, but though defeated at the convention by Deneen, wanted to stump the state for the party. He planned to make all towns from La Salle to Grafton and wired Bartlett and me to come to Springfield to get things ready for the trip. The party was to consist of twenty or thirty people, and I was to sing at each meeting. We had an excellent cornet player engaged for the same purpose. We started from Meredosia and had meetings at every landing and town on the river.

We had a great meeting at Beardstown. Charles Dawes, Frank Lowden, and Governor Yates made the speeches. I sang several times. The governor had his regular reception after the meetings and then returned to the boat. It took a week to fill all the engagements. We landed at Havana on Saturday afternoon. The company passed resolutions thanking Col. Bartlett and myself for our kind attention during the trip.

How Do You Like the Scenery?

The next event in my public career worth mentioning was in connection with the Fish Exhibit at the 1904 World's Fair in St. Louis. Mr. William de Chastignier Ravenel, of the Smithsonian Institution at Washington, had formerly been connected with the United States Fish Commission. He had charge of the fish exhibit and asked our cooperation. We were to take charge of the aquarium. We had the facilities for collecting fresh-water fish and were near St. Louis. The legislature made an appropriation for the purpose and allowed us a liberal amount for our expenses. We were to be part of the government exhibit. There were several experienced fish culturists from the aquarium sent from Washington connected with this display. They were all fine fellows, and I became quite intimate with them in the six months I was associated with them. The Fish Exhibit was one of the great attractions of the fair. We had all appliances for the hatching of fish. We received fertilized eggs daily from the different hatcheries for the purpose of giving the public the benefit of observing the art of artificial propagation. Our exhibit was visited by thousands daily. Among the most distinguished visitors were President Roosevelt and his daughter Alice. The President was very keen in taking in every detail. He was familiar with the work and seemed to enjoy his visit with us. Almost every prominent person in the country would be seen there and many prominent foreigners. It seemed that our exhibit was more attractive than any other. Our work went on smoothly until one day the machinery got out of order. The pumps failed to work, and it was impossible to aerate the water in the tanks. Air had to be supplied in the water to keep the fish alive. The receptacles not being large enough to supply oxygen sufficient to keep the fish alive more than an hour or so, it had to be supplied continually artificially by a mechanical device made for that purpose. Well, the machine failed to work for several hours. The fish began to come to the top, and before we could adjust things properly, more than half the fish died. We lost no time. Messengers were sent to all parts of the country as well as Puerto Rico, Cuba, and Jamaica to make collections. In about a month, one would not have known anything out of the ordinary had occurred.

This was a very pleasant six months for me. It gave me an opportunity to meet and cooperate with all the eminent fish culturists of the country, and the knowledge I gained was worth a great deal. When the fair was ready to close, Mr. Conway, one of the best superintendents of the aquariums of the country and the man who had charge of the one at Detroit, attended to the disposal of the fish. They were given to anyone who would take care of them. I have seen Mr. Conway several times since then, and he is still the good-hearted fellow he was when we worked together at the fair. We were presented with medals of honor some months later in acknowledgment of our services. We had plenty of work awaiting us at the close of the fair. We got busy collecting fish from the overflows for distribution.

Applications were piled up during the six months we were at St. Louis. The river was in fine condition for our work, and before the season closed, every application was filled to our great satisfaction. Politics were on again, and Charles Deneen was elected governor with the whole Republican ticket.

The legislature convened in January. The governor presented the names of Col. Bartlett, Henry Klein, and myself for confirmation. We reorganized our board for the third time. Mr. Klein was a wholesale leather dealer from Chicago and quite a politician, but he knew nothing of fish. He seemed to want to take a hand in all that was going on. His main object for going on the board was to have Fox Lake stocked with fish, as he had a summer home there and had made promises to everyone that the lake would be taken care of. So we were compelled to make good. He seemed to be a pleasant man, but kept us busy satisfying the demands of his friends. Affairs went on as usual until spring. The governor was anxious to know about our work, and so we made arrangements to take him on the river. He met us at Havana with his family, in a few minutes boarded the boat, and was off for St. Louis. They were delighted with the boat and river and seemed to appreciate everything. The trip lasted four days, and on leaving for Springfield the governor thanked us for himself and family. Mrs. Deneen told us she was delighted with the trip and never enjoyed herself any better.

One trip I recall involved a party made up of [Chicago] Mayor Fred Busse, Dan Campbell, the postmaster of Chicago, Joe Haas, the Cook County Circuit Court clerk, Adam Wolf, the Cook County treasurer, Chief of Police Shurtleff Peters, Sheriff William Reddick, and Cook County Republican Committee Chairman Judge Willard M.

McEwen. This was one of the liveliest parties we ever had. They were with us three days, and we wished it had been longer. Fred Busse was one of God's noblemen, and everyone who knew him admired him. He never forgot anything. His hand was in his pocket all the time. No one could pay for anything when Fred was in the party. Another trip I will make a record of may be of interest. The party included Congressmen Joe Cannon and William B. McKinley, Fred Smith, of Peoria, Attorney General Howland J. Hamlin, and State Senator Martin Bailey. This party was out for a good time, and they had it. After breakfast, they called for cards and chips. A six-handed game of national reputation called poker was inaugurated; rules of the game: deuces wild. They started in and played till noon, ate dinner rapidly, and requested me to get the table ready again. There was no time for storytelling. They were at it again until suppertime. After eating a sumptuous meal, Cannon said: "Commodore, get the table ready." I said: "How do you like the scenery?" He said: "I haven't seen anything but deuces." They played until 2 A.M. It was amusing to watch the game. They showed such good nature: no matter whether winning or losing they were all jolly and having the time of their lives. I don't know how much was won or lost, but it went up to three figures. But what did these men care? They were all good friends and enjoying themselves. We left them after four days at Peoria. They remembered the crew with a handsome contribution. William Nolden was my mate. He gave them every attention and saw that the supplies were adequate and of the best. Nolden was one boy in a thousand and could always be relied upon. I understand he is now pilot on the *Bald Eagle,* running from St. Louis to Peoria. Our parties came on continually. It seemed that almost every prominent man in the state looked forward to a trip on the *Illinois.* We had three months we could use for that purpose, as we did not begin to make our collections until late fall.

A Nice Little Chat with the President

A deep-waterway project was under way at that time. The object was to dredge the Mississippi and make a twenty-foot channel from Lake Michigan to the Gulf. Several prominent engineers were employed by both Missouri and Illinois to investigate the possibility of this proposition and report to the governors. An appropriation was made by each legislature to cover expenses. Then came a rumpus between Missouri and Illinois. St. Louis claimed that the sewage of Chicago flowed down the drainage canal through the Illinois River, polluted the water in the Mississippi River at St. Louis, and made it unfit for use. Suit was begun by the state of Missouri in the United States Supreme Court to enjoin Chicago from emptying sewage into the drainage canal. The governor ordered us to be in readiness to take aboard the parties he appointed to make the investigation. The object was to take in every town on the river, get all the information from the fishermen relative to the difference in the condition of the river before and after the drainage canal flowed into the Illinois River, and to take all the testimony from all persons, including ourselves, as to the effect on the fish life since the drainage canal changed its course and emptied its contents in the Illinois River.

The personnel of the party included Attorney General Hamlin, Chicago attorney W. Todd, of the Drainage Board, Isham Randolph, Drainage Board engineer, and attorney Cory Johns. There were also two or three other engineers and two more lawyers. They made a thorough investigation in every town and landing on the river, and the evidence seemed mostly in favor of the Illinois side of the case. Col. Bartlett and I were examined, and I think our testimony saved Illinois, as we both testified that since the canal emptied into the Illinois, the volume of fresh water from the lake cleared it to such an extent that the fish were in better condition than previously. The river was three feet higher than before. Temperature was much lower, and in the hot months, July and August, there was an absence of decayed aquatic life and the thousands of dead fish which had created a stench that could readily be noticed whenever passing one of these estuaries or lakes. Changing the course of the river has eliminated all this and, in my opinion, is a great benefit to all concerned. In a few weeks, the case went to the Supreme Court and was decided in favor of Illinois. Justice David J. Brewer said if fish could live in that water, people could drink it.

A short time after this trip, William Lorimer wanted the members of the legislature to inspect the river with a view to having a water measure put through. The governor ordered us to meet the senator at Peoria. We did so. There were about forty in the party and only twenty-four beds to accommodate them. Well, we piled them in anyway. I could not assign the rooms without showing partiality, so it was first come, first served. I gave my room to the senator, which pleased him. After supper they started to play poker. Some went to bed and slept until midnight, when he was routed out and another took his place. So they made this shift. All slept part of the night and played poker the rest of the night. They were a jolly crowd—all members of the legislature. Nolden and I changed watches and managed to get some sleep in the two days. We were in St. Louis when Lorimer was to be the principal speaker at a banquet given in the interest of the deep-waterway. It was one of the finest I ever attended. In opening his speech, Lorimer paid me a fine compliment for the way they were treated on the boat under my supervision. He said I had even given up my bed to him. He made a splendid speech in behalf of his pet project. The committee left St. Louis by train for Springfield or home. Lorimer went to Chicago.

The principal event of the deep-waterway craze of the year was that of President Roosevelt's personal investigation of this mammoth enterprise. He made arrangements to have a party start from St. Louis and go as far as Memphis. About twenty boats were engaged for the grand event—congressmen, governors, senators, prominent men of all walks of life were to make up this demonstration in the interest of the deep-waterway. Our boat, being the fastest on the river, was selected as the pilot boat. St. Louis was in gala array. Flags and banners were floating everywhere in honor of the president. Our boat, with an extra pilot, took the lead at the signal of the harbor master. We glided slowly down the river until the fleet was organized for the trip. Bands were playing on most of the boats, and the air seemed to be full of enthusiasm. As we rode down the old Mississippi, we kept a respectable distance apart all night. One could hear music from the other boats. The sight was beautiful at almost every landing—fireworks and the booming of guns in honor of the president. It was a fairylike carnival, a sight never to be forgotten.

Our first trip was to be at Cairo. All the way down, people were waiting all night to pay tribute to their president, the foremost American of the age. We arrived at Cairo on time. The demonstration was amazing, with bands playing and cannons roaring. Thousands of people were waiting, including the state militia. My son Sidney, then captain of Company M of Champaign, greeted me. The flotilla landed one by one. The president was escorted to the city park by militia, mayor, and council. He spoke for an hour, and after being entertained by the citizens of Cairo he was escorted to the river amid cheers and the waving of flags. You could see by this demonstration how much he was loved by the people. Afterward from the harbor master I gave the signal, and our boat whistled for the start. In a short time the flotilla was on its way. A boat belonging to Cairo took the liberty of going ahead of my boat and racing. The boat had no connection with the flotilla. It was just a piece of nerve: they wanted to show the president how swift they were. This annoyed Mr. Roosevelt, and he had us signal the boat, ordered it out of the procession, made a complaint to the harbor master at Cairo, and had his license taken away. The same demonstrations all along the river each day showed the president's popularity. A tremendous crowd awaited us at Memphis. Every factory, every steamboat let forth all the whistle power it possessed, and then some. The governor of Tennessee and his staff with a military escort met the president at the boat. He was carried to the square and made a speech in the evening at the Wigwam, which was packed. By his reception, one would never imagine there had ever been any trouble between North and South. Another big reception took place after the meeting. The city was illuminated by a splendid display of fireworks. I had a nice little chat with the president at the hotel, after which I made ready to depart. I intended going home by train and so made all arrangements for coal and supplies for the boat to make her trip home. Some of the party went back on the *Illinois.*

They Made Believe They Were Sorry

I arrived home at Urbana the next day and was glad to be with my family again. The cigar business was going along as usual, and my business was established. There was always a demand for my cigars. I could have disposed of a much larger product, but was handicapped by the labor question. It was impossible to get cigar makers to remain in Urbana, the town being dry and most cigar makers not being members of the Prohibition party. Nothing of any consequence occurred in the next two years, but for some reason the friendly feeling that existed with the Fish Board formerly was now on the ebb. I saw this and made up my mind that, unless I could have the whole support of the commission and the governor, I would resign. I was trying my best to have the accounts which were incurred go through my hands before being approved. This the board objected to. I was president, and originally a resolution had been passed, giving me the authority. I spoke to the governor about it and told him I thought I should be upheld. In case anything went wrong, I was the one who would be responsible. All he told me, however, was to settle it among ourselves. That was impossible as there were two against one, and all authority would be taken from me.

Things went on in this way for a year or so, when in October President Taft, who was deeply interested in the deep-water project, was induced to make a trip down the Mississippi, by the promoters of this enterprise. The governor called me by phone and said he would like me to turn the boat over to Engineer Isham Randolph and his family for that trip. This was our season for collecting. We had at least six hundred applications for fish, and we had to use the boat for at least two months, or abandon our work and disappoint our applicants. I made this statement to the governor and told him that the party could get passage from St. Louis to New Orleans for fifty dollars each, on one of the best boats on the river. My appeal was to no purpose. He insisted I should have the boat at St. Louis for the Randolph party at the appointed time. There was nothing for me to do but obey orders or resign. I was not quite ready for that, so I met them and our boat was detailed as pilot on account of our speed. When all was in readiness, the flotilla started, and nothing out of the ordinary occurred until we neared Vicksburg, when we were signaled by a boat which was stuck on a bar. We hastened to the rescue and found the passengers were U. S. senators and congressmen. Senator William J. Stone of Missouri and Governor Ashton C. Shallenberger of Nebraska were in the party. I don't think there was ever a more distinguished lot of statesmen together at one time except in the House or Senate. I took them on our boat, as Governor Shallenberger was to make the opening speech at Vicksburg. We got them a splendid meal, and I sang several songs. Governor Shallenberger looked at me and asked if I lived in Champaign. I said: "I live in Urbana." "Well, well," he said, "I used to go to school there, and I am sure I heard you sing *Pinafore* several times." I told him he was right. We had several hours of real enjoyment and reached Vicksburg at 8 P.M. The party passed a resolution of thanks on leaving the boat. Governor Shallenberger wrote me a fine letter a few weeks later and sent me his picture.

The same evening the boat started down the river. My guests were not very congenial, and I was pleased when we reached New Orleans. Mr. Randolph informed me that the governor had given him charge of the boat, so I left the party at New Orleans. I left orders with my faithful purser, William Nolden, to make a record of the up-trip. I then left on the Illinois Central for home. It took the boat fifteen days to return, too late to make any collections—which made it necessary to disappoint six hundred applicants for fish and put the state to the extra expense of almost two thousand dollars, which was to be deducted from our meager appropriation. I saw the governor a few days after my return and told him what I thought, that I was only a figurehead and president in name only. I had worked hard for fourteen years and had advanced the Fish Commission to a standard that was recognized as one of the best in the country. I had neglected my own business and for twelve of the fourteen years had received no salary, only my actual expenses paid, and I knew there was a conspiracy to shove me out of all the authority I was entitled to as president of the board. I therefore asked him to accept my resignation at once. He refused, told me I was excited, and asked me to call a board meeting. I did so and had the board meet me in Chicago. I explained matters and said I was tired of the whole business, as there was no harmony and my orders were not carried out. I was positively through. It made no difference whether the governor accepted my resignation or not. I refused to serve any longer. They made believe they were sorry and asked me to change my mind, but I said I intended going to Europe to see my sons who were studying there. We parted on friendly terms, and I returned home an ex-president of the Fish Commission with a great weight off my mind.

The result was as I expected. When Governor Deneen was in office a few months, he had an expert investigate the accounts of the commission and called an extra session of the legislature for the investigation. They found money misappropriated and fraudulence, no records of money collected for fines, and total inefficiency. Resignations were demanded at once. I had seen this coming while I was on the board, and I thank God I came out of it with clean hands. My wife and I sailed for Europe a few weeks later to visit our sons, Julius and Sol. We remained with them four months at Budapest and returned with Sol, leaving Julius to continue his studies.

Samuel Rosinger

DEEP IN THE HEART OF TEXAS

When he died in November 1965, a few weeks short of his eighty-eighth birthday, Samuel Rosinger had been a Texan for more than half a century. Eighty at his retirement from the pulpit of Temple Emanuel in Beaumont in 1957, he had been the rabbi of his congregation for forty-seven years. Only Henry Cohen, of Galveston, saw a longer tenure of service in Texas.

Curiously enough, notwithstanding their association with the Reform rabbinate, neither Cohen nor Rosinger was an alumnus of the Hebrew Union College. Each had moved into Reform Judaism from more traditionalist beginnings. Cohen had studied at Jews' College in London; Rosinger had been ordained at the Jewish Theological Seminary of America in New York City.

For decades Samuel Rosinger functioned as a Conservative rabbi. It was only in 1930 that he became a member of the Reform Central Conference of American Rabbis, and until 1947 he continued to maintain a concurrent membership in the Conservative Rabbinical Assembly of America. He is one of the few rabbis to have belonged simultaneously to both groups.

In 1958, under private auspices, Rabbi Rosinger published My Life and My Message, *a hefty volume which included an essay entitled "My Life." I have not used that version of the essay, however. Instead, it is a manuscript version submitted to the Archives by Rabbi Rosinger in the early 1950s which appears here, revised somewhat and annotated.*

❦

I was born on December 21, 1877, in Tibold-darocz, a small Hungarian agricultural village nestling in the foothills of the Carpathian Mountains. My father's name was Moritz and my mother's Hannah. I was named Samuel in memory of my paternal grandfather. I am grateful to him for this name, for the prophet Samuel has been my choice biblical hero, and his supplication, "Speak, O Lord, for Thy servant heareth" [1 Samuel 3:10], has been the motto of my ministry.

Father earned his livelihood from cultivating a small farm and from the commission for selling the villagers' produce. He had to work very hard to provide for his family of eight children. Mother, however, "looked well after the ways of her household" [Proverbs 31:27], and efficiency experts could have taken a lesson or two from her economic management. She sewed, mended, knitted, washed, ironed, cooked and baked, fed chickens, stuffed geese, and milked cows. She was blessed with a sense of scrupulous cleanliness, and our little thatch-roofed cottage was always spick and span. She whitewashed it inside and outside and painted its tamped earthen floor with a solution of black clay, and adorned the center of the living room with a large Star of David enclosed in a scalloped circle. She was the first to rise and the last to blow out the kerosene lamp, even after her five daughters had grown up and relieved her of most of the household drudgery. Mother was a pious soul of sweet disposition who brought up her children with tender kindness and infinite patience, imbuing them with love and reverence for God and training them in the observance of their ancestral faith.

There were twelve to fifteen Jewish families in our town, all of modest means, who kept up a congregation. Their spiritual leader was the *shochet* [ritual slaughterer]. In addition, the congregation had to maintain a teacher to instruct the children in Hebrew and secular subjects, for the public schools in the rural communities were strictly denominational; and considering the meager wages the congregation could afford to pay, the position was usually filled by incompetent amateurs. Therefore my parents decided to send me to the neighboring town of Saly (pronounced "Shy"), where the Jewish school was conducted by a government-licensed teacher. Thus I was not yet ten when I left the paternal roof and set out on the career of a wandering Jew. In this school I made rapid progress and became the favorite student of my teacher. I was a voracious reader, and the teacher supplied me with books from his library that widened the horizon of my knowledge far beyond the school curriculum.

I was going on twelve years when an event took place which determined my future career. There was a family in Saly that had stemmed from a famous rabbi, Chayim K'tzay. This ancestor bequeathed to his children a large library of printed Hebrew books as well as a great number of thick tomes of manuscripts containing his voluminous correspondence with the rabbis of Hungary on an infinite variety of legal and ritual problems. Other volumes dealt with the explanation of knotty talmudic passages and still others with homiletical interpretations of the Bible. I can still see before me the beautiful, pearl-type handwriting running in close parallel lines in glossy ink on the yellow parchment leaves. This forebear also left a good deal of worldly goods for his family, which they invested in a landed estate of considerable size. At the time I entered into the orbit of Chayim K'tzay's progeny, four families shared in the income of the estate.

Now, according to the testament of this learned sire, in each generation one of his male descendants had to be educated in a rabbinical school, and after marriage his task was to settle down in the library and pore over the books so that the study of the Torah would never cease among his offspring. And if there were no male descendant to carry out this will, then a scholar had to be grafted onto the family tree by marriage. One morning such a scholar visited our classroom. He had married a beautiful girl of the K'tzay clan, and after spending a few years in the seclusion of the family library, he decided that he would select a few diligent students from the Jewish school and would teach them advanced Hebrew after school hours. He chose for his experiment three boys recommended by our teacher, and I was one of them. School let out at four o'clock, and the scholar—we called him Reb Zecharyah—arranged with us to be at his library at half past four to settle down to advanced Hebrew studies. He told the local selectees that he had already conferred with their parents and gotten their consent to the arrangement. I told him I was certain that my parents, too, would be satisfied. At the appointed time the trio was at the library, and our new master addressed us thus to my best recollection:

"Boys, you are a holy seed, children of the patriarchs of blessed memory. Of all the nations of the earth, the Lord has chosen our people as the sacred vessel into which to pour His spirit, the Torah, revealed to our fathers at Sinai.

You were present and I was present as well, as the souls of unborn generations, to witness this miracle, and your voice and my voice joined in the unison exclamation, 'All that the Lord has spoken we will do and we will obey' [Exodus 24:7]. To fulfill this vow and to carry out this pledge, we must study the Torah as it has been given us in writing and interpreted by tradition. For the Torah is our life and the length of our days and we must meditate in it day and night [Deuteronomy 30:20; Joshua 1:8].

"Now, even as our people are the chosen of the nations, so you are the chosen of the pupils of the school. Thus you are the chosen of the chosen and, in a manner, are fit, even as the prophet Elisha, to receive a double portion of the divine spirit [2 Kings 2:9, 13–15]. Now, I am willing to pour into you the knowledge I have learned from my teachers and from those great sages and luminaries who have stored up their wisdom in the volumes which crowd this library. But I want you to know, you must take this work seriously. It must be *Torah li-sh'mah,* a study for its own sake, a voluntary effort, a labor of love. Then it will not be a burden to you; on the contrary, it will lift you up, it will give your soul wings. You will not be tethered to this material world, but soar in the realm of the spirit."

And he illustrated to us the elevating power of study by the following parable: "When the Lord created the birds, he did not furnish them with wings. They could hop and run with great speed but could not fly. The beasts of prey took advantage of these weak creatures and wrought havoc among them. Thereupon the birds assembled and prayed: 'Dear Lord, give us a weapon to protect ourselves against the rapacious animals that threaten to destroy us.' The Lord heard their prayer and sent upon the earth a shower of wings. The birds picked up the wings and carried them in their beaks. But instead of being a blessing, it proved a burden to them. Yet, since the wings were a gift from heaven, they pressed them to their hearts as an expression of their thanks. And doing this day by day, the wings grew to their bodies and they soon learned the right use thereof. Similarly, my boys," our master continued, "if you will comply with the commandment 'And these words which I command thee this day shall be upon thy heart' [Deuteronomy 6:6], you will find that the words of the Torah will furnish you with wings and lift you higher than any bird can fly."

The earnestness of our master impressed us very much, and we resolved to study as hard as humanly possible. But, alas, he underrated our ignorance and overestimated our capacity, and the result of our labors was anything but satisfactory. We had no opportunity to rehearse together the lesson he had taught us, and our recitation the next day was a sorry performance. Each of us rememberd some part of the assignment, but none could recall all of it. After weeks of experimentation, our master came to the conclusion that a way had to be found for us to spend the night together so that we could help each other unravel the intricate passages of the Talmud that we could not do individually. And he found the way without any difficulty. The estate had quite a number of small cottages, located in the neighborhood of the school and the synagogue. These three-room dwellings were usually occupied by the peasants who worked on the estate as sharecroppers. One of these cottages happened to be empty, and our master sequestered it for us. It was furnished, and all our parents had to supply was bedding. We liked the idea of being on our own and enjoyed the untrammeled freedom that had come to us.

After my bar mitzvah, our schoolteacher informed Reb

Zecharyah that we three had acquired all the practical secular knowledge that he could teach us; thereupon, our master persuaded our parents that they dedicate us entirely to the study of the Torah under his direction. However, since he could not devote to our instruction more than the forenoon, our parents furnished him the means to engage a *yeshivah bachur,* a student of a rabbinical college, to serve us as a tutor. We were fortunate in securing the invaluable assistance of a saintly young man who knew the tractate of the Talmud we were studying practically by heart, and who had infinite patience with us in repeating without end the lessons assigned to us, until we could recite them to our master's great delight and satisfaction. Our concentrated rabbinical studies continued for an additional two years, when a crushing tragedy put a sad end to it.

My master's young wife contracted the lingering sickness of typhus, and though famed physicians were called into consultation by the local doctor, she failed to respond to their medicine; nor were the tearful prayers with which we, as well as the whole congregation, battered the gates of heaven of any avail. After lingering for many weary weeks, lovely Hannale joined the angels of heaven and left behind a disconsolate husband and a six-year-old girl. With all his faith, all his piety, my master could not become reconciled. He was desolate and prostrate with grief. I was also confused and perplexed. I asked myself: Why did the Creator, who had lavished on Hannale so much beauty, charm, and loveliness, cut her life off in the prime of her youth? A sculptor would not have shattered such a superb statue. A painter would not have destroyed the canvas of such a masterpiece. A gardener would not have uprooted a tree in the full glory of its bloom. Since then, however, I have learned that it is not for us mortals to question, but to accept the dispensations of God. In the words of Job [1:21], "The Lord gave and the Lord hath taken away. Blessed be the name of the Lord."

After the days of mourning were over, our master told us: "Boys, I have passed through a trial and tribulation from which it will take me some time to recover. I will have to devote a good deal of my time to my orphan child and will have to find some means to earn a livelihood, as I want to conserve her share of the income from the estate in its entirety. Therefore, much as I regret it, we will have to part company and sever the pleasant and profitable relationship we have maintained for over three years. You have received sufficient training and absorbed ample knowledge in the Talmud to be advanced and independent students in any of the yeshivas. I hope that you will build upon the foundation I have laid for you a godly life, and that you will ever sanctify and glorify your Father in Heaven!" With tears in his eyes, he shook hands with us, embraced and kissed us, and retired from the library. This was the last time I saw my beloved master in the land of the living. I corresponded with him until the First World War severed mail connections with Hungary. I owe Reb Zecharyah a gratitude which I could never repay, and I will cherish his blessed memory to my dying day. Unfortunately, I was the only one of the trio who continued his studies and became an ordained rabbi. The other two joined their parents in business.

God Showed Me Switzerland

Of the yeshivas where I continued my rabbinical studies, the one that appealed to me most was in Mezo Csat, where the saintly rabbi and renowned scholar Shrage Zevie

Tannenbaum maintained a large college. Next to Reb Zecharyah, he was my most beloved teacher. There are personalities who possess a magnetic power of attraction of which they are as unconscious as Moses was of the radiance of his countenance [Exodus 34:29]. This rabbi, notwithstanding his greatness and though advanced in years, mingled freely with his students. His heart and home were wide open to his disciples who wanted to confer with him. He saw to it that his indigent students received a sufficient stipend to subsist on. Here I settled down to my studies with the old verve and vigor, and at the age of sixteen, the rabbi conferred upon me the signal honor of *chaver,* "associate," as a reward for my diligence. My father, whose Hebrew education was quite limited, was very proud of me when I was called to the Torah with this title prefacing my name.

Let me record here an act of my holy rabbi of Mezo Csat that has become indelibly engraved upon my mind. One night fire broke out in the synagogue, and an old Catholic priest whose *parochia* was nearby was the first to notice the smoke issuing from the building. He alarmed the neighborhood, broke open a window, and at the risk of his life brought to safety the Torah scrolls from the smoke-filled sanctuary. The next day the rabbi, heading a delegation of his congregation, called on the priest and expressed heartfelt thanks for his heroic act in rescuing the most precious religious treasure of the Jewish people.

Shortly thereafter the aged priest took sick. When the rabbi was apprized of it, he ordered psalms recited for his recovery in the house of study as well as in the synagogue. And when the priest passed away, the rabbi told the students: "This venerable priest was one of the saints of the nations of the world. He saved us from the great calamity of having our *sifré torah* [pentateuchal scrolls] consumed by fire. Let us render honor to his memory by attending his funeral in a body." And that funeral was truly catholic, not in the denominational, but in the universal meaning of the word.

After leaving Mezo Csat, I studied in yeshivas located in cities where there were secondary schools that gave me an opportunity to catch up with my secular studies. Then I entered the rabbinical seminary at Budapest, where I studied under Moses Bloch, Wilhelm Bacher, and Ludwig Blau. I remained there but a couple of years, for the wanderlust had seized me and urged me on, even as it had prompted the first wandering Jew: "Get thee out of thy country and go unto the land that I will show thee" [Genesis 12:1]. I am ever grateful to the Lord that Switzerland was the land which He had shown me. Switzerland is not only unexcelled in scenic beauty, but is also a most cultured country and an ideal republic. Mind you, its population is composed of three distinct nationalities, German, French, and Italian. Each speaks the language of its national origin and maintains an autonomous administration of its canton, and yet all three are united in a federation and get along most harmoniously. Even during the First and Second World Wars, when the three countries that border on Switzerland were engaged in a bitter war, Switzerland, instead of being embroiled in their killing contest, devoted her energies to lifesaving. She offered a sanctuary to the thousands upon thousands of refugees who managed to escape from the shambles of the belligerent countries.

In Switzerland I registered at the University of Bern and plunged into the study of philosophy under the brilliant Ludwig Stein. He was an eloquent speaker and had to give his class lectures in the large assembly hall of the university in order to accommodate all the students who were eager to hear him. I also took an intensive course in Bible study. Strangely enough, in the yeshiva the Bible is neglected, notwithstanding that the Talmud is basically an interpretation of the Bible. Again after two years my wanderlust, which now I called "divine discontent," moved me to pick up my tent and settle in Berlin, Germany. At the Kaiser Friedrich Wilhelm University I continued the study of philosophy and German literature. Had anyone foretold at that time, in 1902, what would happen to German Jewry but thirty years later, he would have been considered a fit inmate for an insane asylum. I myself heard Ludwig Geiger, son of Abraham, an assistant professor at the University of Berlin, make the statement in a large assembly: "The German government would be fully justified in canceling the citizenship of any German Jew who is a member of the Zionist Organization." Again my "divine discontent" whispered to me most alluringly: "You have seen enough of old Europe. Why not jump across the ocean and see what is going on in the New World?" And so in the spring of 1904, after receiving the cordial greeting of Lady Liberty on Bedloe's Island, I landed at Ellis Island with a gold coin worth ten dollars in my pocket, representing all my worldly wealth. I was quite proud of myself for entering the land of golden opportunities with a gold piece in my possession.

Space does not allow me to retail the diverse ways in which I managed to subsist during the years of my peregrinations, but the following story will give an inkling of it. Socrates was found one day standing before the show window of one of the most expensive, fashionable stores of Athens, gazing intently at the luxury articles displayed there. Soon a large crowd gathered, wondering what could have attracted the philosopher's attention in the assortment of fineries. Finally, one of the crowd asked him: "Sage, what dost thou intend to buy in this shop?" And the sage answered, "I have no use for any merchandise shown here. My purpose in looking at this display was to find out *without* how many things a person could get along and still be happy."

After my arrival in New York, I stayed with a relative who lived on the East Side and, fortunately, had a large empty cellar where I could escape from the deafening noise of the nearby elevated trains. Even after I had made up my mind to leave for America, my common sense told me to defer the study of English until I would be in a country where it was a living language. Otherwise I would have acquired an accent difficult to get rid of. I recall the shock I experienced when I first laid eyes on *Webster's Unabridged.* I was wondering how I could lay up even a small part of that thick tome in my small brain. Yet, I started the task with a pocket German-English dictionary and grammar, with the help of the three schoolchildren of my relatives whom I taught Hebrew and German; and they in turn not only listened patiently to my reading chapter upon chapter of their history books, but also corrected my mispronunciation. I made enough progress to converse haltingly and understand on the whole the lectures at the Jewish Theological Seminary, which I entered in the fall of 1904. When I first entered the Talmud class, I was astonished to find there a woman student. Upon my inquiry, I was told she was none other than Henrietta Szold, who pursued talmudic studies under the greatest talmudic scholar, Professor Louis Ginzberg.

Of learned women every period of Jewish history offers illustrious examples. The prophetesses and the "wise women" of the Bible, the erudite wives of the talmudic sages, and the daughters of medieval rabbis who lectured to the students of the yeshiva from curtained bay windows, all furnish a telling proof of the futility of the effort of the misogynic Eliezer, the son of Hyrcanus, to confine woman's wisdom to the distaff [Sotah 3:4]. Yet, even in these ultra-modern days, it was certainly a unique experience to behold a Jewess, and an American product at that, attending one of the most abstruse courses which a theological institution can offer young men preparing themselves for the ministry.

Yet had that female theological student been anyone else, I would have regarded her as a freak or faddist whose whim was to excel in a field which, in modern times, no other member of her sex had attempted to enter. But Miss Szold's position as secretary of the Jewish Publication Society and translator of many important Jewish works from German fully accounted for her desire to be equipped with knowledge to penetrate into the original sources of Judaism.

Some years later I was even more surprised at Miss Szold's appearance in wild and woolly Texas than at her attendance at the Jewish Theological Seminary. Scholarship was, after all, her element, and therefore she could afford to venture upon the vast sea of the Talmud. But with her modesty, simplicity, and naturalness, she was not cut out for propaganda work which, especially in this borderland of civilization, required the slapstick methods of a man and not the hysterical temperament of a woman. Yet Miss Szold's Texan tour in 1912, notwithstanding the utter lack of theatricality in her personality and method, was a success of the most enduring kind. The Hadassah chapters she organized in many towns, including Beaumont, have grown from strength to strength and have made vital contributions to the work of healing and redemption to which she dedicated her life.

Princes in Israel

At the seminary, my favorite teachers were Solomon Schechter, Joseph Jacobs, and Israel Friedlaender. Schechter, president of the seminary, usually went off on a tangent which was, as a rule, more interesting than the main line of his lecture. His sudden demise in November 1915 cast a spell of deep-felt sorrow, not only over the American Jewish community, but also over scholarly circles in every part of the globe. For the deceased had the distinction of being not only a great but also a well-known scholar, a combination rarely to be met with in the realm of genuine scholarship. Popularity in the sphere of knowledge is generally bought at the price of profundity. The man of learning who desires to reach the laity is supposed to skim the surface of his subject, and refrain from delving too deep or soaring too high for the average intelligence of his public. Professor Schechter, however, had the rare gift of presenting the most intricate problems of Jewish theology and rabbinic literature in such a lucid and fascinating style that he satisfied scholar and layman alike.

Schechter's scholarship had, moreover, another and a very important aspect. It won not only the admiration of the Jewish world, but also commanded the highest respect of Christian theologians who, at least in the English-speaking countries, obtained the first clear presentation of Judaism from his masterly essays. He contributed more to the true comprehension of the Jew by the outside world than a deluge of popular tracts or Jewish pulpit oratory could ever hope to accomplish. His voice, without being harsh, never assumed an apologetic tone for Jewish concepts and principles. He manfully stood up for traditional Judaism, which, in his admirable exposition, appeared in a new light and revelation.

Even greater, however, than the charm of his style was the magnetic power of his personality. Humility, the touchstone of greatness, was the brightest jewel in the diadem of his character. He possessed not that cultivated humility which leads to conscious self-abjection, but that natural unassumingness which renders the truly great almost childishly insensible of their importance. In speech, habit, and manners he was informality and unconventionality personified. In his relation to the students of the institution which he presided over, he displayed a spirit of camaraderie. They had free access to his study, books, home, and heart. He often encouraged the struggling student by referring to the vicissitudes of his own life as a student when, to quote his own phrase, he had been satisfied with a pair of leaky boots and patched trousers, a crust of bread, and a book.

His influence upon the development of Judaism in America is inestimable. He established Conservative Judaism upon a firm footing, moderating thereby both the radical tendency of Reform and the rigidity of Orthodoxy. By bringing to light the hidden treasures of Judaism, he showed that the Synagogue is rich enough in spiritual resources and need not go begging and borrowing inspiration from the Church. He demonstrated that religious progress cannot proceed along the line of least resistance, that conviction cannot walk hand in hand with convenience, and that rationalism in religion may as much lack rhyme and reason as hysteria. And, on the other hand, he condemned with equal severity the unholy zeal of the Orthodox who desired to transplant the Judaism of the Russian Pale, unmodified and unmitigated, to American soil. He branded as criminal the selfishness of the older generation of immigrants who cared only for their own salvation and who, though idly bewailing it, did not actively prevent the estrangement and defection of their children from Judaism. His Conservatism was not a compromise but a conciliation of conviction with conditions; hence he asked for no change of principle or practice, but of policy and procedure. He was a creative force in Judaism, performing constructive work of the highest caliber, and though death had removed the master builder, his fellow craftsmen and disciples would continue the rearing of that monumental edifice of Judaism, the foundation of which he laid upon the bedrock of tradition.

I mourned in Professor Schechter a teacher and friend to whom I owed not only a goodly part of my education, but also the finding of my bearings in my delicately difficult calling. All those who knew Schechter, either by personal contact or by the touch of his gigantic intellect as it revealed itself in his immortal works, lament his passing in the words of the Scripture: "There is a prince and a great man fallen this day in Israel" [2 Samuel 3:38].

While the genius of Jewish scholarship was still brooding disconsolately over the death of Solomon Schechter, another one of Israel's great sages was called away from the land of the living. Dr. Joseph Jacobs, the polyhistor, the man of whom it can literally be said that "nothing human was foreign to him," joined his illustrious friend in the celestial academy in 1916. The loss his death meant to the literary world in general, and to Jewish scholarship in particular, was eloquently described in the glowing appreciations which his learned associates and friends contributed to [the February 4, 1916, issue of] *The American Hebrew,* of which periodical he had been the distinguished editor.

My relation to Dr. Jacobs was of a most peculiar character. He was my English teacher at a time when I could scarcely battle, or batter, my way through a page of good English prose without the powerful aid of a diamond-type pocket edition of Webster, which I carried with me as religiously as soldiers are reported to have hugged prayer books in World War II. Nothing testifies to his greatness and humility more touchingly than the patience which he, the accomplished master of English style, mustered for the instruction of a class of foreigners in elementary English. He had also been Schechter's English teacher and had come over from England to serve as an English editor of *The Jewish Encyclopedia*. Registrar was his official position with the seminary, yet knowing that future preachers would have to use the English language as their tool, he volunteered to teach a class in English composition and to give students the benefit of his expert knowledge.

Unfortunately, we were too ignorant to realize his greatness, else we would have better appreciated him. The curriculum of our alma mater in conjunction with our university studies was so crowded with sacred and secular subjects that had we theological students had our whole time at our disposal, we would have had work aplenty. Most of us, however, had to subsist on the income derived from tutoring, which compelled us every now and then to infringe upon our studies and absent ourselves from one of the lectures. We usually perpetrated these time thefts against those members of the faculty who were feeble disciplinarians and kept no regular record of absences.

Joseph Jacobs was too good-natured not to be taken advantage of. He was, furthermore, too much of a scholar to be—not a good teacher, for that he was in the best sense of the word—but a stickler of a schoolmaster who is more of a policeman than a pedagogue. Hence his class—which was never large, as the native-born students deemed it below their dignity to attend it—often dwindled down to a diminutive size. Jacobs, either realizing the dire necessity that kept his pupils away from his lectures or not attributing greater merit to an attendance by disciplinary pressure than conceded by the adage "You can lead a horse to water, but you cannot make him drink," never complained of or resented our absences. He was too humble to construe them as a personal insult. He rarely, if ever, referred to his works or achievements as a scholar.

I, either realizing more my ignorance or being actually more ignorant of English than my classmates, very seldom missed his lectures. One afternoon his class consisted of my lone self. Upon entering the room, he looked around in surprise at the great vacancy, then he recited the following lines of the divine Milton so loudly that at their conclusion we both burst forth into a hearty laugh:

> *So spake the seraph Abdiel, faithful found*
> *Among the faithless, faithful only he;*
> *Among innumerable false, unmoved,*
> *Unshaken, unseduced, unterrified,*
> *His loyalty he kept, his love, his zeal.*
> (*Paradise Lost,* Book V)

To my humiliation, be it said, while I understood the allusion, I did not know the source of the quotation, as I then lost my way in works of lesser classicality than *Paradise Lost.*

I owe my Jewish journalistic activity, whatever its worth may be, to Joseph Jacobs. Shortly after graduation, I sent him an article which he received very favorably and published in *The American Hebrew.* I still treasure his letter which encouraged me to future efforts. I have also preserved a few half-baked English compositions with his corrections. The primitive and rudimentary character of these exercises and the painstaking effort which he bestowed upon them are a pathetic proof of his scrupulous conscientiousness in the discharge of his duty.

I could freely turn to him for information throughout my career, being ever certain of his ready response. My last correspondence with him dealt with the elimination of the "Children's Page" from *The American Hebrew*. I deplored the disappearance of the page which—I wrote to him—I myself was enough of a child to enjoy, and which induced children to read a Jewish paper. In his reply, he fully agreed and sympathized with me. However, a newspaper being a business enterprise, in its management sentiment has often to give way to financial considerations.

In [the death of] Schechter, I lost a teacher and guide, but in [that of] Jacobs I lost a benefactor who lavished upon me his vast wealth of wisdom with unstinted generosity. May the bread of knowledge which he cast upon the waters be found after many days in the activity of his numerous disciples who sat at his feet and drank in his words!

As to Israel Friedlaender, I was disconsolate when the press reported his tragic death [at the hands of Ukrainian brigands] in July 1920. Oh, that such a brilliant mind, such an eloquent speaker and such a profound scholar should have fallen victim to ghouls while engaged in the performance of his mission of relief to his destitute brethren in the Ukraine! Schechter and Jacobs had already enriched Jewry and humanity with the bountiful harvest of their scholarship, but Friedlaender had but sown, and his precious life was brutally cut off before he could gather the fruit of his labor. The only answer to such baffling questions that could comfort the heavy-laden heart, I found in the following passage of the *Book of Wisdom*: "But a righteous man, though he die before his time, shall be at rest. For honorable old age is not that which standeth in length of time, nor is its measure given by number of years; but understanding is gray hairs unto men, and an unspotted life is ripe old age. Being found well-pleasing unto God . . . therefore he was translated. . . . Being made perfect, in a little while he fulfilled long years" [Wisdom of Solomon 4:7–10, 13].

The Good Lord Answered My Prayer

In 1908 I received my Master's Degree from Columbia, was ordained, and married Miss Gertrude Kaelter, who, all unknowingly, had no doubt been the cause of my "divine discontent." My first pulpit was Temple Sholom in Toledo, Ohio. Comparatively speaking, it was a new congregation that I took hold of. I was only their second rabbi. The temple had ample facilities for a large religious school, and I succeeded in obtaining faithful religious teachers. I also organized a weekday Hebrew school and a young people's Judean League, and I was "raring" to make the temple hum with religious activities. During the "honeymoon" enthusiasm ran high, attendance was excellent, and the future looked bright, but after a few months I realized that the ardor of the congregation was not a bush which burned without being consumed [Exodus 3:2], but a straw flame which gives a dazzling light, but lasts no time. I was not yet used to empty pews and to a small audience composed of the faithful remnant and the bodyguard of the rabbi. I worked very hard on my sermons. I followed the advice given to our class by our teacher, Joseph Mayor Asher of blessed memory, that we write out and memorize our sermons, for looking in the eyes of our audience instead of at the manuscript, we could impress them so much more with what we had to say. But I had far more empty pews to look at than human eyes, and I smarted very much at the indifference of my congregation.

After two years of unremitting effort, I realized that I could not breathe life into the dry bones of my congregation; therefore, even though the board reelected me unanimously, I resigned my position. That I acted wisely was proved by the dissolution of the congregation just a few years after my departure. Before leaving Toledo, I went into the temple to bid farewell to that institution which witnessed my vain struggles and futile effort and understood my heartaches and disappointments, and before the open ark I poured out the sorrow of my heart in a flood of tears before the Lord.

I had no other position in prospect, but I had three months' time in which to look for one. In those days, smaller congregations secured rabbis by advertising their vacancies in the Anglo-Jewish weeklies. In one of these national weeklies an ad appeared which read, "Rabbi wanted by Congregation Temple Emanuel of Beaumont, Tex. He must be a good mixer. Applicants may be graduates either of the Hebrew Union College or the Jewish Theological Seminary. Salary $1,500." The Anglo-Jewish press poked fun at this ad, advising the congregation to engage a bartender and not a rabbi. I disregarded the colloquialism of the ad and applied for the position. To my great joy, I was invited for a trial sermon with all expenses paid. I shall never forget that trial sermon; it was a trial of the severest kind. To give that sermon, I had to travel over 1,200 miles in August, the hottest month in the South. My train missed connections in New Orleans, and I had to spend the night in the St. Charles Hotel—alas, not in peaceful slumber, but chasing mosquitoes. My room had no screens, but it had a four-poster bed, covered with a veillike material. I thought that this was a colonial-style ornament, and being extremely tired, I removed the canopy covering, hit the pillow, and fell asleep. About midnight I awoke to the tune of a dissonant symphony emanating from a swarm of "skeeters" stinging my body and sucking my blood. Then I realized the purpose of the netting, but I could not readjust it to shut out the nefarious pests.

According to the train schedule, I was supposed to arrive at my destination Friday morning. Now, here was Friday morning, and I had before me a dusty all-day ride in a day coach on a train that stopped at every flag station. It finally lumbered into the station at Beaumont an hour and a half late. I was met at the depot by the president and treasurer of the congregation. They took me to a nearby hotel to brush up and whisked me to the temple. The sleepless night, the humid heat, and the long travel exhausted what I thought was my last ounce of energy, and if my exterior showed my limpness and languor, I must have cut a sorry figure when I ascended the pulpit. Before starting divine service, I am in the habit of turning to the ark and offering the supplication, "Heavenly Father, open the gates of heaven to our prayer." On this occasion I added the fervent prayer, "and give Thy faint servant strength to endure this trial." And the Good Lord answered my prayer. As soon as I started to read the service, I became oblivious to my fatigue and delivered my sermon with assurance and conviction in my voice. Sabbath morning I spoke to the women in a lighter vein, and Sunday I was elected for a term of two years. In thanking the board for their confidence in me, I gave them to understand right then that they were engaging not a lackey, but a leader whose specialty was religion. And Judaism is not a petrified creed, but a way of life; its interpretation and application must be left to the rabbi's judgment. Such a situation presupposes a free pulpit.

I am happy to say that my congregation has accepted this condition and has lived up to it. I can express my convictions without fear that I might step on somebody's toes. Whether my people agree with me or not, they know that I walk in the light of truth as it has been given me to see it. To make the pulpit free not only to myself, but also to the congregation, at the end of my first two years I told the board: "We need no formal contract, but let this verbal agreement be binding upon us. If I want to leave you, I will give you six months' notice; if you want to get rid of me, do likewise." This loose agreement has kept us together in peace and harmony for forty years. At the celebration of that anniversary, the congregation bestowed on me a lifetime tenure.

After I had moved and settled down in this oil town, I inquired of the chairman of the committee to secure a rabbi whether he had received many applications. And he showed me quite a batch, some from men who had much longer experience, others with doctors' degrees. And I asked him, "What made you decide to invite me?" And he answered, "I liked your beautiful handwriting."

Very Much Alive

About a quarter of a century ago, a well-known Jewish writer gave a lecture in my community. And he asked me: "What heinous sin have you committed that in expiation you have buried yourself in this hole?" I told him that, far from being buried, I was very much alive. We had in Texas a very active *kallah* [scholarly group], for the annual meeting of which I had prepared a paper ever since its organization. I was an editorial writer for *The Texas Jewish Herald* for many years. Throughout my ministry, I have been intimately associated with movements of social uplift and civic betterment of our city. I have served as president of the local chapter of the Red Cross, of the Jefferson County Tuberculosis Association, of the Municipal Hospital, of the Rotary Club, of the Beaumont High School Parent-Teachers Association, and other humanitarian institutions.

As the fruit of my labors in the social-service field, let me mention the Jefferson County Tuberculosis Hospital, which I was instrumental in establishing both for white as well as colored patients. It has restored to health hundreds upon hundreds of industrial workers who contracted this contagious disease in the great oil refineries of which our town is the center. I was the chairman of the board of this institution for twenty years.

When my congregation was ready to build a new temple, I persuaded the board to engage Albert S. Gottlieb, an expert on synagogue architecture, who designed for us not a functional freak, but a house of worship, every feature of which represents the chief characteristics of our faith: solemnity, dignity, grandeur, and, withal, simplicity and clarity. Its six large art windows depicting the prophets of Israel are the work of Zeev Raban, of the Bezalel School of Jerusalem, and are peerless products of revived Jewish art.

When celebrating my fortieth anniversary, my congregation presented me with a trip to Israel. This visit to the Holy Land represented my life dream. When I was introduced to David Ben-Gurion, I told him: "When I came to my congregation, they were anti-Zionists, but I converted them to Zionism, and they rewarded my effort with a trip to Israel." And the brilliant prime minister answered:

"Rabbi, you have done a commendable work, but that was only the beginning of the task incumbent upon you. When you return home, you have to convert them to be Israelis."

I remember the paper a Reform colleague read before the Central Conference of American Rabbis in 1908. It was entitled "The Rabbi's Problems in Smaller Communities,"* and his introductory sentence was: "The first and foremost problem of a rabbi in a small congregation is how to get out of it." I am grateful to the Lord for having cast my lot in a small community where I could enter into an intimate relationship with my congregation and serve them as teacher, guide, counselor, and comforter. Now I am bringing up the third generation, and I love them and they love me as do my own grandchildren. I am at the sunset of my life, and one cannot see anywhere a more gorgeous, breath-taking sunset than one sees on the prairies of Texas. Once, while I was watching this wondrous pageantry, I wove this allegory upon the loom of my imagination: Flowers depend for their growth and coloring on the sunshine. From morning to evening the sun pours its golden rays upon them all along its circuit. Now before the sun finishes his day's work, the flowers of the field and forest, mountains and valleys all want to offer him a parting gift in gratitude for the blessing he has bestowed upon them. The rose offers the color red, the daisy yellow, the violet blue, the marigold gold, the morning glory purple, and other flowers every color of the spectrum. And the sun takes these gifts and paints with this riot of color the western horizon.

So also my spiritual children upon whom I invoked God's blessing at their birth and in whose hearts I implanted the precious seeds of Judaism, confirming them in

*See *Central Conference of American Rabbis Year Book*, XVIII (1908), 50–51.

the tenets of our holy faith, and uniting them in the holy bond of marriage—they offer me the gift of their love and appreciation in the form of personal service to the institution through which I dedicated my life to them. My spiritual children serve on the board, they are the teachers in my religious school, they form my volunteer choir that sings not only with their art, but also with their heart. I have received, not only from my congregation but from my whole community, so many kindnesses and courtesies and honors that I would have to live twice as long as my allotted span to reciprocate even a fraction of them. I praise God daily for having placed me in a position in which I could serve Him by serving my congregation and my community.

The Rav-*ess*

A spiritual daughter of mine with a penchant for verbal coinage felt the need in the English idiom for a word corresponding to the Yiddish *rebbitsin* [rabbi's wife]. Going back to the Hebrew root of the word rabbi, she minted the brief and euphonious Hebrew-English hybrid "*rav*-ess."

My *rav*-ess is not that self-effacing type of a spouse who would use her life as oil with which to lubricate the machinery of her husband's religious organization. Nor is she that submissive spirit who would encourage the sisters of the congregation to consider her as a community servant. Independence is bred in her bones. She is her husband's partner and not his echo or shadow. She chooses her friends according to her predilection. She assumes the kind and amount of religious work that is agreeable to her. She is as much of a volunteer worker as any member who stands close to the rabbi and takes an interest in his work. She guards zealously the dignity of her husband's position and resents and repels any imposition on his good nature by the ignorant or arrogant. And, withal, she is loved and respected by all, and during a period of forty-five years she has maintained a most amicable relationship with great and small. And even as the "virtuous woman" of the Bible "she worketh willingly" [Proverbs 31:10–31] and renders an invaluable service to the congregation. She is my most efficient religious-school teacher and is the premier of the "Kitchen Cabinet," as I facetiously call the group of women who prepare the repasts for the many occasions when the congregation or its auxiliary organizations entertain in the Temple Center. She also renders an important service to the congregation by being the severest critic of my sermons.

She has brought up our four children to righteous manhood and refined womanhood, and she managed my modest salary so skillfully that we could give all four a college education. The gracious Lord has, indeed, blessed our domestic life with harmony and happiness. I penned this tribute to her on the flyleaf of the Bible she uses in her classroom:

To Gertrude
Of the virtuous woman's ABC
You have complied with every letter;
Nay, that paragon of a female
You have even gone one better.

True, in one art she excelled,
You have been quite lax:
You never sat at the distaff
Nor spun wool and flax;
Yet, you have labored harder
Than she of the strong arm:

For you have served as a
Religious schoolmarm.

Let this Book of Books be
My gratitude's token,
For words, no matter how
Eloquently spoken,
Could not express the debt
I owe you for the help rendered,
And the spirit of love
In which it was tendered.

The Mystic Magnetism of Texas

I would be utterly unworthy of the title of honor and distinction that goes with being called "a Texas rabbi" had I not caught the contagion of bragging about the glory and grandeur of my great state. Here follows a small and an inadequate eulogy that I have penned on this subject.

There is something in the atmosphere of Texas that attracts and holds. Perhaps it is the vastness of the state's area and the variety of its soil and climate that carries a strong appeal. Then there is the warmth of Texas that manifests itself, not only in the climbing mercury and the semitropical vegetation, but also in the accelerated heartbeat of the southern people, in the cordiality of their hospitality, the fervor of their friendship, the glow of their faith, and the ardor of their loyalty.

To a man blessed with an independent soul, Texas has an irresistible appeal on account of the ruggedness of its people, who still retain distinct traces of their pioneering ancestry, with their quaintness and picturesqueness, and have not yet become obsequious slaves of conventions and standardization. Furthermore, Texas, with its sparse population and undeveloped natural resources, represents the future, and one who does not regard life as fixed and stationary, but as a steady growth, finds great fascination in linking his fate with this youthful state and sharing the adventures of its romantic unfoldment and the changing fortunes of its colorful development.

The mystic magnetism which Texas exerts upon one by the vast reaches of its prairies, the matchless beauty of its skies, the luxurious growth of its tropical vegetation, and the warm heart of its people explains the secret of the long tenure of service of the Texas rabbis, and accounts, very largely, for my lifetime incumbency with my congregation.

My Righteous Convert

Of late, the Central Conference of American Rabbis has given serious consideration to the idea of publicly inviting Gentiles dissatisfied with their faith to embrace the mother religion, Judaism. Now, the gates of Judaism have never been shut to the righteous proselyte who, without any ulterior motive but pure conviction, was willing to accept our faith. That the number of such proselytes must have been considerable before the rise of Christianity we may safely infer from one of the eighteen benedictions recited in each of the three daily traditional services—a prayer, dating back to the second century, which reads: "Upon the righteous and the pious and the elders of Thy people Israel, and the remnants of their scribes, and *upon the righteous proselytes,* and upon us . . . may Thy tender mercies, O Lord, be stirred." Yet, in later centuries, converts were discouraged. In the *Shulchan Aruch,* the sixteenth-century code of Joseph Caro, we have this law relating to proselytes: "If a Gentile applies to us for admission to our faith, we should inquire of him about his motives. We should tell him that we Jews are oppressed, persecuted, and proscribed— and that suffering is our lot. If he answers, I know it, and yet I consider it a privilege to join them, then he is worthy of being accepted" [*Yoreh Deah* 268:2].

My righteous convert has fully complied with the conditions laid down by the ancient code and moreover has borne with heroic fortitude many trials with which the Lord has tested the purity of her motives.

Her first trial came very early. "Mary Howitt" (a fictitious name) is a talented musician and earns her living by teaching piano and serving as an organist in a church as well as in our temple. She was an attractive girl and married a fine young man who, in spite of receiving a clean premarital bill of health from a reputable doctor, contracted tuberculosis shortly thereafter and, after lingering for two years, passed away. Mary mourned his death with that consuming grief which is shut up in the heart and seeks no relief in outward manifestations. She remained loyal to his memory by not marrying again.

Mary had served as our organist for about fifteen years when she asked me to teach her Hebrew so that she could understand the meaning of the service for which she rendered musical accompaniment. She learned Hebrew rapidly and used to follow me attentively while I was reading the Hebrew portion of the ritual. Afterwards, she borrowed books from my library on Jewish history and religion, and upon returning them asked me to elucidate many points that were not entirely clear to her. This went on for a number of years when one day, upon bringing my books back, Mary startled me by the statement: "Rabbi, I have carefully listened to your sermons these long years and studied the books I borrowed from you thoroughly. As a result, I have decided that Judaism has the right interpretation of the Bible, and that Jesus was only a teacher, not the son of God in any other sense than that we are all the children of one God, who is our Heavenly Father. Therefore, I have made up my mind to adopt Judaism as my religion, and I want you to convert me and accept me as a member of your congregation."

"But Mary," said I, "we are not a missionary people, and we do not seek converts. Our teacher Moses told us: 'It is not because of your multitude that the Lord has chosen you' [Deuteronomy 7:7]. I never dreamed that your study of Judaism had any other purpose than familiarizing yourself with the foundation of Christianity. We respect all religions and believe that heaven is large enough to hold all good people. Therefore there is no reason why you should not remain in the faith in which you were born and reared."

"Rabbi," she countered, "I am not a fickle woman who makes hasty decisions. I have pondered over this matter for months and months. I have no husband or children, and I must have a God to pray to and lean upon; and that God is the Invisible, yet ever-present God of Israel."

"Mary," I answered her, "you may pray to and lean upon the God of Israel without conversion. He is the God of all nations. 'The Lord is nigh to all who call upon Him, to all who call upon Him in truth,' says the Psalmist [145:-18]. Furthermore, you must take into consideration the feelings of your parents; more especially your father whom you adore. He would be distressed to death if you were to change your religion."

This last argument had a restraining effect upon Mary. After some hesitation she said: "I will yield temporarily to my rabbi; but I want you to know that I am a Jewess, heart and soul, even if I have to keep it a secret for a while. I will continue to study my new religion, so that when I formally pledge my allegiance to it, I shall be fully qualified and worthy of the privilege."

After a few years, Mary's father passed away, and I formally accepted her into the faith of Israel, adding to her name the name of the model convert, Ruth, who refused to leave her bereaved mother-in-law, but said: "Thy people shall be my people, and thy God my God" [Ruth 1:16]. I wish that every native Jewess had as wide a knowledge, as profound a love and appreciation of her ancestral faith, as my righteous convert.

"Whom the Lord loveth, doth He chastise, even as a father chastises his son" [Proverbs 3:12]. Ruth Mary has shared unsparingly the fate of her adopted people, whom, according to Isaiah [42:1-4, 24-25; 43:1-2], the Lord chose in the crucible of affliction. Due probably to overwork and malnutrition, a common habit with lone women, her health became undermined and she had to undergo a series of operations to clear up an ear infection which threatened the loss of her hearing and the ruination of her means of livelihood. Her auditory nerves were actually affected, but finally she regained her acute hearing completely.

A few years later she had to have one of her breasts removed. I am in the habit of visiting my sick members before they are wheeled into the operating room and of asking them to recite the prayer: "Into Thy hand, O Lord, I commit my soul when I sleep and when I awake; the Lord is with me; I shall not fear." In the case of Ruth Mary, I supplemented the prayer with the encouraging words: "Ruth Mary, faith in God nestles in your heart. He has redeemed you from many evils, and I am confident that He will continue to be your keeper."

Whereupon Ruth Mary unbuttoned her gown, and on the very breast which the surgeon's knife was soon to remove, there was lying a little *mezuzah* [amulet containing the *Shema:* Deuteronomy 6:4–9; 11:13–21]. I could not help but turn aside and dry the tears which flooded my eyes. The suspected lump proved benign, and Ruth Mary, though maimed in body, was without blemish in her soul.

The supreme test of faith for Ruth Mary came when she contracted the dreaded disease of crippling polio. After so many visitations, perhaps even a saint's faith would have been shaken. Ruth Mary, however, accepted even this trial-of-trials in the spirit of the Book of Proverbs [27:6]: "Sweet are the wounds of a friend. . . ." She was laid up for over two years, and for the first time in her long tenure as our organist, she could not serve on the High Holy Days. We sorely missed her, for she put not only her art, but her heart into her music. We received from her on Rosh Hashanah [New Year's Day] the following letter:

To my Rabbi and his dear Wife:
    May you be inscribed for a good year in the Book of Life. As our New Year approaches, I want again to express my appreciation for your friendship and influence in my life. In my recent experience, I realized, more fully than ever before, how much Judaism and our God mean to me. Our God is a merciful Heavenly Father, who never places upon us troubles too great to bear. With His loving arms about us, He gives us the strength to face whatever happens. My faith in the God of Israel is firmly rooted in my heart, and not even one born in Judaism with its rich heritage could cherish this faith more than I.
    My heart is aching because I cannot take my place in the temple for divine services. I certainly shall be with you in spirit, and I will be reading the prayers

here at home. Please extend my best wishes for a good year to the congregation that I love so much.

I read this letter to my congregation. There was not an eye but that was moist with tears.

Ruth Mary's boundless faith in the God of Israel was well placed. He brought about her full recovery. We pray the Lord that He, to use the words of the Psalmist [90:15], "make her rejoice according to the days He has afflicted her, according to the years she had seen evil," so that she may serve as an incentive and inspiration to the faithful remnant and as a ringing rebuke and reproach to those of our people who neglect and even despise their priceless heritage.

The Most Precious Gift

The incident I shall now relate occurred in the early years of the First World War, before our country had entered that cataclysmic conflict. At that time, it was very difficult to make American Jewry realize the tidal wave of misery and misfortune that had engulfed the six million Jews of the Pale, trampled underfoot by the Russian and German armies. At the approach of Yom Kippur [Atonement Fast], I made up my mind that I would put forth a supreme effort to arouse my people to the magnitude and urgency of the help needed. I am happy to recall the response of ten thousand dollars that my fervent Kol Nidre [Yom Kippur night] appeal received from the Jewish population of our town, numbering then about seven hundred souls. I still treasure a letter of thanks, signed by the late Jacob H. Schiff and Henry Morgenthau, Sr., for the magnificent gift of the small Jewish community of Beaumont.

At an early hour Yom Kippur morning, one of our

young working girls paid me a visit. She was an orphan and had to depend on her meager wages for her livelihood. I had no inkling of the reason for her untimely call, but welcomed her cordially without an indication of my surprise at her presence. "Rabbi," she said in a halting voice, "I have brought you a donation for the Jewish war sufferers. I cannot give you much in money, but here is my jewelry, left to me by my blessed mother." And she handed me a little sack containing a couple of rings, earrings, a brooch, and a bracelet.

I was touched to the core by the generosity of my visitor. I was reluctant to accept her heirloom gift, and yet I could not turn it down without offending her. As if by inspiration, I found a way whereby she kept her jewels and could make a liberal contribution to the war sufferers. I told her I would ask a jeweler to let me know the monetary value of her gift, and she could pay that sum in small monthly installments.

She accepted this compromise. Hers was the most precious gift that I have ever received for philanthropy in my long ministerial career. And whenever wealthy people contribute to charity a paltry sum, representing less than a crumb of their abundant means, I recall the generosity of blessed Henrietta Lowenstein, and I pity the poor rich, whose hearts are too obdurate to thrill and throb with the joy of liberal giving.

Abraham Asked a Question

Let me conclude this biographical sketch with a brief summary of my philosophy of life, which I have distilled from the wisdom of our sages and my personal experiences.

Ever since I have been mature enough to think of the problems of human existence, I have trained myself to look at the positive side of life. I know that all is not well with the world, that evil is rampant abroad, that injustice wrings bitter tears from the victims of our imperfect social system, that life has its shady and seamy sides, and that sorrow, suffering, and misery sound very discordant notes in the symphony of the universe. Yet, withal, there is so much goodness, kindness, and sweetness, and such an abundance of beauty, grace, virtue, and wisdom in the ordinary course of life, that a person whose mind is not morbid will turn his face as the sunflower toward the source of light, which renders these divine blessings visible, and not in the direction of darkness, where the pall of gloom hangs over all.

I believe that the Almighty has placed us in this world not to censure, not to cavil and criticize, but to construct and correct, to build and improve, so as to make this sphere a better and fitter place to live in. Hence, I have adopted for my motto the maxim of our sages: "Judge every man in the scale of merit" [Abot 1:6]. Instead of searching for the flaws and foibles, let us try to find the good and noble qualities in our fellowmen. When viewing a landscape, let us not fix our gaze on the few ugly spots which detract from its beauty, but feed our eyes on those sights which fill us with delight and rapture.

There is no perfection on earth. "There is no man on earth who doeth good and sinneth not" is the verdict of the Bible [Ecclesiastes 7:20]. Yet our shortcomings, far from discouraging us, should serve as an incentive to higher things. Failure disheartens the feeble, but spurs the strong to renewed attempts. Who will gainsay the truth voiced by Tennyson:

I hold it truth, with him who sings
To one clear harp in divers tones,
That men may rise on stepping-stones
Of their dead selves to higher things.
("In Memoriam": Prologue)

Whenever I visit a big, strange city, where I get lost in the maze of streets and avenues, I usually single out a tall, centrally located building which towers above other structures and use it as my compass by which to find my directions in the confusing traffic arteries. No matter in what outlying district of the city I move about, as long as my eyes can see the top of the tall building, I can orient myself and find my way. This world is naught but a huge, strange city into which we are placed at our birth, and unless we set up God as the towering ideal of our lives, as the compass by which we determine our going out and coming in and as the pivot around which our whole existence revolves, we lose our bearings and move around aimlessly.

We have been sent into this world, and we do not know why. Yet, the human mind is inquisitive and searches for a satisfying answer to the why and wherefore of man's existence. Speaking by and large, there are but two solutions of the riddle of life. Either we are here by chance or by the will of a directing intelligence. Either we are tossed about in this world as aimlessly as the seared leaf is driven before the autumnal wind [Job 13:25], or there is a divinity that shapes our ends and guides our destinies.

Let the pseudoscientist and the half-baked thinker presume a godless world. My horse sense tells me that if a claptrap of a shack is not the work of chance, but of a builder, how much more does our marvelous universe presuppose an Architect of supreme wisdom and intelligence?

"The heavens declare the glory of God, and the firmament showeth forth His handiwork" [Psalms 19:2]. There is a deeper truth in this scriptural statement than in all the labored speculations of philosophy. One glimpse of the majestic sky lends me surer guidance than all the fine theories which scientists have spun on the looms of their brains.

True science, gaining an ever-increasing knowledge of the universe, discerns a directing intelligence behind it. The time will come when science will discover not only manifestations of intelligence, but also revelations of benevolence in the world. The universe is governed not only by law but also by love, and behind the cosmic forces which keep the universe in balance, there is a compassionate heart that beats with tender love for the humblest creature that breathes on earth. In the midst of all the doubts and uncertainties of life, in the flood of all the confusing and conflicting theories evolved by scientists, in all the flux of this ever-changing world, cling to the Rock of Ages, and you will find safety, security, and stability.

Have you ever observed a tree, laden with a rich yield of fruit? Have you noticed that the branch which bears the most hangs the lowest? Is not the bough, bending almost to the breaking point under the burden of fruit, symbolic of a soul bent under the heavy load of grief and sorrow? Rich in harvests, indeed, are the afflictions that are sent upon us from heaven. Clear skies, bathed in sunshine, are pleasant to behold; yet, unless clouds gather and descend upon the earth in refreshing showers, the vegetation dies of aridity. Barren is the soul that has never been moistened with tears; hard is the heart that has never been softened by sorrow. It is in the body wracked by pain that the wellsprings of compassion open up, and it is in the breast pierced by sighs of agony that the reservoirs of genuine sympathy are contained. Therefore, it is not for man to question the dispensations of Providence. Our implicit faith in divine justice must admit of no doubt, no matter how strongly assailed we are by the sordid realities of life. We must reconcile all discrepancy between facts and faith by asking in the words of Abraham, the father of faith, the question that has only one answer: "Shall the Judge of all the earth not exercise justice?" [Genesis 18:25].

It is in such a reverential and submissive spirit that we should seek to find a meaning and a purpose in every misfortune that befalls us. We cannot pierce the veil. We cannot comprehend the divine plan. Yet this much we know: the innocent do not suffer in vain. Divine truth grows out of the soil drenched with martyrs' blood. The tears of the righteous quicken the earth more than the dew of heaven. Out of the broken and contrite heart flow the healing waters of love, charity, kindness, and helpfulness. The scalpel of the surgeon hurts, yet heals. The storm destroys, yet cleanses the atmosphere. Pain is not a measure of punishment, but a purification. Cast in the crucible of suffering, we emerge free from the dross of selfishness. Adversity is the balance in which God weighs His children. The man and woman of character and faith and worth will not be found wanting.

Even as the rays of the sun have to pass through the raindrops of the clouds in order that their hidden colors may appear in the resplendent beauty of the rainbow, so also the life of man has to pass through the teardrops of sorrow and suffering in order that its hidden beauty shall become manifest. It takes the darkness of the night to reveal the splendor of the sky. While the firmament is bathed in sunshine, the pageantry of the stars is invisible to the eye. So also it takes the somber shades of adversity to set off the grandeur of life and reveal its hidden powers, its unscaled heights and unfathomed depths.

It seems that we have not yet reached, or perhaps even approached, that stage of spiritual development which would enable us to appreciate fully the blessings of prosperity. Plenty and piety do not always go hand-in-hand. Abundance of means seldom makes for the life abundant. Wealth often weakens our moral fiber. We lean more on money than on manhood. It is the sweatbeads of painstaking toil, the anguish of hardships and misfortunes, the tragedy of shattered dreams, of frustrated hopes, that bring forth our reserve strength, our hidden resources, and all those spiritual treasures which are laid up in our hearts and minds.

I am convinced that were we in a position to trace the enduring blessings and imperishable values of life to their original sources, we would find that we drew them from the bitter waters of the fountains of adversity.

Morris M. Feuerlicht

A HOOSIER
RABBINATE

Morris Marcus Feuerlicht (1879–1959) spent nearly half a century in the pulpit of the Indianapolis Hebrew Congregation and —concurrently, of course—thirty-one years on the Butler University faculty. It is hardly surprising that the Indianapolis Times *thought him "one of the true assets of the State of Indiana." To read the memoir which he wrote in the early 1950s is to wonder whether anyone has ever been more of a Hoosier. Yet Morris was a native Magyar. A year before his birth in Tokay, his father, Jacob Feuerlicht (1856–1920), had been ordained a rabbi at the Pressburg Hochschule. Morris was scarcely more than an infant when the Feuerlichts settled in the United States.*

Jacob Feuerlicht had begun by upholding the pieties of the Jewish past; his son was an exemplar of Jewish modernity, an incarnation of the synthesis that emerged during the early 1900s between American aspiration and Jewish perspective. It is not without significance that Morris Feuerlicht's best-known publication appeared in 1926 under the title The Influence of Judaism on the Founders of the Republic.

❧

I happen to be the last survivor of a class of ten graduated from the Hebrew Union College in 1901. All ten of us were also graduates of the University of Cincinnati, in a day when there were no pre-"medic," pre-law, pre-cleric, or other selective combinations of courses such as prevail in the universities of today. We were required to take a straight belletristic course which included Latin, Greek, French, and German before our ordination as rabbis became valid. Our ordination exercises as rabbis were presided over by the saintly Moses Mielziner, professor of Talmud, who had been serving the Hebrew Union College as acting president since the death of Isaac M. Wise in the spring of 1900.

The baccalaureate address was delivered, appropriately enough, by Henry Berkowitz, of Temple Rodeph Shalom, Philadelphia. I say "appropriately" because, if there was any one man in the American rabbinate of that period who seemed to all ten of us peculiarly to embody all the ideals and purposes to which we were being dedicated, that man was Henry Berkowitz. Like bridal couples standing with rapt attention at the marriage altar, but who, in the ecstasy of the moment, will soon enough have forgotten the literal text of the proffered counsel, we sat enthralled, yet indelibly impressed with the fact that here was a man who in his own career and person radiantly exemplified the very things whereof he was speaking. It was not so much the sincerity and eloquence of the man and his specific text of the moment that impressed us; it was, rather, our instant recognition of him as a perfect embodiment of that rabbinic leadership which Isaac M. Wise had envisaged in the establishment and development of what he preferred to call American Judaism. Indeed, men like Henry Berkowitz and his early contemporaries among the alumni of the Hebrew Union College set the pace and the pattern for building up what all wings of Jewry today unite in calling American Judaism. And we of the class of 1901 thought of ourselves as beginners in a second generation of that upbuilding process.

It should be remembered that this was a period when, for the most part, the ancient Judaism of the fathers in America was still confused and unsettled in a contemporary world that was itself unsettled and confused. The Hebrew Union College, founded in 1875, sent forth its first graduating class of four in 1883. Solomon Schechter and the Jewish Theological Seminary of America had not yet appeared upon the American scene. Yeshiva University and its kindred localized facsimiles were not yet contemplated. A United Jewish Appeal, though deeply rooted in Judaism, was not thought of as a probable or even possible necessity. Despite Theodor Herzl and the traditional Jewish liturgy, undertakings like the Hebrew University, Zionism, and Israel, at least in their more purely nationalistic aspects, were not yet being hotly debated. The full force and numbers of East European Jewish immigration had not yet set in. Jewish ritual, liturgy, and practice, in whole or in part, were still continuing in many spots in the Old World vernaculars. This was the spiritual climate into which the earlier alumni of the Hebrew Union College were graduated.

Sitting immediately next to me during the entire eight years of our student careers prior to graduation was Henry Englander, of blessed memory. Our lifelong friendship thereafter was inevitable. Englander's first pulpit was Ligonier, Indiana, at the northern end of the state; my own first rabbinic post was that of Lafayette, in central Indiana. Although the congregation had been in existence since

1848, I was the first alumnus of the Hebrew Union College to occupy its pulpit. Both Lafayette and Ligonier were within easy traveling distance of Chicago. Shortly before Englander and I accepted our respective positions, Dr. Emil G. Hirsch, of Temple Sinai, was presenting a course of lectures before the student body in the old college chapel on West Sixth Street. We asked his counsel in the pending negotiations with Lafayette and Ligonier. He urged our unhesitating acceptance with the suggestion that, since both cities were so close to Chicago, we might, while concurrently serving our respective congregations, continue postgraduate studies at the university, where he was professor of rabbinic studies. Accordingly, on assuming our posts, we proceeded to arrange for regular weekly visits to the university. On our first meeting with Dr. William R. Harper, president of the university, the suggestion was advanced that, since the department of Semitics had just been opened, there was an eagerness to enroll as many qualified students as possible. Abram Hirshberg, serving Temple Sholom in Chicago, joined us later, as did Louis Wolsey, then of Little Rock, Arkansas, during our summer vacation periods.

Englander and I attended classes for two full calendar years, leaving our respective Indiana homes about 4 A.M. every Monday to be on hand for classes in Chicago at 10 A.M. We continued on this schedule until Englander left Ligonier to assume a new post with the congregation at Providence, Rhode Island, where he resumed his postgraduate studies both as student and associate professor at Brown University, and thence, having obtained his doctorate, proceeded to Cincinnati on appointment by his alma mater as professor of Bible and medieval exegesis. For my part, I continued the graduate work with all residence and credit requirements satisfied at Chicago until, in the fall of

1904, I transferred from the Lafayette pulpit to that of the Indianapolis Hebrew Congregation. I still continued my weekly visits to Chicago, however, and was about to begin a doctoral thesis with the cooperation and supervision of Dr. Harper himself, when his sudden and untimely death in January 1906, together with the mounting requirements of my new pulpit in Indianapolis, intervened to terminate this particular phase of my academic career.

I felt somewhat compensated for this technical deficiency some years later when I served in Indianapolis as professor and lecturer at the School of Religion of Butler University, where for a period of twenty-three years it was my privilege to give instruction for a few hours weekly to graduate ministers of various Protestant denominations in the essentials of Judaism and the beginnings of Christianity. This was quite an innovation in Jewish-Christian relations at that time, although it has since been carried on in many similar institutions elsewhere throughout the land. I mention all this because in the course of my many years in the ministry I have been frequently asked, like many others among my colleagues: "How do you like to be called, Rabbi or Doctor?" I have always (perhaps gratuitously) replied: "My rightful title officially and professionally is 'Rabbi,' but personally, socially, and generally, I prefer plain 'Mr.'"

It Hath Been Told Thee, O Man, What Is Good

When I entered upon the active duties of my first pulpit in Lafayette, the spiritual climate of the period appeared to reflect itself with special favor upon the sociological rather than the theological aspects of religion. The liberal pulpits of America, both Jewish and Christian, were calling loudly for a kind of religion that should be not merely spiritual and moral in theory, but also ethical and social in practice. The true function of the pulpit and of religion, it was emphasized, was to remind men not alone to serve their God, but also to serve their fellowmen; indeed, the highest service to God was best reflected and expressed in a corresponding service to man. Back, therefore, to the religion of Israel's prophets. Not so much ritual, or form, or ceremony, but: "It hath been told thee, O man, what is good, and what the Lord requireth of thee: only to do justly, to love mercy, and to walk humbly with thy God." This was the eloquently insistent text and theme, particularly of the American Jewish pulpit of that period. Of course, rabbinical and academic scholarship on the part of graduating rabbis was by no means ignored, but more particularly it was the social service aspects of the ministry that were pressed upon the rabbi's attention.

Accordingly, several members of our class of ten volunteered, even before ordination, for some form of social service in connection with the organized charities then operating in Cincinnati. Immigrants in large numbers from Eastern Europe were beginning to seep into the Middle West, and what was then called a neighborhood settlement house, patterned after the famous Jewish Educational Alliance of New York, was established in Cincinnati. The traditional and sporadic methods of the age-old forms of Jewish social service had, of course, long been operating here but were just then being coordinated and reorganized into the more compact and technically perfected forms of what is now called modern scientific charity. My own choice and first experience in this kind of social work was that of teaching elementary English to the newly arrived immigrants at the Cincinnati settlement two nights a week. One of our number, Solomon Lowenstein, chose service with the lately organized, or reorganized, Cincinnati United Jewish Charities, whose executive director he became after a brief period in the ministry and from which he rose to become a leader in both the Jewish and non-Jewish National Conference of Charities (now Social Welfare). Others of our group, and of later Hebrew Union College classes, carried on in this same field of executive and administrative social work along with their regular local rabbinic service. Some even reached out as far as arbitrators and umpires in labor disputes, usually at the invitation of local labor and industrial groups.

I mention these things here because it was during these early years of the present century that most, if not all, of the widespread Jewish and national social and charitable agencies of our current day had their organized beginnings. Older traditional forms of public, private, and personal charity among Jews and non-Jews alike were being reappraised and were giving way to what was then called, sometimes sneeringly, organized "scientific" charity. Local relief and benevolent societies were being transformed into "associated charities," "social service agencies," "community chests," and the like. Most significant in all such changes, perhaps, in the field of social service, both Jewish and non-Jewish, was the fact that the basic motivation of social service itself was being gradually, but nonetheless definitely, lifted from the lower level of condescending relief and almsgiving by the so-called privileged to the under-privileged, to the more equal and dignified status of *tsedakah*—the traditional Jewish and prophetic concept of a mutual and precisely even justice between man and fellow-man. This, to me at least, appeared to be the spiritual climate to which the social work of that period was tending and in which it was actually operating. In the creation of that climate, I venture to think, the contemporary rabbis of that day played a notably significant and important role.

In my own case, I know, this altered motivation was a conscious and persistently dominant factor. At the insistence of Professor Charles R. Henderson, then head of the sociology department in the University of Chicago, Abram Hirshberg and I undertook to write two chapters on "The Jews" in his forthcoming book *Modern Methods of Charity* which Macmillan published in 1904. Hirshberg did a twelve-page chapter on the Jews of America; I contributed one of twenty pages on the Jews of Europe. This book of Henderson's, undertaken with the assistance of Edouard Munsterberg, of Berlin, "one of the first authorities in the world in this field" (Preface, p. xi), was the first compendium of its kind which, according to Henderson, considered the charities of the Jews important enough to be included in a comparative study of the subject.

But my interest at this particular stage of my rabbinate was not entirely academic or literary. Shortly after my installation in my first pulpit at Lafayette, I attended the second meeting of the National Conference of Jewish Charities in Detroit, Michigan, which had been organized the previous year at Chicago by such men as Emil G. Hirsch, Leo N. Levi, Lee K. Frankel, Max Senior, Max Herzberg, and others. It was at this Detroit meeting that I was approached by Max Senior, of Cincinnati, one of the prime movers in the organization and modernization of our Jewish charities on a national scale, with an invitation to accept a proposed scholarship in Jewish social studies. The young candidate should be one who, as Senior put it, "knew how to wear a dress suit." I do not recall that I was exactly flattered by the invitation in this form, but after consultation with Lee K.

Frankel and others on the spot, I respectfully declined it. The late Jacob Billikopf, an undergraduate in sociology at Chicago, was then approached, and the invitation was accepted by him, with results that have since become historic in the annals of American Jewish philanthropy.

Lafayette, a community of about sixty Jewish families at that time, provided a rather limited opportunity for modernizing its existing social services. Its chief problem, like that of most other communities of comparable size, was the almost daily visit of some itinerant *schnorrer* [beggar] who seemed to come from nowhere and everywhere, and always had some innocent tale of personal tragedy and woe to tell. He was one of those ubiquitous and not unpicturesque characters in our American Jewish life that a Zangwill of another day would have delighted to portray in an American version of his *Children of the Ghetto*. The usual victims of such visitors were the rabbi, the local ladies' benevolent society, and the few scattered merchants along Main Street. The *schnorrer* would pocket the more or less nominal proceeds from these sources and thence betake himself by one means or another to the next adjacent town with similar results. Sometimes he came with an advance list of his prospective victims obtained from among the more successful of his predecessors on earlier visits.

The elimination of this type, along with the settlement of immigrants forwarded by the lately organized Jewish Agricultural and Industrial Aid Society in New York (then the chief port of entry), constituted the initial problems which the National Conference of Jewish Charities was formed to solve. Also, at this time, the various existing national and district eleemosynary institutions like orphan asylums, homes for the aged, tuberculosis sanitoriums, and similar institutions, had their respective local representatives collecting annual contributions from the Jewish community. The combining of all these agencies was in most instances responsible for the organization, or reorganization, of what are today known as our local federations or associations of Jewish charities. These local federated Jewish charities, in turn, have become in more than one of our American cities the inspiration and model for the larger non-Jewish organized charities of the general community. While I do not have the precise historical data at hand, I believe it is generally accepted among social workers that the first Community Fund in America was that of Cleveland, Ohio, organized in World War I days through the efforts of a native Hoosier, Martin A. Marks, a leader in both the Jewish and general social activities of his community. And while it is true that the National Conference of Social Work antedated by some years our own National Conference of Jewish Charities, I like to think of our present-day Community Fund as one of the distinctive contributions of Judaism, and especially of American Reform Judaism, to the general communal and civic life of America.

The influence of our Indianapolis Jewish federation was similarly effective outside of its own parochial field. Early in its career, a campaign against usury and the evils of moneylending by loan sharks was undertaken, although there were very few Jews locally engaged in this sort of business. The non-Jewish tradition persisted here as elsewhere, however, that this was somehow a peculiarly Jewish business. It was reported to the board of the federation that the Rothschild Bank in London, England, had resolved at the turn of the century to combat both this tradition and the evil itself by investing some of its funds in the building of apartment homes for the poor that would bring a return of no more than 4 percent profit. The experiment in England proved to be successful. Inspired by this example, our federation embarked upon an anti-loan-shark campaign and succeeded in getting our state legislature to enact a bill prohibiting any kind of usurious or unreasonable interest in moneylending. At the same time, a few members of our board privately decided, along with a small number of like-minded non-Jewish neighbors, to organize a public welfare loan company to lend money at a rate of interest lower than that currently prevailing among the private local companies. This, too, proved to be successful, as in the Rothschild instance—so successful, indeed, that some years later, when its management became too burdensome for the originators, the business was sold to a private group on the sole condition that the rate of interest be continued as originally planned. Another piece of legislation for which the Jewish federation was directly responsible was the enactment of a state law making it mandatory for children, or the next of kin, to care properly for aged and disabled parents.

All this was, of course, highly encouraging to me in my personal activity and interest in the field of Jewish and public social service. Accordingly, while still hard at work within my own congregational area, I was urged to enlist in wider social activities outside. I was especially interested in the work of our Marion County juvenile court, which had been established a year prior to my residence here. This court was, despite the rival claims of Chicago and that of the nationally known Judge Ben B. Lindsay in Denver, the first court of its kind in the country. Its claim to priority lay not only in the chronological fact that it was the first public court devoted exclusively to the handling of delinquency among juveniles, but also in its unique volunteer probation system, whereby delinquents brought before the court were turned over to the probationary care of qualified volunteers among our citizenry.

Both the court and this volunteer probation system became so popular in the community that when its first presiding judge, George W. Stubbs, a lovable one-armed veteran of the Civil War, was up for reelection, he was the only successful candidate on his party ticket in a landslide victory of the opposition. During Judge Stubbs's incumbency, and during the comparatively short period of the voluntary probation system's existence, I was delegated to various counties and cities of the state to explain the virtues and advantages of the Marion County juvenile court system. The success of Judge Stubbs at the polls was in large measure attributed to the activity of the Children's Aid Association, whose membership was comprised of the Volunteer Probation Officers Association. I accepted the presidency of the Children's Aid Association and served for twenty-one years, until its merging with two other local social organizations to form the Indianapolis Family Service Society, which, in turn, became the nucleus for the formation of the Community Fund. During the life of the Children's Aid Association, it was its purpose and policy to serve as both auxiliary to the juvenile court and also as the chief voluntary agency for the establishment of baby clinics, milk pasteurization, playground and recreation facilities for children, and the like. Fortunately, by the time its work was taken over by the Family Service Society, all these functions had been incorporated and continued by the city, thus perpetuating the original purpose for which the society had been organized. From the presidency of the Children's Aid Association, my social service road led to appointment to membership on the County Board of Welfare, thence to the presidency of the Indiana State Conference of Charities (now the State Conference of Social Welfare), and then, as its first Jew, to the six-member State Board of Charities (now the State Welfare Board).

When I left Lafayette to begin my new work in the capital city of the state back in the fall of 1904, I found an enlarged opportunity for just this kind of modernized social service. Local conditions were especially favorable. The Indianapolis Hebrew Congregation consisted of some two hundred families, most of whom were resident within an area of a few blocks near the home of James Whitcomb Riley, who was the common friend of the neighborhood. Founded in 1856, it was, though not the oldest, certainly the largest congregation in the state, situated in its exact geographic center, an inland city moreover, through which most of the *schnorrers* of the land were compelled to pass, either by passenger or freight car, to reach their constantly movable destinations. As soon as they reached town, their immediate goal was the home of the rabbi, my predecessor Mayer Messing, a kindly, genial personality, who had held the office for thirty-seven years and, like the vicar in Goldsmith's *Deserted Village,* was known to love just such impoverished itinerants. He was assisted by the Ladies' Hebrew Benevolent Society, the only organization to care for the community's indigent and needy. Its energetic president was the personable and unforgettable Eliza Leopold, herself possessed of none too excessive earthly riches.

At the same time, several of the national Jewish institutions had their volunteer local representatives to collect annual contributions and dues from members of the community. For instance, Sol S. Kiser represented the Cleveland Orphan Home and the Denver Hospital; Henry Rauh, the Montefiore Home for the Aged in Cleveland; and Louis

Newberger, the recently established National Farm School and the Jewish Chautauqua Society. With the exception of the Ladies' Benevolent Society, it was felt by all these agencies that much time and energy and money could be saved by a pooling of their common interests. Thus was born the Jewish Federation of Indianapolis, the first of its kind in the land among cities of comparable size. Gustave A. Efroymson, president of the congregation, was elected president of the new federation. To me was assigned the task of formulating its constitution and bylaws, a composite of similar laws framed shortly before by the larger federations of Cincinnati, Chicago, and St. Louis, but adapted to meet the smaller and more particular needs of our own community. In contradistinction to the larger metropolitan organizations, however, we took a special pride in designating ours as a "Jewish" federation, uniquely, we thought, among similar societies elsewhere. We purposely omitted any reference to "charities" in the title, both because we believed it to be more strictly in keeping with Jewish philanthropic tradition, and also because we wanted to broaden its scope to include *all* local Jewish organizations—social, educational, and civic—outside of the purely synagogal. No wonder, therefore, that our Ladies' Benevolent Society had been thrown into panicky fears of its being displaced—as shortly thereafter it was—by the proposed new organization. The good ladies who up to this time had had an almost complete monopoly in supplying all local charity needs were quick to rally husbands, sons, and brothers to their protesting side, and the community was thrown into turmoil. But not for long. By the time of the next general meeting of the federation, about a year later, all was again peaceful and calm. The Ladies' Benevolent Society quietly passed out of the picture, as we had clearly, though not willfully, expected, and even those who had been most vehement in their opposition were ready to admit that a good forward step had been taken.

Redeemable in the World to Come

The first annual meeting of the federation to which I have just referred remains an especially vivid one to me. Julius Rosenwald and Judge Julian W. Mack, who was then sitting on the federal bench in Chicago, had been particularly active in supporting and organizing the national federation movement, and they volunteered to come down to help us. Their mere presence, of course, was itself enough to encourage and fortify us. Among other things, they suggested that, in our efforts to improve and strengthen our new social service program, we make a combined and determined effort to do away with the wasteful and extravagant practice, then universally current, of sending flowers on the death of a friend or loved one, and replace it with a contribution of their equivalent cost to the federation, or some equally worthy cause. The suggestion found immediate favor, and its consistent execution here in Indianapolis, both within and without our Jewish group, may be said historically to have dated from that meeting. But, in addition to their presence and addresses at our meeting, both Rosenwald and Mack remained over the following day, an exceedingly hot one in June, to help in soliciting new memberships and also to increase the contributions of members already signed.

It was here that I experienced one of the earliest rebuffs and humiliations of my ministerial career. I had been assigned to accompany Rosenwald for an interview with a possible prospect, a well-to-do clothing merchant on our main business street. The merchant, something of a misfit, had been known to boast of his frequent and "generous" doles of quarters and half-dollars to all the *schnorrers* that came his way, and was therefore particularly emphatic in his opposition to our "newfangled" idea of charity organization. Apparently not knowing or caring who Julius Rosenwald was, the man listened in poker-faced silence to our plea; then, without a word, he curtly ushered us to the door. My righteous but voiceless indignation can be imagined. Rosenwald, however, in his gentle and benignly characteristic way, merely shrugged it off with the comment: "You know, as in any old and historic group of people, you'll find the extremes of the best and the meanest of the human species among our own."

The promised results of our federation campaign were quickly forthcoming, both in financial returns and in the solution of pending "cases." One of the first of the latter was that of a newly arrived immigrant with a family of six children. His only material possessions consisted of an old huckster's wagon and an equally aged horse, and he suffered from incipient tuberculosis. The good ladies of the Benevolent Society had been helpful, of course, but could only supply him and his family with their well-meant sympathy and periodic baskets of food. With this early case on its hands, the federation immediately forwarded the father to the Denver Hospital for Consumptives and provided regular and systematic care for his family at home. After he had had a brief stay in Denver, the father's physicians there recommended that his physical condition had improved sufficiently to permit his return home, provided that our federation could furnish him with housing somewhere out in the open, where his medical care and treatment might be continued. All this was satisfactorily arranged by the newly organized federation and in a manner which completely won the hearts of our erstwhile rebellious Benevolent Society. To summarize the story, the father in due time was cured, lived until late in his seventies, and he and his family, quite in the fabulous tradition of Horatio Alger, prospered sufficiently to become not only material and civic assets to but even benefactors of the community that had earlier befriended them.

Shortly before the Jewish Federation was formally organized in the fall of 1904, about a dozen members of the community met to establish the Nathan Morris House, a local equivalent of the neighborhood settlement movement then growing in popularity in the various congested sections of the nation's metropolitan cities. In the spring of 1904, Nathan Morris, a prominent local attorney, had died a heroic death attempting to save the lives of members of his family during a fire that destroyed their home. After rescuing several of them, he returned to the burning building to deliver its last survivor, a little nephew, alas, only to perish himself along with the child. The Jewish and general community were shocked and deeply grieved. To honor his memory, therefore, the Nathan Morris House was established. From it there developed a splendid group of earnest social workers, who subsequently transferred their headquarters to what later became known as the Jewish Communal Building, at 17 West Morris Street.

Although we in Indianapolis had never had a congested section anywhere nearly as large as those of our larger cities, the federation was able to purchase a large wooden structure that had been used previously as a sort of public assembly and gymnasium for the general neighborhood and called it the Jewish Communal Building, to house the activities of both the federation and the Nathan Morris

House. It was insisted that the name *Communal* be emphasized, because, rightly or wrongly, we in Indianapolis held
the notion that much of the social service being rendered
by the neighborhood settlements of that day was inspired
and consciously motivated by a feeling of social superiority
on the part of rich to poor, of privileged to underprivileged. We wanted to avoid every semblance of any
such condescending or patronizing attitude. We sought to
make our settlement house as realistically democratic as
possible in the purely communal sense of the term. *All*
members, rich and poor, privileged and underprivileged
alike, were to be full and equal participants in all its various
and manifold activities. All were to be charged a nominal
and equal membership fee, and all were eligible to be officers, club leaders, instructors, and so on, regardless of
which side of the tracks they may have hailed from. Rather
proudly we believed this to be the first settlement of its
precise nature in cities of comparable size, and it was so
acknowledged and accredited in his dedicatory address by
the late Boris D. Bogen, then head of the United Charities
in Cincinnati and president of the National Conference of
Jewish Charities.

The death of Nathan Morris and the tragic circumstances in which it occurred profoundly stirred the entire
community. The obsequies were held from our temple, in
whose construction he had taken a keen and active interest
just a few years earlier. The funeral address was delivered
by Morris's close friend and colleague John L. Griffiths,
consul general to London under his—and Morris's—friend
President Benjamin Harrison. So universally and deeply
moving was Griffiths's address on this occasion that some
twenty years later it was included in a compilation of the
best American orations under the title *Select Orations* in

"The Macmillan Pocket Classics" published in 1924. Among many other things in this noble tribute to a noble man, Griffiths said:

> When we think of Nathan Morris in the years to come, and we must needs think of him very often, it will be of a friend who was catholic in thought, tolerant in speech, and generous in impulse and deed—of one whose heart went out in warmest sympathy to the weak, the defenseless, and the suffering, of one who gave as freely of himself (and this is always much the larger gift) as he did of his means to relieve the unfortunate. . . . I sometimes think we do not appreciate the debt we owe to the Jewish race: The Jewish household is the best example we have, perhaps, of pure and holy family life. The persecution, injustice, and cruelty to which the Jewish people have been subjected through the centuries has bound the members of their families together in the most perfect loving union. Nathan Morris was loyal to his race, but wholly free from the prejudices and bigotry and race tradition. He led a life which levelled all distinction between Jew and Gentile. He had the virtues of his race, and they are many.

I had never met Nathan Morris personally, since his death occurred a few months before my arrival in Indianapolis, but shortly after assuming office here, I was assigned the address at public exercises dedicating a memorial in his honor. This memorial was in the form of a simple yet imposing fountain for man and beast at the intersection of Massachusetts Avenue and Walnut Street, and was the result of funds contributed by friends and fellow members of the American Bar Association throughout the country. The fountain served its benevolently useful purpose on that spot, one of the busiest in a city of peculiarly busy intersections, for many years, until the general traffic changes from horse and buggy to automobile necessitated its removal. Unfortunately, due to these changes and the not altogether unexpected public neglect of a later generation, the Morris monument has never been replaced and remains today, like many another of its kind, only a fond though still benevolent memory.

The work planned by our Nathan Morris House was in due course absorbed and continued by the Communal Building. But about the same time it was felt by many of the more prosperous that a similar institution might serve an equally useful and even necessary purpose in their geographic part of the community. Our own temple membership had been discussing just such a project for a number of years in connection with the contemplated building of a new temple edifice. At long last, in the fall of 1925, a temple-site and building committee was appointed. This committee was instructed to go ahead with plans for the selection of a site suitable for the erection of a building, or buildings, on the order of what was then called an "institutional synagogue," initiated a few years previously by the temples of Rabbi Moses J. Gries in Cleveland and Rabbi Leo M. Franklin in Detroit. Our local idea, however, was to expand and if possible to improve upon both these structures. While the latter were already operating successfully in their respective communities, with a sanctuary-auditorium and religious school permitting worship plus educational, social, and *indoor* recreational facilities, we had the ambitious thought of adding *outdoor* recreational facilities, such as tennis courts, a baseball field, and even a miniature golf course as well.

Chairman of the site and building committee was Sol

S. Kiser, who promptly communicated with an architect, none other than Albert Kahn, of Detroit, architect of the Ford buildings in Detroit and elsewhere, inviting him to come down and survey the situation. When Kahn came, a full day was devoted to a search for available sites, and we tentatively agreed upon a lot at the southeast corner of North Meridian and Fortieth Streets. This lot measured 300 feet in frontage and 600 feet in depth, quite adequate, we thought, for our pretentious purposes, including parking. Incidentally, it should be gratefully recorded, Mr. Kahn, internationally renowned and busy though he was, very graciously declined to accept any return for his service other than his railroad expenses.

Albert M. Rosenthal, though physically handicapped at the time, accepted the chairmanship of our finance committee. He proceeded with his task along a rather unique and unusual line—unusual at least in a fourth-generation Reform synagogue. He asked that he be permitted to preside at a meeting immediately following our Yom Kippur Eve service, which was to have an appropriate sermon for the purpose by the rabbi. Then in the old-fashioned way of Orthodox *schnoder*ing, he would offer for "sale" to prospective bidders what he was pleased to call "*tsedakah* bonds" (charity bonds) purchasable *ba-olam ha-zeh* (in this world), but redeemable *ba-olam ha-ba* (in the world to come). These he had had printed in advance in standard commercial form, and they were distributed among the assembled congregants with the cautioning admonition that, it being Yom Kippur, all the business details usually accompanying such a transaction were to be avoided.

The response of the congregation was galvanic. With practically no preliminary organization, such as is customary in similar financial campaigns, the assembled membership pledged a total of $187,000, a sizable sum for that time. There were eight "big gift" pledges of $10,000 each, and two for $15,000 each. It was planned to follow through with a solicitation of several of these initial big givers for increases of from $10,000 to $25,000, and an encouraging beginning to that end was already being made when, unhappily, Rosenthal's physical condition became aggravated, and he was forced to abandon his enthusiastically accepted task, to be followed not very long thereafter by his untimely and universally mourned death.

But this was only the first of the congregation's obstacles in its new temple project. In the fall of 1929 began the country's Great Depression. The congregation's membership, along with the rest of the country, was grievously affected. The prospect, or even possibility, of redeeming the solemnly made Yom Kippur Eve pledges diminished to nil; among them a jealously guarded and zealously hoarded temple sisterhood fund of ten thousand dollars. At a formal meeting of the congregation, quite in the Kol Nidre spirit, all pledges were canceled, and thus the congregation's new temple project lay dormant, to be resumed by a later and more prosperous generation.

Disappointing though this experience was, I was not disheartened. The usual activities within the old structure were not interrupted. From time to time the walls needed refurbishing, the old furnace needed to be replaced, and the basement was entirely renovated to accommodate the largest attendance in the history of our religious school. The attendance at worship continued to be good, stimulated perhaps by the economic depression as well as by the sentimental memories which the old building inspired. The building, indeed, though only about a quarter of a century old, had already developed an interesting history. The Indianapolis Hebrew Congregation had been founded in 1856, and this was its second edifice. The first, built in 1866, had been dedicated by Isaac Mayer Wise. This first structure was purchased and used by an Orthodox congregation, Ohev Zedek, which some years later merged with a newly organized Conservative congregation into the present-day Beth El-Zedek.

Prior to 1866 my congregation's first meeting place was in an upstairs room on East Washington Street, rented from the owner, John M. Judah, a son of Samuel B. Judah, of Vincennes, the famed attorney, friend of Henry Clay, and speaker of the Indiana Assembly in 1830. The elder Judah had been one of the first Jews to settle in Indiana in the early part of the nineteenth century; he had come there from the East, of a family well known in American Revolutionary days. He married out of the faith in Vincennes, and his children were reared as Christians. John M. Judah, his son, was quite conscious of his Jewish descent and even proud of it, because, as he once told me, it afforded him the double pride of being descended from the two most historic groups in history. It was for this reason, no doubt, as the congregation's minute book reveals, that he consented to allow the rental of his room at a "discount" in a period which found the congregation confronting financial distress. This pride in his partial Jewish descent, however, was apparently not shared by his brother Noble B. Judah, of Chicago, widely known attorney for the Marshall Field Company and at one time the American envoy to Cuba. Some years ago, when a reader inquired as to whether Noble Judah was a Jew, the B'nai B'rith magazine, *The National Jewish Monthly,* printed Judah's curt reply, in which he emphatically denied that he ever had any Jewish connection whatever.

Mary, Martha, and Dorcas

I have said above that the present building of the congregation, its second, has had an interesting history. It was the last of many synagogue buildings throughout the land dedicated by Isaac Mayer Wise prior to his death in 1900. It has a number of magnificent memorial windows, almost completely covering three sides of the auditorium. One of these is a memorial to Moses Eckhouse, donated by his widow, Emma, who felt it especially appropriate to depict in heroic size the descent of Moses from Sinai as described in Exodus, Chapter 34. It is a glorious specimen of the stained-glass artist's work; it glows with a thrilling brilliance, especially when the midafternoon sun shines through its variegated coloring. But just before this window was permitted to be installed, a furious controversy arose within the congregation. Many voices protested that the installation of this kind of memorial was contrary to Jewish tradition—that it was a violation of the Second Commandment of the Decalogue. After much debate and argument, a congregational meeting decided to appoint a committee to confer with Dr. Wise and ask his counsel. The committee returned, reporting that Dr. Wise had said he could see no present danger of such a window tempting even the most indifferent of Reform Jews to idolatry. Accordingly, the window was installed, and the temple building, window and all, was duly dedicated by Dr. Wise before a unified and contented congregation in the spring of 1899. So far as I know, this was the first memorial window with a personal figure in any synagogue, Reform or Orthodox, in the country. A similar memorial in honor of John Hay, secretary of state, was installed some years later by Keneseth Israel Temple of Philadelphia, in recognition of his success in abrogating the Russo-American treaty of 1832 because of the tsar's refusal to honor passports issued to American Jews.*

Isaac M. Wise's decision about memorial windows brings to mind a curious personal experience of my own in connection with the *kashruth* of personal figures in synagogue art. For many years both before and after my ordination as rabbi, it was my periodic custom to visit the grave of my sainted mother in the cemetery of Congregation Mishkan Tefillah, in West Roxbury, Massachusetts. My father, of blessed memory, was rabbi of this traditionalist congregation at the time of my entry into the Hebrew Union College. A small wooden chapel with plain glass windows had long been used for the conduct of funeral rites at the congregational cemetery. On one of my visits I noticed that this older building had been supplanted by a more pretentious stone structure, one which had stained glass windows along both of its sides. Each of the windows portrayed a New Testament heroine with her name impaneled at the bottom: Mary, Martha, Dorcas, and the rest—what a strange phenomenon in an Orthodox Jewish cemetery! Upon inquiry, I learned that, a short time before, a local Presbyterian church, after erecting a new structure of its own, had disposed of its old building at a bargain to the Mishkan Tefillah congregation, which bought and transferred it in toto. There it stood in the cemetery, windows, names, and all! Apparently no one in the congregation had noted anything incongruous about this until I called it to the attention of the cemetery committee. When I next visited

---

*Actually, Hay died in 1905, six years before the treaty's abrogation. What Rabbi Feuerlicht had in mind was Hay's so-called Rumanian Note of 1902, objecting to Rumanian governmental Judeophobia on the ground that it stimulated an undesirable immigration to America. See *Publications of the American Jewish Historical Society*, XV (1906), 54 ff., and XXIV (1916), 80–83.

the cemetery, I observed that the windows with their New Testament figures were still the same, but in the place of Mary, Martha, and Dorcas the names Miriam, Sarah, Rachel, and Deborah had been substituted! Such was the Boston Orthodoxy, in the first quarter of the twentieth century, of what later became known as New England's largest and most representative Conservative congregation.

The incident I have described here occurred about the time that the late great Solomon Schechter transferred his residence from Cambridge, England, to New York. My personal experience with this kind of Orthodox Judaism came somewhat more pointedly on my very first meeting with Dr. Schechter himself right here in Indianapolis. On assuming the presidency of the Jewish Theological Seminary of America in New York, to which he had been called by the rapidly growing Conservative groups along the eastern seaboard, he brought back with him, as a senior student of the seminary, Charles I. Hoffman, attorney and editor of *The Jewish Exponent* of Philadelphia, who about a year before had given up his reputedly successful law practice to enter the rabbinate. After Hoffman's ordination as rabbi, he was assigned to his first congregation, the United Hebrew Congregation, which had just recently been organized in the heart of Orthodoxy in Indianapolis. It had assumed the name *United* because it was presumed to be a composite of Indianapolis Jews, who had come from their various European hinterlands and who could now start afresh in America as a sort of melting pot and at the same time establish just the kind of Judaism which Dr. Schechter had been promulgating in his plea for a "catholic Israel."

Indianapolis was regarded as a particularly promising prospect because of its proximity to Cincinnati, the headquarters of American and "Isaac M. Wise" Reform. Accordingly, the new congregation set about to make both the inauguration of its new rabbi and the dedication of its newly acquired house of worship (an old church building) an occasion of great and historic éclat. Dr. Schechter was invited to dedicate the synagogue and also to install his favorite disciple. Although not yet due for installation in my own new pulpit until the following week, I was invited to offer an introductory prayer and some welcoming remarks in behalf of the older Reform congregation. Naturally I was complimented and happy to accept, and in my politest English, mixed with an occasional word of classical Hebrew, and all the while with an eye focused on Dr. Schechter, I presented what I thought was the only appropriate welcome the occasion permitted—the joy which we, of a sister congregation, although the Reform temple these many years, still genuinely felt at the advent of a new congregation enlisted in the cause of our common, grand old faith of the fathers: "Behold, how good and how pleasant it is for brethren to dwell together in unity" [Psalms 133:1]. To my disappointment but not dismay, Dr. Schechter was not enthusiastic. "How does it happen," said he in his characteristically kind and benevolent way, "that all you Cincinnati men always use the adjective and stress *Reform?* Why not have just an unadjectived Judaism?"

The exercises were being conducted on a Sunday afternoon in a small brick building which the congregation had purchased from its original church owner and had renovated to meet the synagogue's traditional ritualistic and normal needs. Since the building had no balcony, men were seated on one side, women on the other, and all wore headgear. That same evening the festivities were resumed at our Reform temple in the form of addresses, followed by a social reception. The meeting was designed, quite in the spirit of Dr. Schechter's "catholic Israel," both as a welcome to the new congregation and its rabbi and also as a personal tribute to Dr. Schechter himself. The temple was well filled with its own members in their usual everyday attire, in mixed seating, and of course without headgear. All was quiet and expectant when suddenly both Dr. Schechter and Rabbi Hoffman appeared, marching from the rear of the auditorium to the pulpit. Although the fashion books decreed such attire for Sunday impermissible, both were in full formal swallowtail regalia, but crowned by black circular skullcaps (the present-day *yarmelke* was not yet universally prevalent in American Conservatism).

The sight of such extraordinary attire in a Hoosier environment was striking enough in itself, but to watch the short, pudgy, Santa-Claus-like figure of the world-renowned rabbinic scholar Solomon Schechter with his benign, ruddy face and white-bearded, leonine head alongside the tall, gaunt, brown-bearded and cadaverous Charles I. Hoffman in a Reform congregation appeared to border on the grotesque. The host congregation was nonetheless most respectful and cordial, and the evening proved to be harmonious, religiously as well as socially, for all.

On the following day, I was due in Chicago for my regular weekly schedule at the university and with Dr. Emil G. Hirsch. I described the event to Dr. Hirsch, who listened with special interest. He had been engaged for some time in controversy with Dr. Schechter and some of the latter's East Coast Reform sympathizers like Jacob H. Schiff and Louis Marshall, on the general theme of the new "Schechterian Judaism," and he used both his pulpit and *The Reform Advocate,* of which he was editor, as vehicles for

ventilating his violent and characteristically sardonic opposition. The Indianapolis incident was just the right sort of
grist for his grinding. He wrote a brilliant editorial entitled
"Swallow-Tailed Judaism," in which he scornfully satirized
the modernistic Schechter-Hoffman swallowtail incident in
Indianapolis as peculiarly symbolic of the kind of Judaism
that was seeking to infiltrate itself into the American synagogue. Imagine, roared the editorial, the ludicrous performance of "Neo-Orthodoxy" in the form of "Schechterian
Judaism" attempting to guarantee the future of Judaism in
America by a mere change of costume from medieval *kaftan*
and *payoth* to modern stiff shirt and swallowtails!

Unfortunately, the festive exercises accompanying the
installation of Rabbi Hoffman and all the glowing promises
of loyalty to "Schechterian Judaism" made in the presence
of its founder in Indianapolis suffered a severe anticlimax
within the same year. Shortly after his formal installation,
Hoffman began a series of tirades both from his pulpit and
in the Philadelphia *Jewish Exponent,* which he continued to
edit, against Reform as practiced in Cincinnati, and especially nearer home here in Indianapolis.

His tenure in Indianapolis was brief. At the end of his
first year he resigned to assume a new post in Newark, New
Jersey. The congregation which was to initiate a healthier
Judaism in Indianapolis, and indeed in the whole Midwest,
had not yet paid him his salary for the year, and he was
compelled to resort to legal procedure to collect. He placed
the matter into the hands of a colleague of earlier days,
Louis Dembitz, of Louisville, the uncle of Justice Louis D.
Brandeis. The congregation's case was entrusted, ironically
enough, to Louis Newberger, board member of my Reform
temple and also a friend of Dembitz. Happily, the case was
settled without reaching the courts.

Sic Transit Gloria Rabbinica

The present building of the Indianapolis Hebrew Congregation has acquired historic interest on other grounds than its memorial windows. In the course of the first quarter of this century, its pulpit was occupied, usually at a regular Friday evening Sabbath service, by well-nigh all the country's distinguished rabbis, and on other occasions by nationally and internationally known laymen. I recall the visit of Chaim Weizmann, later the first president of Israel, about the year 1928. When I learned that because of his personal business interest in the Commercial Solvents Company at Terre Haute he would frequently pass through Indianapolis, I invited him, on behalf of the congregation, to speak from my pulpit during some regular Friday evening service, on his next visit to Terre Haute. He very graciously accepted. I suggested to him that ours was a free pulpit, and he could feel free to speak on any phase of Zionism, even political, if he chose to do so, despite the predominantly non-Zionist composition of the congregation. This was, I believe, his first appearance as a participant in any Reform liturgical service in the country, and while he did not explicitly say so, he seemed to enjoy it. His address was a simple plea for his favorite cause and was presented in a manner and with a content that could neither alienate nor antagonize even the rabid anti-Zionists in his audience.

Of course, there was a heavy contingent of local "professional" Zionists in attendance. These were headed by Daniel Frisch, who a few years later, was to rise from a local to the national leadership of American Zionism as president of the Zionist Organization of America. His rise to the presidency of the ZOA, while meteoric, did not surprise our local community. He started as a more or less obscure figure among us, a moderately successful businessman, but with a ubiquitous—and frequently mischievous—activity in local Jewish affairs. Although without formal education, he had a remarkable native mental capacity and was ambitious to be the proverbial *macher* [big shot] in any and every Jewish organization with which he associated himself. His central interest, however, was political and national Zionism. In this he was fanatically intolerant of all opposition, especially from Reform non-Zionists. In his earlier career, he had pioneered for a brief period in Palestine, whither he had migrated from his native Rumania. On one occasion, a dinner at our local Talmud Torah to which I had been invited as a special courtesy to the principal speaker, a leading Reform colleague and high officer in the national Zionist organization, Frisch, directly pointing his remarks at me, shouted: "A Reform Jew cannot be a Jew at all unless he is a Zionist. This goes for all Jews, whether in America or elsewhere." He later moderated the letter of this public declaration, if not its spirit, when he assumed the presidency of the ZOA—primarily no doubt because of the complicated diplomatic relations the involvements of his new office demanded.

Another notable guest of our pulpit was Israel Abrahams, English rabbinic scholar and a co-founder of the World Union for Progressive Judaism. He was making a tour of some of the larger communities of America, and Indianapolis was on his itinerary. A considerable audience of Jews and non-Jews greeted him, attracted no doubt by the theme of his address which had been announced as a lecture on Judaism in the early Christian period. As a social courtesy in connection with his Indianapolis visit, we managed to provide him with at least two incidents of local historic interest.

On the day after Governor Thomas R. Marshall of

Indiana was elected vice president, along with Woodrow Wilson as president of the United States, I took Abrahams into the governor's office to meet the new vice president-elect. Marshall, in his accustomed genial way, gave us a good half hour of his exceptionally busy day. Abrahams was especially complimented and pleased with this brief meeting, affording him, as it did, a notable example of our simple American and Hoosier democracy. Leaving the governor's office, we toured the city to "see the sights" in a large Marmon automobile especially built for Louis Newberger, attorney for the Nordyke-Marmon Company. Newberger himself accompanied us and suggested that we visit the federal court, to allow Mr. Abrahams to witness American court procedure. At the moment the man on trial was John J. McNamara, charged with having set off the bomb which had caused the death of some hundred spectators in a labor demonstration out on the Pacific Coast. The three of us were ushered to seats in the same row with the defendant, Abrahams sitting immediately next to McNamara, but completely ignorant, of course, of both his neighbor and the crime of which he was accused. Abrahams looked on and listened as intently as the defendant. On leaving the courtroom, Newberger and I were curious to know his reaction. We jestingly asked if he knew how actually close he had been to the commission of an enormous crime. When informed who his immediate neighbor had been, he blinked and said: "Well, it was certainly an experience, even if not exactly a distinguished honor."

A few years later, Indianapolis was honored by the visit of another famous English personality, David Lloyd George. He, too, was on a tour of America shortly after World War I, in which he had played so significant and important a role. His itinerary did not permit more than a single day for his Indianapolis visit, and so his schedule here was completely occupied by engagements and appointments with every sort of organization and group that might conceivably have some pertinent claim upon his attention. Prior to his departure for America he had written a number of articles on the subject of anti-Semitism. The articles, syndicated and published in American newspapers, were highly laudatory of Jews, their patriotism and achievements, and were designed to counteract the defamatory propaganda being circulated in Europe and America during the postwar period. We Jews of Indianapolis along with those the country over were naturally gratified by the publication of these articles, because Lloyd George's reputation for good will toward Jews and underdog minorities in general had long been quite universally established, and more especially because, so far as anybody knew, his articles attacking anti-Semitism had not been solicited or suggested by Jews.

Many minority groups along his planned American itinerary felt it peculiarly appropriate to accord him their own particularistic group honors in addition to those proffered by the majority general population. One such minority group was the Welsh Society of Indianapolis, which undertook to handle the local details of Lloyd George's program during his single day's stay here. This seemed proper enough in view of our visitor's Welsh ancestry. What was my surprise, however, to learn that the president of this society was Morris Jessel, a wholesale dealer in meat supplies and a Jew "in good standing" both in the synagogue and in the general community. "Wouldn't it be nice," said Jessel on the telephone, "if we Jews of Indianapolis joined the Welsh in some kind of special tribute to David Lloyd George?" "It certainly would," I agreed, "but tell me, how do you, a Jew, happen to be president of the Welsh Society?" "That's easy," he replied; "I was born in Poland, decided to visit Wales on my way to the United States. There I met my wife-to-be, who, with her family also born in Poland, had been resident in Wales for a number of years, and our children were born in Wales. My wife and I are the only Jews in the local Welsh Society, and they elected me president; so here I am, a Jew, and an American, and president of the Welsh Society."

At a meeting of our temple board, I conveyed Mr. Jessel's suggestion, and it met with instant and enthusiastic approval. Since our time was limited, I was authorized to prepare a suitable testimonial in behalf of all the Jewish organizations of the city as well as of the temple. Accordingly, we designed as our testimonial a plate of gold in the form of a Magen David, a six-pointed star, eight by eight inches, the center to be inscribed with the words from 1 Samuel 17:49–50: "And it came to pass, when Goliath the Philistine arose, and drew nigh to meet David . . . David hastened and ran toward the army to meet the Philistine . . . and smote and slew him." Our problem then was how to fit the presentation of this testimonial into the already overcrowded schedule of the day's program. Every available moment had already been preempted. The program's *pièce de résistance* was to be a mass meeting in the evening, at which the guest of honor was to make his address responding to the city's official welcome. Although we were magnanimously proffered the opportunity of squeezing in a moment for our purpose, we did not think this would be fair to the various other groups with similar special purposes. The Welsh Society had its luncheon, presided over by Meredith Nicholson, Hoosier novelist and author. He, too, offered to make way for us, but we declined for the same reason. Finally, it was decided to catch our honoree

just as he and his wife and daughter Megan were leaving
the city in their special car at the Union Station.

Accompanied by an entourage of our temple board
and the half-dozen or more presidents of the city's congregations, we climbed the stairs onto the platform of the
railroad car. Lloyd George, of course, had been apprised of
this in advance; and so, together with his family, he came
out to meet us. Under the circumstances, the ceremony of
presentation was necessarily brief and informal. After a
word of reference to the biblical inscription on the Magen
David and its peculiar historical aptness, I could not resist
the added remark that even its outward expression in the
form of a Magen David held a double significance, in that
it embodied both his own name David and, by a mere
transposition of vowels, also that of his daughter Megan.
He received the gift laughingly and warmly, then very
earnestly said that since it had come from a Jewish group he
appreciated the token all the more, because throughout his
entire career, public and private, in war as in peace, he had
consistently and honestly tried to live up to the ideals of the
ancient Hebrew prophets. Our brief ceremony ended, the
train sped away, leaving behind memories of a strenuous
but happy experience in local Jewish history. My own part
in it as an ardent admirer of the "Little Welsh Giant" was
meager enough at best, but was not yet concluded.

A few weeks later, after Lloyd George had returned to
his home in England, the London *Jewish Chronicle* sent a
reporter to interview him about the experiences of his visit
to America, more particularly with its Jewish community.
As reported in *The Chronicle,* he said that he and his family
had been universally welcomed and heartily received. The
part about the Jewish community was particularly gratifying. Then, in an otherwise unmistakable reference to our

testimonial in Indianapolis, he said he was especially appreciative of the "presentation made by the Rabbi of *Philadelphia*"! *Sic transit gloria rabbinica!*

The Heat of the Day

The year 1916 marked the centennial of Indiana's admission to the union. To help in contributing to its local celebration, the National Conference of Jewish Charities, concurrently with the National Conference of Charities, held its annual meeting in Indianapolis. This was quite an event for our Jewish community, since it was only a few years previously that our local federation had been organized and joined with the larger organization as a constituent member. Since our temple annex was too small to accommodate the assembly, the auditorium of the sanctuary was used for the opening meeting. The governor of Indiana, Samuel Ralston, and Father Francis H. Gavisk, president of the National Conference of Charities, were among the welcoming speakers, and both confessed to a sense of nervousness because it was the first time that either of them had ever been inside a synagogue.

Also in attendance was Jacob Gimbel, of Philadelphia, then president of Gimbel Brothers and the oldest of the sons of Adam Gimbel, whose first store had been established in Vincennes, Indiana, in 1842. Gimbel said he had come to attend the meeting both out of a feeling of Hoosier nostalgia and because at the moment he was especially interested in a kind of social service that might be helpful in formulating a policy of mutual assistance among the employees of his company. His presence in Indianapolis afforded me the opportunity of asking about some of his reminiscences of early Vincennes, especially about its then most noted citizen, Samuel B. Judah. Gimbel had been a young boy then, but he still had some vivid personal recollections of Judah. He remembered that Judah had been in the habit of coming into the Gimbel store daily and, in the proverbial cracker-barrel style of Hoosierdom, would join in debating political and other issues of the day. One day, while Judah was thus engaged, a dark-looking itinerant drifted in expecting a handout. Judah was about to respond with a silver coin when he looked the stranger in the eye and asked from what part of the Old Country he hailed. "From Spain," answered the stranger, whereupon Judah withheld his proffered coin and scruffed the man out of the door with the remark: "Your people once kicked my ancestors out of their country; I'll do the same to you."

Another event to be accredited to the temple building's history was the first and only meeting of the Central Conference of American Rabbis held in Indianapolis, in 1906. Joseph Stolz, of Chicago, was then president, and although I had been in my new pulpit only a year and had only shortly before been admitted to C. C. A. R. membership, he asked if I thought Indianapolis could be prepared to accommodate the next meeting of the conference. I answered affirmatively, though with some mental reservations. Not only was I a newcomer in the city, but a convention of such nationwide Jewish significance was also a new experience for the community. Moreover, the annual meetings of the conference were usually held in June, and Indianapolis, being an inland city, was known to be a pretty warm spot in the summertime. In spite of all this, the conference was held here, and proved to have the largest attendance of its history up to that time. I was honored, as the host rabbi, with the privilege of welcoming the conference.

The evening was insufferably hot. In opening my address, I likened Indianapolis's eagerness to welcome so distinguished a body to the enthusiasm with which, according to tradition, the patriarch Abraham was accustomed to greet every stranger passing the door of his tent, and quoted the familiar lines from Genesis: "And the Lord appeared unto Abraham . . . as he sat in the tent door in the *heat of the day;* and he lifted up his eyes, and lo, three men stood over against him; and when he saw them, he ran to greet them . . ." (Genesis 18:1–2). Familiar enough, indeed almost hackneyed, as that passage was to my audience, it struck them as being so obviously and literally pertinent at the moment and in the premises that it was greeted by an unrestrained roar of laughter. Even the usually motionless face of the venerable Dr. Kaufmann Kohler, honorary president of the conference, who was seated on the platform, broke into a broad and rollicking grin. I do not recall that this particular meeting of the conference accomplished anything so extraordinary as to make the name of Indianapolis historic in C. C. A. R. annals, but it certainly gave our community a historical luster it continues to cherish. A large photograph of those in attendance, most of whom, alas, have long since passed away, hangs both as a memento and as a memorial in our vestry.

Another interesting name to be associated with our temple pulpit was that of Wong Kai Kah, Chinese ambassador to the Louisiana Purchase Exposition in 1904. Although the exposition was being held in St. Louis, Wong chose Indianapolis as his family home for the duration of the fair because he wanted his children to attend our local public schools. Having met him at the home of one of our temple members with whose family he had developed an intimate friendship, I invited him to speak from our pulpit on the history and status of Jews in China. The prospect of an educated Chinese, who was also slated to be his country's next ambassador to the Court of St. James's, in a Jewish pulpit at a regular Sabbath evening service attracted a full attendance. He had not proceeded very far with his address, however, when suddenly every light in the building went out. In the complete darkness of the moment, and while those nearest the exits skirmished about for candles in the neighborhood, I tried to allay the confusion by reassuring the audience that it would not be long before we should once again learn *ex Oriente lux.* Within minutes, a few candles were collected and lighted when, sure enough, the electricity was back in operation, and the "light from the East" was resumed. As a souvenir of the occasion, the congregation presented him with a set of Graetz's *History of the Jews,* and since the presentation was made on a Christmas Day, which in that year fell during the week of Hanukkah, we had the flyleaf inscription read: "From a Congregation of Jews to a Buddhist on a Christian holy day!"

During the first of my three years' tenure in Lafayette, the congregation had voted me a salary of fifteen hundred dollars, which in those days was considered a fair wage for a young rabbi just out of school. In each of the two succeeding years, this was increased by a hundred dollars, in compliment, it was officially explained, to my "successful leadership." About this time, the Union of American Hebrew Congregations was beginning to carry out another of the original purposes of its organization: that of establishing congregations and religious schools in the smaller, still unorganized communities of the country. I took on for this purpose Kokomo and Logansport, Indiana, both about fifty miles from Lafayette. Each of these had about a dozen Jewish families, and biweekly services were conducted.

It was in Logansport that I was paid what I have since

come to regard as one of the bluntest, but pleasantest compliments of my pulpit experience. The young rabbis of that time, like those of today, were frequent recipients of compliments, discriminating and otherwise, from congregants, especially after their sermons had been delivered. "Doctor, that was a wonderful sermon you delivered today," was a familiar phrase then as it still is today; and then, too, as today, many a young rabbi allowed himself to accept such statements at their face rather than their real value, with results that not infrequently were just about as dubiously flattering to his personality as they were to his subsequent pulpit career. In my own case, though by no means unsusceptible or indifferent to the common weakness, I deliberately and studiously tried from the very beginning of my ministry to be on guard in all such situations. I tried consistently to build up a sort of cautious if not always tactful resistance, even though I well knew then, as I do now, that from the viewpoint of the pew, it does not always "pay." Accordingly, I was not altogether prepared when, after our biweekly services in Logansport were beginning to get into swing, I was approached by three members of the congregation immediately at the conclusion of the service. They said they had been appointed as a committee to ask officially that I make my sermons longer! Sermons in synagogue and church alike, whether good, bad, or indifferent, were proverbially long in those days. I felt inwardly, therefore, that among preachers I was being really complimented in a unique way. On later reflection, however, my triumphant sense of self-satisfaction was somewhat tempered.

Our services were held on Sunday evenings in the basement of a church, which had graciously tendered its room for the purpose. The church would hold its own service a half hour later in the auditorium upstairs. We had neither choir, music, nor even copies of the *Union Prayer Book*. All we had was the weekday service-text from the *UPB*, with which I would start the service and then deliver the sermon, usually a repetition of the sermon given my congregation in Lafayette on the previous Friday evening. The sermon rarely exceeded twenty minutes in length. Thus the total time of the service, including sermon, was about thirty-five minutes. It can be readily understood, therefore, why a small group of Jews who never had held a religious service before should suddenly feel an acute sense of spiritual hunger and welcome the opportunity of satisfying it adequately. Their grievance in this case seemed a just one. Knowing some of the individuals in the congregation as I did, however, I had a sneaking, though perhaps unwarranted, suspicion that they may have felt they were not "getting their money's worth," inasmuch as I was being paid the munificent sum of ten dollars per visit for both my service and expenses. Taking all things into account, I still like to boast that this official request of the Logansport congregation makes me the rightfully proud possessor of a compliment rarely, if ever, paid to a pulpiteer of church or synagogue anywhere.

The first decade of my ministry was largely a period of personal and professional adjustment. In 1909, five years after my induction in Indianapolis, I married Mildred J. Mayerstein, a member of my first confirmation class in Lafayette. She was the daughter of Maurice M. Mayerstein, who was born in Cincinnati but removed in early boyhood to Lafayette, where his father settled as a tutor in public school studies. A sister of Maurice's, Selma, was for many years teacher of German in the public high school of Lafayette, and another sister, Hennie, was for a like period secretary to the dean in the department of agriculture at

Purdue University. Maurice Mayerstein was the first Jew to attain prominence in the history of Indiana journalism. From news and office boy with the Lafayette *Evening Courier,* he rose rapidly to become its owner and publisher until his early and untimely death at the age of forty-two. The *Courier* was then one of the oldest and best known of Indiana's newspapers. Its staff of writers during the Mayerstein regime boasted such later eminent names as Booth Tarkington, George Ade, George Barr McCutcheon, and the cartoonist John T. McCutcheon.

A few years after Mayerstein's death, and while I was already well set in my Indianapolis post, I was confronted with my first serious challenge to leave the rabbinate. The owner of Lafayette's morning paper, one of the state's most influential politicians, was eager to possess the evening paper as well. The city's Chamber of Commerce, comprising both papers' principal advertisers, was resolved to balk his ambition. For commercial as well as personal and political reasons, they were suspicious of his motives, and inasmuch as there was no member of my wife's family either equipped or available at the time to take over the *Courier*'s management, the chamber, at a full membership meeting called for the purpose, made the formal proposal that I take over as editor and manager of the *Courier.* To fortify their proposal, they added the suggestion by the Jewish members of the chamber that I could at the same time return to my old pulpit and thus serve in a double capacity as newspaper editor and rabbi. I confess I was strongly tempted, but since the situation demanded an immediate decision, I definitely and firmly answered in the negative. As things eventuated, the decision proved to have been a happy one all around. For my part, I felt quite content and happy in Indianapolis, and I ventured to think that here lay the most promising field for such success as my limited powers might hope to achieve in the career to which I had been dedicated. Within the next decade I was faced with five similar invitations to leave my Indianapolis pulpit for larger fields of action.

By this time I had come to appreciate the wisdom of the plea: "Lord, my heart is not haughty, nor mine eyes lofty; neither do I exercise myself in things too great or in things too wonderful for me . . ." (Psalms 131:1). I make no pretense to modesty or self-depreciation when I say that, from the very beginning of my ministry, I have tried conscientiously and deliberately to use that obscure line of the Psalmist as a sort of motto to guide me when walking in the valley of decision or indecision, as the case might be. While no less sensitive than the next man to the normal urge of ambition, or any less vulnerable to the seductive sounds of flattery, I have found this, despite frequent importunities of family and friends to the contrary, to be a pretty safe rule to follow on grounds of sheer physical self-preservation, if no other. Thus conscious of my own limitations and by no means unaware of Browning's admonition, in contradistinction to that of the Psalmist, that "A man's reach should exceed his grasp—or what's a heaven for," nevertheless, I felt from the beginning that I would "fit in" better with the size and conditions prevailing in Indianapolis than I could have done, physically or generally, in some larger sphere of action elsewhere.

Stephenson for President

By appointment of Governor James P. Goodrich and reappointment by succeeding governors, I became the first Jewish member of the Indiana State Board of Charities and Correction and continued as such from 1920 to 1931. This was the period when the Ku Klux Klan was politically regnant in Indiana, as well as in some other parts of the nation. Its recollection still sends a shudder through many an honest and penitent Hoosier heart. While this latest Klan epidemic, like its predecessor in the Civil War era, had had its beginnings in the South, it seemed now to have its seat and center in Indiana. Its "hero" and Grand Dragon appeared in the person of a David C. Stephenson, who had come to Indiana from Texas, and its basic philosophy was that to be a true 100 percent American, one had to be native-born, white, and Protestant. This of course automatically reduced Negro, Roman Catholic, Jew, and immigrant to sub-American status, and in Indiana at least resulted in commercial, social, and political pandemonium. At the same time, moreover, the liquor prohibition amendment had called into being here, as elsewhere in the nation, speakeasy clubs which were quite notorious—except that Indiana still had upon its statute books an old, unrepealed horse-thief detective law dating back to Civil War days, when horse thievery had been quite common, and permitting the wearing of a police badge and gun for the protection of the horse owner.

Stephenson made ready use of these Prohibition-flouting organizations by joining them into a strong collective group which wielded a tremendous political power. For the most part their memberships were made up of "hijackers, roughnecks, and rowdies," who thrived on the illicit liquor traffic of that period. By assuming the garb and grandiloquent pageantry of the Ku Klux Klan, they increasingly added to their numbers, until their enrollment included not only the lawless and rowdy elements, but also many of the illiterate and unwary, and even prominent business and professional people, especially those who may have had

From *The Independent,* November 28, 1925

Ku Klux Klan: "The Light That Fails"

political ambitions of one sort or another. All these were required to purchase the white-sheeted garb of the Klan at a cost of ten dollars, and after signing a formal, high-sounding pledge to defend and protect the Constitution of the United States were accepted as members. The head of this whole potpourri was Stephenson, Grand Dragon of the Indiana Ku Klux Klan, who thereby accumulated such wealth and political power that when challenged by some legal but skeptical group, he was reported to have claimed: "I am the law in Indiana." And for a time he was.

Undercover pamphlets and books—I saw one of the latter—were printed and circulated, grooming Stephenson for the presidency. The general population of the state, more especially the four groups at whom the Klan's shafts were aimed, was terrorized. Public criticism, comments, and even news reports of the Klan's doings could not be found in any of the state's newspapers. Such reports, if and when available, were only those which were brought in by newspapers from outside the state. It was not until long after the collapse of Stephenson's power, as a result of his conviction and life imprisonment on a second degree murder charge, that the whole sordid story of the Klan in Indiana became public knowledge, and then only through a Pulitzer Prize award to one of the Indianapolis newspapers that first published it.

Chief targets of the Klan agitation in Indiana were Roman Catholics, on religious grounds primarily, and Jews, for business reasons usually inspired by envious non-Jewish local competitors. But the curious thing about it all was that the agitation was noisiest in communities where Catholics and Jews were fewest in number, if not altogether absent. My own disturbed state of mind throughout this period can readily be imagined. It was shared, of course, not only by my fellow Jews and the other victims of the Klan propaganda, but also by all the decent and high-minded citizens of the state. In the face of blazing fiery crosses and brazen terrorist tactics, however, they appeared to be able only to stand by and await developments.

Klan terrorism made any kind of active resistance short of rioting and shooting warfare seem futile. Here and there a few voices did speak out. More eagerly perhaps than under normal conditions, I accepted invitations to address service, business, church, and women's organizations throughout the state, groups which wanted to hear some kind of pronouncements from the minority or unpopular side of the subject. And I was supposed to be especially and personally complimented by such invitations, because in only the rarest instances, if any, had similar invitations been tendered to a representative of the other three Klan opposition groups. Of course, I took advantage of such opportunities to satirize the Klan's percentage kind of Americanism, and to appeal to the better judgment and higher patriotism of my hearers. Invariably, the first to come up at the conclusion of the address for a word of appreciation would be some self-announced Catholics, to be followed rather timidly by others.

To show that we in Indianapolis at least were not yet completely intimidated by all this Klan agitation, two mass meetings of protest were held in Cadle Tabernacle, a supposed Klan stronghold. These were addressed by two prominent Protestant ministers, the Rev. Dr. S. Parkes Cadman, of Brooklyn, N. Y., and Bishop Frederick D. Leete, of the Indianapolis Methodist district. Both meetings were sponsored and arranged by a small but loosely organized committee of local Roman Catholics, Protestants, and Jews which ultimately grew into what is now known as the National Conference of Christians and Jews. I believe this to be historically correct, although the minute books of the larger organization may not so record it.

Shortly before the Klan began its virulent operations hereabouts, in Indiana at least, the Central Conference of American Rabbis and the Federal Council of Churches of Christ in America had joined hands in passing formal resolutions to further amicable relations between their two constituencies. The National Council of Catholic Societies had not yet joined the other two. The subsequent union of the three organizations to a similar end was really started in Terre Haute, Indiana, by a mass meeting in the local opera house, organized by Rabbi Joseph L. Fink and the Rev. Dr. John W. Herring, both then of Terre Haute, to protest against the rising tide of Klanism in their vicinity. This meeting proved to be so enthusiastically successful that the two men suggested a similar meeting to the Church Federation of Indianapolis. I was then invited by the Church Federation to select a group of ten representatives of the Indianapolis Jewish community for a luncheon meeting with a similar number of Protestant representatives, at which it was suggested that I preside. I respectfully declined the invitation to preside for two specific reasons: first, I believed the responsibility for such leadership lay primarily and properly with the majority or Protestant group, and second, there was no Roman Catholic representation in attendance to help in achieving our common purpose. With these matters duly adjusted, the meeting thus became the nucleus of an *active* implementation on a local scale of the overall interfaith movement projected by the three national organizations and now known as the National Conference

of Christians and Jews, directed by Dr. Everett R. Clinchy.
Unfortunately and in spite of, if not because of, the tension
prevailing hereabouts at the time, our local efforts were so
loosely and intermittently organized that most, if not all, of
the specific and pertinent official records are unavailable
today, and our title to boast historical priority in this field
of interfaith activity will therefore probably not remain
uncontested.

Despite this deficiency, however, there are many incidents and aftermaths of this turbulent Klan period that can
readily enough be confirmed by extant and authoritative
records. One of these was an interim Marion County election by which a show of hands on the general citizenry's
attitude toward the Klan situation was made possible. The
candidates for office on the Democratic side of the ballot
were all, with one exception, known Roman Catholics. The
exception was Meredith Nicholson, well-known Hoosier
novelist and writer who, for the sake of religious tolerance
as well as party allegiance, permitted his name to remain on
the ticket as a candidate for the state senate. The Republican
candidates, for their part, were all without exception non-
Catholics, and therefore presumably represented the Klan,
since it was generally known that the Klan had long since
been infiltrating itself into the party. To all appearances,
therefore, the issue between Klan and anti-Klan was being
forced upon the voter in such a way as to challenge him at
the polls with a mixture of church and practical politics
which was dangerously close to a violation of his presumably basic Americanism. Nicholson and I were alarmed. The
election was only ten days off, but we agreed to ask our
mutual friend, Msgr. Gavisk, to appeal to the Roman Catholic head of the Democratic ticket, a candidate for Congress,
to withdraw his name with a frank statement as to his reason

for doing so. Father Gavisk agreed that this was not only the patriotic and proper thing to do, but might also prove to be politically advantageous to the candidate himself. Unfortunately, it was too late. The candidate declined on the ground that he had been duly nominated by his party and had already been compelled to incur too much expense in the campaign to forgo the chance of his election. The result was an election in which the entire Democratic ticket, including the lone non-Catholic Nicholson, went down to defeat, and for the nonce the alleged Klan candidates prevailed.

This was one of the very few instances of my ministry in which I felt it not only warranted as a citizen but also my duty as a rabbi to take a dip into the frequently complicated practices of real party politics. A somewhat more dramatic instance, but one involving Jews more directly, occurred during this same Klan period at Muncie, the very head and center of the movement in Indiana. An upstart lawyer by the name of Clarence Dearth had announced himself Republican candidate for county judge on a Klan platform. Here, too, both Republican and Klan sentiment appeared to be in the majority. To offset and, if possible, defeat this candidate, the Democratic organization prevailed upon Adolph Silverburg, a leading lawyer and the outstanding Jew of Muncie, to accept their nomination as Dearth's opponent. Reluctantly he accepted, primarily, as he expressed it, as a matter of party loyalty and plain decency. The organization well knew his sincerity in this, because he had neither the taste nor the need for dabbling in local politics, but he in turn was convinced of his party's honesty in trying to maintain the good name of the city against the threat of Klanism. In the preelection campaign, Dearth ambulated about the county, haranguing his audiences and denouncing his opponent in the most vulgar and demagogical terms. "Do you want a miserable Jew to sit in judgment upon you?" he insistently and shamelessly challenged. The election returns favored Dearth, and Silverburg, as can well be understood, felt bitterly humiliated.

A few weeks later, the handful of Jewish families in Muncie, about fifty in a total population of some thirty thousand, dedicated their small new synagogue. All the city's notables were invited to attend the ceremonies. Muncie had been my monthly pulpit in student days. Accordingly, for this reason, as well as my being rabbi of the temple in the state capital, I was invited to deliver the dedicatory address. Silverburg was chairman of the building committee and in that capacity was to present the keys of the building to the president. In doing so he recited in a loud but quavering voice just a single line for his speech: *"Shema yisroel adonoy elohenu adonoy echod*—Hear, O Israel, the Lord our God, the Lord is One! For that idea," he continued, "I have been crucified." He then handed the keys to the president and abruptly took his seat.

The effect upon the assembly was literally stunning. It seemed as if a wave of mingled shock and guilt was visibly sweeping through and across his audience. My address immediately followed, so it devolved upon me somehow to allay as best I could the very perceptible uneasiness of the moment. I managed to sputter something about our common understanding of Silverburg's feelings in the light of what had so recently occurred in the community. Then I proceeded with my prepared address, reminding my audience, however, that once upon a time, about two centuries ago, Dean Swift had written: "Some people have just enough religion to hate their fellowmen, but not enough religion to love them"—whereupon the mayor of the city, who was sitting directly beneath my eye, impulsively punched his neighbor on the knee and quite audibly remarked: "See, that's just what I've been telling you fellows all along."

Muncie, however, even amid such unflattering incidents, was not yet completely Klan-ridden. It should be recorded that the well-known family of Ball Brothers, glass manufacturers, contributed the unsolicited sum of five thousand dollars to the building fund of the Muncie synagogue. The family contributed a like amount for a similar purpose in nearby Marion. Moreover, in the infamous Dearth episode a day of poetic justice for Silverburg was not far in the offing. Not long after Dearth took his seat on the bench, he was charged with malfeasance in office, was tried, found guilty, and finally removed by a special session of the state legislature called for the purpose. There still persists, however, a strange and malodorous aftermath of Klanism in Indiana, despite this public finding of the legislature. A transcript of the legislature's proceedings somehow disappeared shortly after the single day's trial session, and to this day (1953) has not been recovered. Thus, so far as the state's official records are concerned, the whole Dearth episode remains a historical blank.

A Christmas Card from the Pen

Throughout this stormy period in the mid-1920s, I was privileged to serve as a member of the State Board of Charities and Correction. In this capacity I had frequent occasion to come into closer and more intimate contact with the Klan itself. Ironically, one of these occurred with the organization in Muncie. Here a Mrs. Daisy Douglas Barr, a minister, had been particularly active in Klan affairs. She was reported to have accumulated a considerable sum of money from the sale of sheets and other Klan paraphernalia. To honor her the organization proposed to erect an orphanage to be named the Daisy Douglas Barr Children's Home. According to Indiana law, every such project must have the approval of the State Board of Charities to qualify as a proper institution for safeguarding the welfare of its inmates. I was chairman of the board's subcommittee on children's welfare, with Father Gavisk as my colleague member. The Klan's application, therefore, had to pass through our hands before final ratification by the full board.

When the application reached the office of John A. Brown, successor to Amos W. Butler as secretary, he was inclined to disregard and discard it at once. But on reflection, he decided to pass it on to our subcommittee, believing we would be likely to confirm his inclination anyway. But even to his surprise, I said the application should be permitted to pass, inasmuch as I thought it to be the only decent thing for humankind the Klan was attempting to do. "But what about Father Gavisk?" asked Brown. I replied that I was sure Father Gavisk would concur, whereupon the application was filed in due form, but, as might have been suspected, nothing further eventuated, and the Daisy Douglas Barr Home for Children never reached beyond its initial nominal stage. The same thing happened a little later at Valparaiso, Indiana, when newspapers reported that its university was in financial difficulties and was about to be offered for sale. Immediately, the Klan announced through the press that it was prepared to purchase the institution and continue to conduct it under Klan auspices. But again, as in the Muncie case, the purchase never got beyond its public announcement.

But of all these personal contacts with the Klan, my most revealing and exciting, perhaps, was with the erstwhile "hero" and Grand Dragon, David Stephenson himself, during his incarceration in the Michigan City Penitentiary. While he was serving his sentence here, many of his erstwhile followers were eager to disavow him. A strong and numerous anti-Stephenson faction developed within the Klan itself. He frequently complained of being persecuted and actually mistreated by his jailers, all of whom, he charged, were mere tools of the anti-Stephenson faction of the national Ku Klux Klan, and all of whom, including the warden and board of trustees, were bent on murdering him. When his charges were denied by the warden and the board, Stephenson insisted on his right to appeal to a superior authority, the State Board of Charities and Correction. Accordingly his case was referred to our board.

We visited the prison and interviewed him for two full days. We questioned him on every phase of his Klan activities and leadership. His answers at first were given in characteristically arrogant and dictatorial fashion, but when he was assured that he was standing with his back against the wall and that we were the only official group that could be of any possible relief or help to him, he softened a bit, and we further questioned him about his personal philosophy of life, his belief in God and his fellowmen, and so on. At one point in our discussion he offered to disclose the innermost secrets of the Klan to only two of our six members, a Roman Catholic and a Jew: Father Gavisk and myself! Of course, we spurned his "magnanimous" offer, declaring we were not interested in pulling any Klan chestnuts out of the fire. Altogether, to me, as to the rest of the board, it was, to say the least, a rare and most revealing psychological and social experience, and for a number of years after this two-day meeting I was the questionably proud recipient of a special Christmas greeting from the penitentiary signed "D. C. Stephenson."

One other prison experience while I was a member of the Board of Charities has remained a vivid memory to me. The site of our state reformatory at Jeffersonville was about to be transferred to a new location at Pendleton, but before any such transfer could be made, the new site, according to the law, had to have the approval of our board. The governor, being an ex officio member of the board, joined us in the necessary inspection of the new site. After we had made our tour of inspection, the governor reminded us that we had given no thought to providing for the possible erection of at least three homes for reformatory chaplains. Turning first to Father Gavisk, the Catholic member of the board, he observed: "We'll need one for you"; then to the Protestant minister, "and one for you"; and finally, but hesitating a moment as he faced me, he said: "Oh, I forgot, we'll not need any for your people." I thanked him for the subtle compliment, and on the following Yom Kippur Eve, I recalled the incident from my pulpit to illustrate the difference between ethical and legal morality, which I was using as my sermonic theme. When I repeated the governor's compliment to us as Jews, I added parenthetically: "But of course, I did not tell the governor that you and I know Jews who may even be in the synagogue tonight but should be in jail, though they are not." Despite the solemnity of the occasion, the congregation, in the familiar folkway fashion of our people, reacted with a "knowing" burst of laughter, and I knew then, as they did, that the point of my sermon had been successfully delivered.

I Am a Jew

Mention of the "swallowtail" incident in connection with Dr. Solomon Schechter's visit to Indianapolis in 1904 brings to mind several other incidents with a similar serio-comic touch. Ever since the Civil War era, when Indianapolis was one of the first and nearest of the northern cities of refuge for slaves fleeing from the South, the Negro population of the city has been relatively very large. Except for politicians with motives of their own, the white population generally appeared to take very little interest in their welfare. A year after taking up my residence in Indianapolis, Dr. Frank S. C. Wicks, an officer of the American Unitarian Association, was installed as minister of the recently organized local Unitarian church. I was invited to participate in his installation ceremonies, and we became fast and lasting friends. We agreed that something ought to be done to arouse the local population to an awareness of the need for ameliorating the conditions prevailing among our colored neighbors. The National Association for the Advancement of Colored People was just then being organized on the East Coast. One of its founders was the highly reputed liberal Oswald Garrison Villard, grandson of the famed abolitionist William Lloyd Garrison.

Dr. Wicks arranged a meeting in his church to be addressed by Villard. The modest church, with a seating capacity of three hundred, was filled with local colored folk. Villard, Wicks, and I were the white exceptions. To demonstrate our democracy, as well as out of courtesy both to speaker and audience, Wicks suggested that he and I, as well as Villard, appear at the meeting in the fashionable tuxedo attire of that period. However well intentioned this was esthetically, the sight of three whites thus attired in a friendly yet completely black company in ordinary neat though everyday attire was, to say the least, conspicuous enough to border on the grotesque. This did not disturb me, however, until Villard reached a point in his address when he casually and, as I thought, quite gratuitously and obviously to win favor with his audience remarked that the Negro deserved an attitude and treatment by the white community just as sympathetic as—and indeed *more so than* —that accorded the Jew. I winced at the statement, particularly since it appeared to be a deviation from his text, and I was sorely tempted to challenge his meaning in open assembly, but decided it was best in the premises to hold my tongue *mipne darche shalom* [for the sake of peace]. In any case, I left the meeting rather disillusioned, if not actually chagrined, by the quality of liberalism expressed by one who was universally accepted and acclaimed as one of the foremost of the nation's liberals.

A few years after this meeting, I had local occasion to compensate for my disappointment by participating in what I considered to be a purer and truer kind of liberalism. Julius Rosenwald had let it be known that he was ready to help in improving the condition of the nation's Negroes with his historic offer to contribute the sum of $75,000 for every $25,000 collected by Negroes in any city of the country for the erection of a local colored Young Men's Christian Association. Such a Y.M.C.A. had just been organized in Indianapolis and was struggling along in dire need of funds. The organization, therefore, appealed to its older white brother Y.M.C.A. for help in taking advantage of Rosenwald's offer. A meeting was called by the white Y.M.C.A.'s board to see what could be done about it. I was invited to attend. Whether rightly or wrongly, I suspected that the invitation was tendered to me not so much in tribute to Julius Rosenwald as a fellow Jew, but as a representative of the local Jewish group which might be counted on for potentially generous contributors, like Mr. Rosenwald himself. There had been some current and unfriendly whispers here as elsewhere that Rosenwald's offer was probably prompted by business as well as purely philanthropic motives, since he was at the time president of the nationwide mail-order firm, Sears, Roebuck and Company. I confess that I attended the meeting in a fully sympathetic and cooperative, but somewhat belligerent, mood, at the same time fearful lest, if I were called on to speak, any belligerency of expression on my part might endanger the success of our common project.

Among those present, about twenty-five in all, were representatives of the various denominational groups, many of whom were well known nationally as well as locally. One of these was a wealthy citizen, a moneylender by vocation and widely known for his religious activities, but not quite so well or favorably known for his generosity. I do not mean to be unfair to his memory, but he appeared, to me at least, to be a figure right out of Dickens: short, thin, with long nose, sharp eyes, sunken cheeks, always ready of speech, and always, out-of-doors as well as in, topped with black skullcap—a sort of potential Christian counterpart of the Jewish moneylender as the prejudiced medieval tradition usually still portrays the type. On spotting him I felt my belligerency rising to the surface, and so when duly called to make some remarks, I sallied forth like a Shylock: "I am a Jew; so is Julius Rosenwald. You are Christians being asked by fellow Christians of another color for help in the name of Jesus, also a Jew. Julius Rosenwald is here proffering his bounty to Christians not only in deference to the teachings of Jesus, but also because, as he himself has declared, he is literally and specifically seeking to obey the ancient command of his forefathers: 'Remember that ye were once slaves in the land of Egypt.' If a modern Jew like Julius Rosenwald living in twentieth-century America can still look for inspiration to the slavery days of ancient Egypt, cannot we today unite as Jews and Christians to help fellow humans who are still more or less slaves despite our vaunted modern freedom?" I did not then, nor do I today, imagine that I saw a tinge of redness in the faces of some of my hearers. I do know they were none too enthusiastic in their reception of my remarks, but to their immortal credit, it should be said, they followed through with their project, and in due course a substantial building for the colored Y.M.C.A. was erected. Two or three years later a companion structure for colored women was erected, also with the help of Julius Rosenwald. Although his name is rarely heard nowadays in connection with these two structures, Rosenwald, on a later visit to the city, had the satisfaction of seeing an enlarged photograph of himself in the office of one of them.

I have spoken earlier in this narrative of the large and special role assumed by my generation of Hebrew Union College alumni in both the Jewish and non-Jewish social service areas of their several communities. Theoretically, at least, and in their moral objectives, social service and social justice are not very far apart. In the Jewish tradition, indeed, they are synonymous. It is not difficult, therefore, to understand why in many communities of the land a rabbi should be called upon to act as an arbiter or mediator in local labor disputes. But what a novelty, what an interesting historical phenomenon in the traditional functioning of the rabbinate itself! For centuries it was common enough to see and expect a rabbi to act, either alone or with his *beth din* [his rabbinical colleagues convened as a court], as mediator, arbiter, and judge *within* his own communal jurisdiction. But now in instances too numerous to be regarded as negligible or insignificant the rabbi is called upon to settle disputes and make peace between man and man *outside* his congregational or communal jurisdiction. Verily, this is America, and verily, too, this may be claimed as one of the historic triumphs of Reform Judaism, and more specifically of the Hebrew Union College, in the progress and evolution of Judaism itself!

Here in a Worthy Cause

In the early years of the present century, Indianapolis was known as a strong antiunion labor town, despite the fact that several of the nation's biggest labor unions, like the Miners', Carpenters', Teamsters', and others, had their central offices here. A powerful group of industrialists resolved to keep the city as free of unionism as possible. Strikes and threats of strikes, therefore, were not infrequent hereabouts. Shortly after my installation as rabbi, I was asked to participate as a speaker at a mass outdoor meeting to be held in the courthouse square by the streetcar workers, who were threatening to strike against the local transit company. I accepted the invitation, although at the moment neither I, nor anyone else for that matter, had at hand any very precise or accurate date. I must confess at this late date, and after some experience in these matters, that the dramatic idea of a rabbi addressing thousands of underprivileged people out in the open must have figured in prompting my acceptance. In any case, on the day following the meeting, I was visited by Henry Kahn, a member of my congregation and also of the industrialist group opposing all such labor agitation. Kahn was known to me and in the community generally as a kindly employer as well as a bighearted person, and he did not attempt to rebuke, but rather to counsel and caution me. His visit was received in that spirit.

I single out Kahn in this connection because a few years later he was himself, as the head of a nationwide clothing manufacturing firm, confronted with a similar strike threat by his own employees, a goodly number of whom were coreligionists. In this case I was contacted by a Mr. Lefkowitch, a union organizer from the East Coast, who asked that I in turn contact Kahn with a view to softening him in his known antiunion position. I replied that I would be glad to do so and that I was sure Kahn also would be glad at least to confer with him, provided I too were given the opportunity to confer in the meantime with both Kahn and his employees. All this being duly agreed to by all parties concerned, a meeting of the employees was held, and the strike was averted. Despite my meager efforts to that end, however, I later received, with Lefkowitch's "compliments," a copy of his trade magazine article mercilessly lampooning me as an ignorant, meddling Reform rabbi.

The day came later when, in a period of general business decline, Kahn's firm was itself involved in financial difficulties. This time another union, Sidney Hillman's clothing workers, entered the picture, and with the union's reasonable cooperation and proffers of assistance, the firm's problems were successfully solved. From then on, Kahn, an erstwhile antiunion controversialist, became a correspondingly staunch union sympathizer. From experiences such as these I learned soon enough that there are plenty of controversialists around, even on the underprivileged side of a labor dispute, people willing and eager to use a rabbi, if necessary—especially if he be young and enthusiastic as I was at the time—to advance their own particular interests, regardless of merit in any given case.

One such instance occurred about 1925 and involves an incident which, though minor enough in itself, concerns a name that has since appeared conspicuously and many times in the nation's public prints. It was that of Louis Budenz, a member of a prominent local German Catholic family, one-time editor of a Communist newspaper, and now professor at Fordham University. Shortly before the incident to which I refer, the Central Conference of American Rabbis, the National Federation of the Churches of Christ in America, and the National Catholic Welfare Council had simultaneously and each in its own way adopted a resolution proffering their services in the amicable and peaceful adjustment of disputes between employer and employee anywhere in the land. There was no specific medium or machinery for immediate implementation of the resolution, so far as I knew then or know now, except the usual parliamentary committee or commission created by each of these organizations to help effectuate the general purposes of social service and social justice. About this time, however, there were rumblings of dissatisfaction among the employees of our local Real Silk Hosiery Mills, then reputed to be the largest of its kind in the world, and whose chief officials and owners were Jews.

I had not heard of any such dissatisfaction until I was called on the telephone one day by someone introducing himself as Louis Budenz, "representing the Central Conference of American Rabbis." Recognizing the family name, I asked how he came to represent the Central Conference of American Rabbis rather than the National Catholic Welfare Council, to whose constituency I presumed he then belonged. "Well, they are both the same, since I am here in a worthy cause," he answered. "No," I countered, "you know as well as I that they are not the same, even though the cause be a good one. Moreover, having known me personally, you have no need for this kind of strategy for gaining access to my door, especially since you claim your cause to be a worthy one." He thereupon outlined his purpose, which was for me to arrange a meeting between him and the Real Silk officials at which he could propose certain reforms of evils he alleged were then prevailing in the Real Silk Plant. If such a hearing could not be arranged, he feared for the future success of the Real Silk business. He held in his hand and showed me the printed proofs of an article about to be published in a forthcoming issue of a magazine called *Labor,* or some such name, in case no favorable action by the company was taken. It was couched in the harshest and most violent terms designed to injure the sale of the plant's product. Despite this threat, I called William V. Kobin, a high official of the firm. I was confident of Kobin's characteristic tolerance at least in meeting Budenz, but without promise of commitments of any kind. A meeting was accordingly arranged and held. The following day, I was compelled to leave the city for several weeks' absence. On my return home, I was surprised and chagrined to receive a mailed copy of *Labor* containing the article whose printed proofs Budenz had previously shown me. As I have indicated, the whole incident was minor enough in its general interest, but I am relating it here as a heretofore unreported, off-the-record item revealing Budenz's psychological status long before his publicly confessed somersaults between communism and the religious faith in which he was born and reared.

In the period of the First World War, I was pressed

into extraordinary service as chairman of our local Jewish Welfare Board and also as a kind of civilian chaplain at our adjacent officers' training camp at Fort Benjamin Harrison. Simultaneously, it will be remembered, our national United War Relief campaigns were being conducted all over the land. Indianapolis, incidentally, was one of the first localities to follow through with its campaign on a regular monthly contribution basis. Also, it will be remembered, the First World War was marked by the prevalence of two distinct flu epidemics among both soldiers and civilians. The more severe of these epidemics occurred during the closing weeks of the war in 1918. Mine was the harrowing experience of officiating at the burial rites of many unfortunate victims, among them, on a single day, a father and daughter and a young couple I had married shortly before.

It was toward the close of this trying period that I was called in as arbiter in the renewal of a contract between the owners of the three local daily newspapers and the pressmen's union. A committee of the union called with the formal notice that I had been selected by both parties from a thoroughly sifted list of ninety-seven prospects to arbitrate the pending issues, chiefly wages and labor conditions. I could not resist—though I inwardly feared—the responsibility of so flattering an invitation. The proceedings continued daily from mid-October right up to Armistice Day, November 11, 1918, the only intermissions being those necessitated by emergency duties of my office elsewhere. These proceedings were all most illuminating and instructive to me, although they could easily and perhaps just as effectively for our common purpose have been much reduced in time and detail. But everybody in the group of some twenty representatives insisted on making a speech, much after the manner of our congregational and fraternal lodge meetings, so that the complete reporter's transcript alone counted up to two heavily bound volumes of five hundred pages each, at a total cost of eight hundred dollars. Three sets of these volumes were printed and were presented as souvenirs, one each to the Newspaper Publishers' Association, the Pressmen's Union, and the arbiter. The net result of the entire episode was an increase in the union's wage scale, a raise in the price of our local newspapers from two cents to three, and—what seemed especially gratifying to me, because it was the first time in the history of their mutual relationship—agreement by the two groups to commit themselves to the principle of arbitration. Henceforth grievances, complaints, and controversies of any kind were to be submitted for adjustment to a standing committee on conciliation and cooperation.

Twice in later years the two groups were complimentary enough to renew their invitation to me to act as arbiter, but I was compelled to decline because of the increasing tempo of my regular routine. But some seventeen years later, in January 1935, a similar invitation was tendered by two other but kindred groups, namely, the Indianapolis Typographical Union No. 1 and the Closed Shop Division of the Indianapolis Typothetae. This time, however, the invitation was accompanied by information that tended considerably to deflate my ego. Instead of ninety-seven in the list of acceptable availables, as in the early instance, there were now only twenty. Nevertheless, I still felt cocky enough to accept—on the one condition, however, that the proceedings be limited to hours instead of days. It was agreed that two hours would be sufficient to settle the matter. Instead of two hours, however, it stretched to three days.

St. Patrick's Eve

During the earlier half of my many years' ministry in Indiana, I was kept going at a rather strenuous pace with addresses before colleges, high schools, service clubs, women's clubs, professional societies, churches, and the like, non-Jewish and Jewish, in well-nigh every corner of the state. Perhaps the strangest and largest of such audiences was that in Indianapolis in the fall of 1928: a "debate" with Clarence Darrow, held in Cadle Tabernacle, a shambling structure with a seating capacity of about eighty-five hundred. Many years ago as a student I remembered hearing Isaac M. Wise tell of Robert G. Ingersoll, the noted agnostic, orator, and lawyer of an earlier period, who traveled around the country lecturing on the subject "The Mistakes of Moses" and challenging the clergy to debate the subject with him publicly. No clergyman of any significant standing, so it was reported, had accepted the challenge—with the exception of Wise. Apparently Darrow, also an agnostic, resolved to follow Ingersoll's example with a kindred theme: "Is Man a Machine?"

Already nationally known as a labor and criminal lawyer in the 1920s, he took up the cases for the defendants in the sensational murder trial of Nathan Leopold and Richard Loeb in Chicago and the evolution trial, the so-called "monkey trial," of schoolteacher John T. Scopes in Dayton, Tennessee. In both these cases, more particularly the murder trial, Darrow's line of argument was grounded on a purely mechanistic theory of life and the universe, which seemed to be a kind of special "bestseller" in that decade. "Is man a machine?" was, therefore, a peculiarly pertinent and appropriate topic for popular discussion outside the courtroom. So it came to pass that a Lyceum Lecture Bureau out of Columbus, Ohio, undertook to sponsor and manage

Darrow's tour across the country. In many if not most of the cities visited a local rabbi was selected to debate the subject with Darrow, possibly because two curiosities would be more likely than one as a source of attraction at the box office.

Indianapolis was third on his itinerary. Columbus, as the Lyceum headquarters, was first with Rabbi Jacob Tarshish and Cleveland, with Rabbi Barnett R. Brickner, was second. The Indianapolis meeting—it was technically not a debate, since no decision was to be rendered—was widely advertised and attended by a capacity audience. The subject matter of the debate was intelligently covered by all the local newspapers on the following day. There were, however, many unreported little incidents connected with the affair that made it especially memorable to me. Darrow's manager arranged for a breakfast meeting at Darrow's hotel in advance of the big evening affair. This was attended also by Mrs. Darrow, a few of Darrow's local friends, and two or three reporters.

The breakfast had no sooner begun than Mrs. Darrow quite informally, but nonetheless dogmatically, engaged me in argument. Did I really believe in God, in immortality, in a spiritual universe, and so on? I tried politely to listen rather than argue, until Darrow pointedly yet gently asked her to desist. He thereupon turned to me and said: "You mustn't mind if I get rough tonight." "I understand," I answered. "I'll be prepared to give as well as take." My chance came sooner than I expected—in reverse, however.

The full time of the debate was fixed at two hours: thirty minutes each in opening and thirty minutes each in rebuttal. Darrow was the first speaker. His voice was slightly husky, which he explained was due to his campaigning the night before in behalf of the Democratic candidate for the presidency. When my turn came, I opened with the comment that while we all sincerely regretted the huskiness of Darrow's voice, it was equally evident that the "machine needs oiling; it squeaks." He laughed along with the rest; in fact, throughout my day and evening with him, I found him to be a much softer and more mellow personality than all the public accounts of him in the courtroom had pictured him.

From a goodly mass of fan mail that followed in the trail of this Darrow event, one letter was particularly interesting to me. In spite of my frequent contacts with local Roman Catholic friends, I had never heard of the writer's existence in the community. He was a Jewish convert to Catholicism who signed himself "Brother Gabriel," an instructor in the local Cathedral High School. He wanted to express his pleasure and agreement with my presentation in the evening's argumentation and then asked if I would not do him the favor of writing a word of greeting to his Jewish mother in Detroit, who was celebrating her ninetieth anniversary on the following Sunday. Apparently his estrangement from the faith of his fathers had not yet completely sundered the ties he still felt with the faith of his mother.

Apart from the intellectual excitement and sheer fun of it all, I should not be completely frank in here recalling the Darrow experience if I did not add that it also had its useful material reward for me. There had been no written contractual agreement about this on my part. I was merely told in a casual way that I would be entitled to a certain percentage of the gate receipts. The major part of these was to go to Darrow and the promoter. I never learned just what this share amounted to, but it must have been a sizable hunk of cash, considering that it represented receipts from the sale of eighty-five hundred tickets at the usual theater rates prevailing at the time. My own share was $497.75.

A year later Darrow appeared once more in Indianapolis under the same auspices—this time, however, not in a debate, but in a symposium at the National Guard Armory. The three major religious faiths, Protestant, Roman Catholic, and Jewish, were to have one representative each in a thirty-minute presentation of his group's religious beliefs, while Darrow presented his position as an agnostic. Again the hall was filled to capacity, but this time thirty-five hundred as against the eighty-five hundred in Cadle Tabernacle the previous year. Meredith Nicholson presided, and Bishop Edwin F. Hughes, of the Methodist Church and former president of DePauw University, spoke for Protestantism. Quin O'Brien, Chicago attorney (since it was the practice of the [Roman Catholic] Church not to have ecclesiastical representation at a secular meeting of this kind), spoke for Roman Catholicism, and I spoke for Judaism. The audience was a mixture of affiliated and unaffiliated church people, yet each speaker was accorded an equal measure of applause, despite Darrow's negative and iconoclastic viewpoint and also despite O'Brien's rather lopsided presentation of his own case. O'Brien consumed the full thirty minutes of his time by devoting twenty minutes to a repetition of some funny stories quite irrelevant to the premises, and the remaining ten minutes to a recital of a long list of names preeminent in the history of science, the arts, and letters, about most of whom neither I nor, I am sure, the audience had ever heard, but all of whom, he claimed, were devout Roman Catholics. Even Jesus and his disciples, he boldly declared, had all been Roman Catholics.

President Woodrow Wilson, when addressing a public audience of mixed religious and political composition, loved to repeat a favorite anecdote of his attributed to

Charles Lamb. While Lamb was standing on a street corner one day chatting with a friend, someone who was a total stranger to them both passed by. Lamb abruptly and without apparent reason stopped, pointed to the stranger, and said: "I hate that man." "But how can you hate the man when you don't even know him?" asked his friend. "That's just it," Lamb answered, "I hate him because I don't even know him; I can't hate a man I know." The frequent contacts of a rabbi with leaders of other and even conflicting creeds in an American Midwestern community like Indianapolis serve to confirm the psychological as well as moral and social point of that story.

I have already cited Msgr. Francis H. Gavisk and my almost daily contact with him. A particularly rare and yet more or less typical instance of such cordial interrelationships occurred at the home of my good friend Dr. Karl Ruddell, the eminent surgeon. Early one spring morning a few years ago, Dr. Ruddell telephoned to invite me for dinner at his home that evening. I hesitated to accept because of a tentative minor engagement in my day's schedule. Dr. Ruddell, though himself a non-Catholic, was married to a devout Roman Catholic and had been chief of staff in the Roman Catholic St. Vincent's hospital for more than a quarter of a century. He insisted that I rearrange my schedule because, he said, his brother in Illinois had shipped him a large bag of quail, and besides he had already invited eight priests as guests for the dinner. I must, therefore, come to help him out. I had known some of his guests by name at least, most of them younger men of the clergy. They were already assembled in the basement of Dr. Ruddell's home for appetizers when I arrived a few minutes late.

In the doorway of the room was mounted a sizable

roast pig studded with toothpicked strips of bacon. Apparently the guests had conspired to kid a rabbi. Pointing to the decorated pig, their spokesman greeted me with the challenge: "Rabbi, if we give you a special dispensation, will you eat some of that?" Remembering that it was the Lenten season, I felt safe in replying with a counterchallenge: "Suppose we reverse it," I said. "If I as a rabbi give you a special dispensation, will you eat it?" "Sure," they chorused, "we already have our special dispensation; it's St. Patrick's Eve." Thus foiled for the moment—I do not recall ever having eaten ham or bacon anyway—we proceeded to the dinner table upstairs. Our host, Dr. Ruddell, seemed stumped for a moment about asking for the offering of grace, especially since all his guests were clergymen. Should he ask one of the eight priests, he might appear to be discriminating among individuals of the same faith; should he ask me as a rabbi, he wondered whether this would be altogether agreeable to the priests. It was evident that he really meant to be both personally impartial and religiously neutral to all concerned. Finally, he gestured to me, whereupon I started with a challenge of my own: "How many of you men remember your Hebrew from seminary days?" Two or three of the priests muttered something about not even remembering the alphabet. "Permit me, then, to offer grace in the same language and precisely the same words your Lord and Savior was in the habit of using when he sat down to break bread: *Baruch attah adonay elohenu melech ha-olam ha-motzi lechem min ha-aretz*—Praised be Thou, O Lord our God, King of the Universe, who bringest forth bread from the earth. Amen." Their respectful acquiescence indicated that their kidding had finished.

A trivial incident this, and rather flippant in the long historical perspective of our faith, yet significantly illustrative of the distance we have traveled since the bitter and humorless days of cruelly enforced polemics between Catholic and Jew in medieval Christendom. I also like to recall this incident in particular because it happens to be a factual version of an apocryphal story of similar tenor, long and widely circulated among our contemporary Catholic, Protestant, and Jewish laity. It has been my experience, as well as that of many another rabbi, not infrequently to be in a company of mixed religionists when someone in the group would delight to repeat the story of a bishop seated next to a rabbi at a banquet where ham was being served. "When will you ever eat this?" the bishop teasingly asked the rabbi. "At your wedding," snapped the rabbi. Altogether apart from any interfaith significance, therefore, I am glad to offer this experience of mine at the home of Dr. Ruddell as worthy of record in the archeology at least, if not the history, of humor!

Harry L. Barroway

A PHILADELPHIA CHILDHOOD

The youngster whom Harry L. Barroway (1884–1965) brings to life in the following reminiscence grew up to receive a law degree from the University of Pennsylvania and to be admitted to the Pennsylvania bar in 1905. Three years later, he married Sara Lewis, of Camden, New Jersey, and in 1918 settled in Camden, where before long he resumed the practice of law. During World War II, Barroway entered government service as a lawyer for the Camden branch of the Office of Price Administration.

Barroway's work as an attorney was never enough to satisfy him. He wanted his life to show forth a communal as well as a professional dimension, and so he became a founder and president of Camden's Beth El Synagogue, a president of the Camden Talmud Torah, and a charter member of the Mizpah Lodge of Masons.

At the age of eighty-one, a few months before his death, he set about composing his memoirs. It was, he said, a "labor of love" for his family, and his children—he had four, a son and three daugh-

ters—have preserved them as "a loving tribute to a brilliant mind and a beloved father."

🌷

I was born in a small town on the east bank of the Dnieper River in the Byelorussian government, or state, of Mogilev, situated on the borderline between Old Poland and Russia. The town was called Shklov; the date was Lag B'omer 1884, equivalent in the Gregorian calendar to May 18. The latter date then became my official birthday. Shklov was credited in 1905 by *The Jewish Encyclopedia* with a population of fourteen thousand, some 90 percent of them Jews. Now Shklov, despite its lack of size as size goes in modern city statistics, had considerable influence on the commerce and learning of the Jewish community in the Pale of Settlement, and it probably dated its beginning to the middle of the fifteenth century. It included among its inhabitants some of the most influential and learned rabbis of Poland and Lithuania.

At this point I must be forgiven for indulging myself in a bit of bragging. Chaim Jacob Vidrevitz [1836–1911], who became famous as the chief rabbi of Moscow and was widely known as the "Moskver Rov," was a first cousin of my maternal grandmother. Rabbi Vidrevitz created quite a stir when he came to the United States around the end of the nineteenth century and took over by storm as "chief rabbi" in New York City.

From the commercial angle, the Jews of Shklov carried on an extensive trade in flax and wheat, in lumbering, in the weaving of horsehair, and in the production of bristles for use in the manufacture of brushes. Needless to say, the Shklov Jews engaged in lumbering were not lumberjacks as we know them nowadays; on the contrary, they were on the business side of purchasing standing and growing forests from the landowners. The trees were cut down by peasants from the vicinity, hauled by horsepower to the banks of the Dnieper, lashed together in floats of considerable size, and then floated downstream on the Dnieper to Kiev, the central point of the sawmilling business for all western Russia and Poland. It was in Kiev that the lumber merchants disposed of their products.

The Russian-Polish derivation of my family name, pronounced "Boroway," would indicate that one of my paternal ancestors had had to do with forests and lumbering. Even so, I have no direct evidence that any of them were engaged in the lumbering business. On the contrary, all I know is that my father and his father before him received a thorough talmudic education in the Volozhin yeshiva and adopted the profession of *shochet*—ritual slaughterer.

I remember my father's mother, my paternal grandmother, as in a dream. She seems to have been above the average height for Jewish women of that period and that locale. She disdained to wear a *sheitel* or a wig, had her gray hair always covered tightly with a large kerchief, and spoke softly while patting my head and remarking at the same time how closely I resembled Meisha, my father. She was far from prolific and despite her size and sturdy build gave birth to only two children, my aunt Mahsha Hoffman, who came to this country with her family shortly after we arrived, and my father.

Grandfather Barroway died long before I was born, and my grandmother died while our family, consisting of Father, Mother, two of my sisters, and myself, were living in the Caucasus, in the mountain resort town of Pyatigorsk. Father at that time had obtained the position of *shochet, mohel* (practitioner of the rite of circumcision), and general factotum in the synagogue of the community.

Husbands for Six Daughters

In the winter of 1903–1904, my cousin Saul Joffe took what we called in those days "French leave" (what we now call more succinctly AWOL) from the Russian army, which was being mobilized against Japan. He arrived at our home in January 1904, and so the Russian army's loss was our gain. I never enjoyed a period of my life more than the time Saul spent in our home.

I depart from the strict chronological sequence of my tale in order to introduce Saul Joffe because it was Saul who furnished me with material regarding the maternal side of my family and gave me a clearer, though humorous, perspective of the kind of people they were and how they reacted in various situations. I will not undertake to guarantee the authenticity of these stories, as Saul was a witty philosopher and of necessity his tales are colored by his own lovable character.

According to Saul, our grandfather Shevlin, although descended from a line of well-to-do merchants and learned rabbis, was himself a poor man financially but rich in the acquisition of an honorable character and numerous children. My grandmother Shevlin, despite her diminutive size, helped him procreate and raise a family of six daughters and two sons and was of considerable aid in the operation of two businesses for most of his lifetime. The enterprises consisted of a *shenk,* or country inn, in a suburb of Shklov and a grist mill in another part of the town. The *shenk* was a sort of tavern where the peasants of the vicinity gathered during their leisure, imbibed their vodka, and in varying degrees between drunkenness and sobriety whiled away the time; the mill was used by the local peasantry for grinding the grain they produced.

Bear in mind that this grandfather of mine had six

daughters, very close in marriageable age and none a raving beauty, thus presenting to a good Jewish father the almost unsolvable problem of marrying them off into the proper families and to young men of some promise. The all-encompassing test of a good match was *yichus,* roughly translated as status, either in learning or in wealth. And then again the father of the bride, in order to obtain such an advantageous *shidduch* [match], had to provide a cash dowry and *kest* for at least two years. *Kest* was an institution or custom wherein the father of the bride obligated himself to provide free board and lodging for the couple and whatever offspring came into being during the period of the *kest* [which would usually last until the bridegroom had gained enough tal-mudic knowledge to support his family as a rabbi or teacher].

Now as a matter of fact the six sons-in-law that my grandfather obtained for his respective daughters were tops. Whether or not Saul's vivid imagination carried him some distance further than absolute truth would justify, the story is good anyway. Saul told me that when the time came for his mother, the oldest, to be provided with a husband, our grandfather, who had amassed the munificent sum of three hundred rubles, came forward and endowed the young couple with that nest egg. *Kest* was waived by the groom's family because it was not needed. In due time the second daughter was provided with a man, but grandfather had no other nest egg. So he, the pillar of the synagogue and bearer of a *yichusdik* name, shrewdly touched his first and dear son-in-law for that dowry of three hundred rubles and endowed the second couple with the same funds. And believe it or not, the story goes that Grandpop worked that forward pass on the other four sons-in-law. The story ends with no reward in this world to the six sons-in-law for their generosity and gullibility, but we hope they received their just reward in the next.

I do not want to be guilty of repeating a doubtful story about a grandfather who, according to collateral reports, bore a splendid reputation for honesty and rectitude of conduct. And even though, according to my informant, his motives were laudable, the tragic event that followed the episode of the marriages throws the story into a different perspective.

Six years had elapsed since Grandfather had married off his youngest daughter. He had been relieved of his tough avocation of providing suitable husbands for six daughters; a number of grandchildren had come and were growing up. Life was serene and peaceful for Grandpop and Grandmom when, like a clap of thunder out of a clear sky, misfortune struck. First, my mother lost her first husband, leaving her a widow with two small daughters, aged three and one.

The year was 1871. The Prussians, with Prince Bismarck at their head, forced France to surrender and sue for peace. The aftermath of this was that an epidemic of cholera raged through all of Europe and was especially virulent in the eastern portion. My mother's first husband was an early victim. Fortunately or unfortunately, depending upon your viewpoint, my father's first wife was another casualty. After a year's widowhood Mother and Father were brought together, and a long, happy married life ensued.

As if this blow to the old people was not enough, what followed about two or three years later proved to be the coup de grace to Grandfather's peace of mind and will to live. He lost his son Aryeh in a fire that destroyed the mill and was a different kind of man from then on. Aryeh, the younger of his two sons, was described as a tall, handsome youth of twenty-three and the only child living with his parents prior to his death. The older son, Aaron, had been sent to Odessa and was working for a relative engaged in business in that city. He came home for visits only at infrequent times. So with the marriage of all their daughters and the absence of Aaron from home, the poor old folks were led, in their bereavement, to look upon Aryeh as a veritable only child. Both grandparents completed their lives lonely and forlorn.

There is one more story of Saul's that bears repeating here and that is the story regarding a cousin of Grandfather's whose name was Gimbel, not of the family of countrywide and renowned merchants, but a Gimbel, nevertheless, and probably stemming from the same family roots. Be that as it may, Gimbel is described as a hulk of a man, towering way above the rest of the people of Reshkike. He was the self-appointed bouncer in Grandpop's *shenk,* and whenever a couple of the customers became too drunk and unruly, Gimbel usually appeared on the scene, took hold of the two principal combatants by the scruffs of their respective necks, bumped their heads together not too gently and threw them out onto the roadway. If any of the remaining guests took exception to Gimbel's handling of the first pair, the objectors received like treatment. Usually the size and strength of Gimbel had the desired effect on the remainder, and an atmosphere of peace was restored.

Reshkike was not much more than a hamlet; it probably never contained more than twenty-five or thirty Jewish families, and a great number of them operated inns. The houses were neither too large nor too imposing, but the synagogue was the main building of the town. It housed not only the sanctuary and Talmud Torah, but it was the clubhouse, the municipal building, and the place where all gossip was exchanged and promulgated. It was the place where the men of the community found themselves when not at home.

Grandpop not only operated the inn and grist mill, but was, in the absence of a rabbi, the leader of the synagogue. He led the congregation in prayer, read the Torah at the required times, and at the Rosh Hashanah services blew the shofar. He had a one-man choir, and that was Gimbel. The volume that emanated from the great cavern of Gimbel's throat was so vociferous that it shook the rafters of the sanctuary and stirred up sound waves which on occasion blew out the Yom Kippur candles. That was the quality of Gimbel's voice. Gimbel was Grandpop's choir in the synagogue and his police department on the outside.

No Need for Shochetim

Of my very early years, like most people, I remember little, and an anomalous situation crops up in this connection when I seem to remember something about my mother's *krum* and nothing about our home where I spent most of my first four years. A *krum* is a store, an open-front store. In Mother's case, it was a grocery or foodstuffs dispensary. She sold commodities like salted, dry fish, herring, flour, grits, sugar, salt, and so on. Of course, it was common practice for the wife to operate some sort of a business to feed herself, her lord and master—her husband—and their brood, while said husband occupied himself with nothing more monetarily gainful than wearing out the seat of his pants studying or expounding intricate passages of the Talmud. That hardly applied in Mother's case. When her first husband died and she was left with very little money and two small children to raise and support, she hired an elderly *goya,* a gentile woman, to care for the two girls and, with the little money she could raise, rented a booth on the market square and proceeded to do business as a feme-sole trader.

The marketing system in Russia at the time was far different from our system here and now. There were no corner grocery stores in the Pale or anywhere in Russia at that time. The marketplace was centrally located and was open for business two days a week, on Sunday and Wednesday. Business was confined to the daylight hours. In summer the hours were extremely long, from sunrise around 5 A.M. to sunset about 8 P.M., and in winter correspondingly short.

I think at this point we should make it clear that Shklov was not a *shtetl* in the sense presented by the writer Yudel Mark in the 1965 issue of *The Jewish Heritage Reader.* He describes a *shtetl*—which is the diminutive form of the word *shtot* (the Yiddish for a city)—as a town never containing more than a thousand families, whose lives from the cradle to the grave and whose daily activities from morning to night were controlled entirely by tradition.

This was far from descriptive of Shklov. First, Shklov was far larger than Mark's maximum of a thousand families because in 1905, at the peak of emigration to America, its population was estimated at about fourteen thousand. Second, twenty or twenty-five years before the close of the nineteenth century, the "New Enlightenment" [Haskalah] doctrine had taken quite a hold on the thinking portion of Shklov's population. The most important element of the doctrine was to introduce into education secular studies as well as the study of the Law, Mishnah, and Talmud. That this idea took hold is proven to me by what was done by the parents of all my cousins, both paternal and maternal.

I was pleasantly surprised to find, upon speaking to my cousins of the Joffe, Kroll, and Hoffman families, that while none of them were college graduates, as we would term it, they had all attended the government schools run for the Jews and gained, boys and girls alike, a knowledge of secular subjects. This was a far cry from the old practice whereby only boys were sent to a *heder* or Talmud Torah and from there to a yeshiva, if they merited it, but of secular subjects knew nothing. I repeat that Shklov was not a *shtetl* with the attributes of poverty, unworldliness, and, to a great extent, misery. The people of Shklov were fine, up-standing, intelligent people and were well aware of what was going on in the outside world.

Mother's marriage to Dad brought about no change in her business plans. Father's profession or occupation necessitated his absence from home, because the Pale had no need for more *shochetim*. In fact, the yeshivas produced a surplus of that type of practitioner and few desirable positions were open. It therefore was necessary for young *shochetim* to go far into the interior of Russia to find a desirable job. Moreover, the oppressive measures against Jews during the reign of Alexander III forbade the residence of Jews outside the Pale of Settlement regardless of the religious phase of their work. Mechanics were exempt from this restriction, and since the honing and sharpening of the slaughtering knives was a cardinal requirement for proper ritual slaughtering and the authorities magnanimously agreed that such handling of the knives was a mechanic's job, Father applied for and received a mechanic's certificate permitting the holder to travel and work in any part of Russia. So Father was officially classified an itinerant knife sharpener, with covert duties as a *shochet, mohel,* teacher, and leader in synagogal worship on the side. He labored in

these multifarious capacities for about six months, and as
Mother told it, he started to complain about being so frequently away from his family.

At this point I must pay tribute to my father for the
kind of man he was. He never showed any partiality to me
and my sister, Naomi, over his two stepdaughters, Basha
and Necha. The three girls were now on the threshold of
young womanhood, at ages eighteen, sixteen, and twelve.
At those ages and in those times, serious attention should
have been given to marriage, especially for the two older
ones. But Mother knew that Father's absence was a serious
obstacle to advantageous matches. Mother realized that the
absentee fatherhood had to be ended, and if the truth were
known, she was getting fed up herself with her *krum* business and wanted to return to ordinary maternal and wifely
duties. She therefore proposed that she would pull up
stakes, take the three younger children with her, leave Basha, who was extraordinarily mature, to dispose of the *krum,*
 dwelling, and possessions, and go to Pyatigorsk, an all-
year-round resort in the Caucasus Mountains. There may
have been another factor that prompted Mother in making
her decision. Father's position in Pyatigorsk seemed to be
permanent, his remuneration was better than it had ever
been previously, and the living was far easier in the mild
climate of the Caucasus than it ever could be in Shklov.

Mother had always been a woman of action. As soon
as the decision was made, the four of us were off. I do
remember some childish impressions of our leaving in the
deep snow of late winter and my mother bundling me up
in the sled that bore us to Mogilev, where there was train
service for only a portion of the journey.

I presume that what I must relate to you now is typical
to a more or less degree of all mothers. The love my mother

bore and the self-sacrifices she was ready to endure for her children were most remarkable. Of course, at the time it happened I was too young to appreciate the full import of the act, but in my growing up process, this act of my mother's loomed large in my estimation of her self-sacrificing mold. This happened on the journey from Shklov to Pyatigorsk and is the only event on this journey of which I have even a faint recollection. We had been on the journey for what seemed ages. We must have covered half the route. The snow was deep on the ground. The conveyance was a covered wagon on sled runners. We left the inn where we stopped for the night as soon as the sun was high enough in the sky to lend some small degree of warmth to the four of us huddled inside the wagon. The steam arose from the breath of man and beast alike. Of course, we were all dressed warmly for the journey; all garments were worn double—two of every kind of garment, even to the extent of two overcoats. But despite the warmth of the clothing and the huddling together for mutual body warmth, it was cold. Mother realized that, and off went her *shuba,* an outer greatcoat of some long-haired fur. She made us move even closer together, covered the three of us with the greatcoat, and then asked the driver to stop the sled. She stepped out and, wearing only the single coat, trudged along on the sunny side of the sled to keep from freezing.

This was my mother all through life. She lived for her children. She seemed to endure all troubles and hardships for our sake especially, without the least sign of rebellion or martyrdom. One test came on this journey. Now I do not remember anything in connection with this event; all that I know is what was told to me some years afterwards by my mother and sisters.

We were approaching Rostov, situated in southern

Russia where the Don River empties into the Black Sea, when I developed a very sore throat and high fever. Mother pleaded with the driver to hasten his team and stop at the nearest inn within Rostov's city limits. She put me to bed and called for a doctor. After three or four days my throat had sufficiently cleared, and the fever had subsided to normalcy, to enable us to resume the journey in a much more temperate climate. At times afterwards when Mother repeated the story to me, I wondered whether I had suffered an attack of diphtheria. Mother did not know and, I venture to guess, neither did the doctor.

The Prince Left in a Huff

At long last the journey was ended, and the weary travelers were ensconced in a very comfortable little house off the main street, but in the big heart of a loving father. Both girls were enrolled in the government school. The Jewish portion of their learning my father undertook himself.

In the house set on the lot adjoining ours there lived a non-Jewish family. The head of this household was a fine, middle-class Russian who worked as an assistant postmaster in the local post office. He wore a uniform that made him appear to my young eyes as the general of the army. All government workers in the Russia of those days wore uniforms with elaborate trimmings. I would not be surprised to learn that even the garbage collectors, if they had such, wore uniforms. The family of this man consisted of a wife and three children; the older two, as in our case, were girls in their late teens, and there was a boy, Ivan, about twelve or thirteen. The companionship of this boy had quite an

impact on my upbringing during the three and a half years
our family spent in beautiful Pyatigorsk. Ivanka, despite the
disparity in our ages, took a fancy to me and adopted me
as a younger brother. While my father took charge of my
Hebrew, Ivanka, being in the first year of the local gymnasium when we arrived, became my tutor in Russian. I
should explain that the gymnasium, despite the word's accepted English meaning, was in Russia a training place for
the mind rather than the body; its curriculum was equivalent to our high school and junior college combined. In
restrospect it seems to me that even in those days the Russian system of education in the secondary and college
courses was thorough. They taught and learned the hard
way. Russian educators brooked no shortcuts. The result
was that a boy of thirteen like Ivanka knew as much as the
average present-day sixteen-year-old in the United States
and proved to be an excellent tutor for me.

Nothing that may be considered of interest to a five-
or six-year-old boy and therefore would lodge in his memory occurred for almost the entire first two years of our life
in Pyatigorsk. Everything, I suppose, was routine. My father went about his business quietly and methodically. Necha, the older of the two [step]sisters, sewed and helped
Mother with the housework. Naomi attended the government school, and I, except for the time devoted to Hebrew
and religion in Father's class, was under the control of
Ivanka. The net result of my dual relationship with Ivan as
tutor and companion was that at the time this two-year
period ended, I spoke Russian more fluently than I did
Yiddish.

However, something happened in our family that was
earthshaking and could not escape even me. I mentioned

that Pyatigorsk was a year-round resort. Its equable all-seasons climate, with its hot mineral baths in winter and the mild temperatures of the summer, drew guests and convalescents from all parts of Russia. In the summertime the military band gave concerts in the city park. Retrospectively, what did we from Shklov know about good music or concerts? All the musicians we had ever been acquainted with were the fiddlers and clarinetists who screeched their music "good and loud" at weddings or engagement parties. The people of Shklov did not go in for musicales or even band concerts. My sisters usually attended these Pyatigorsk concerts in the afternoon, and since Necha had a fairly good voice and enjoyed good music, it had become a usual thing in the summertime. Now comes the boy-meets-girl part of this story. It seems that a Georgian nobleman, a prince no less, had seen Necha on a number of these occasions, became enamored of her, and introduced himself to the girls. The upshot was that the prince called at our modest little home on a certain summer evening. He, like a true nobleman, disdained to talk to anyone lower in our family rank than my father. He introduced himself to my father and peremptorily asked for Necha in marriage. Father, to put it mildly, was shocked. He did not wish to hurt the prince's feelings or pride by a flat refusal. So he started off by hemming and hawing that we were Jews and he was a Mohammedan, that our sacred law forbade us to intermarry. But the prince was not stymied by this argument. He very bluntly told Father that she did not have to change her religion. "In fact," the noble prince said, "two other wives that I have at present are Christian girls who practice their own religion faithfully without interference from me or my family." The prince left our home in a mild huff, and the girls never attended another concert.

Small Doses of Poison

Another year passed quite serenely and smoothly, but at the beginning of the following year things commenced to hum. Alexander III, Tsar of All the Russias, acting through the infamous Constantine Petrovich Pobyedonostsev, his minister of the interior,* promulgated the *ukase* or edict that all Hebrews living outside the Pale of Settlement, whether by license or otherwise (except in the case of merchants of the first or highest guild), had to return to the Pale forthwith or at the discretion of the governor-general of that province in which the Jews found themselves at the time.

The pronouncement, when it came, struck like a bolt out of the clear sky. Our family, as well as all other Jews in the town, were stunned. A boy of six or seven years could hardly realize the full meaning of this sudden calamity, but could not help noticing the change in direction of the current of life in our family and even in the community generally. A hectic correspondence with my sister Basha and my Aunt Pesha Stambler commenced. It had to be hurried because, as I understood in subsequent years, it took a letter between two and three weeks to get from Pyatigorsk to Shklov. Orders were sent to Basha to dispose of the store and the home at any price and accompany Aunt Stambler and her family to America. The Stambler family consisted of Zussman Stambler, Aunt Pesha's husband, and three boys: Charlie, who a few years later married Naomi, the

---

*Pobyedonostsev's official title was chief procurator of the Holy Synod.

youngest of my sisters; Morris, and Harry, later to become Dr. Harry A. Stambler.

At this point I want to pay tribute to Basha, a most wonderful girl of twenty-one then, and to become one of the kindest, sweetest characters I have ever known. Just think of what a heavy burden was placed upon a girl of twenty-one. She carried out the duties imposed upon her without a protest or without complaint. I have used the word "imposed" advisedly, because she was, in the every-day meaning of the word, imposed upon. That is my considered opinion. Basha arrived in America about three months before the rest of her immediate family to await our arrival.

You will recollect that the implementation of the edict for the Jews' eviction, or whatever you wish to call it, was left to the discretion of the respective governors-general. I suppose that the governor of the Caucasus district was trying to act charitably when the orders to the individuals were spaced over a six-month period. It turned out to be a case of injecting small doses of poison over a period of time. The ultimate result to the victim is death, but in the meantime the body is debilitated and helpless. That was the case with the small Jewish community of Pyatigorsk. With the receipt of the orders, communal activities had drawn to almost a stop. Every family was busily engaged in its own problem of finding ways and means of getting out, deciding when or where to go. Although most of the community had not as yet received its notice, no one was waiting for the fateful day.

My father's income had almost ceased, and the little he had laid aside was dwindling fast. At that it was fully four months, I was told, before we received sufficient funds for the journey. We sold or gave away our meager belongings to non-Jewish neighbors, principally the very friendly ones from next door, and commenced our long trek to America, the Golden Land.

It was the early part of November when we left, and the weather in Pyatigorsk, I was told, was still mild and balmy, but by the time we reached the Prussian frontier, Mother and the girls had to unpack to get to our heavy winter overcoats. Due to the difference in the respective seasons and the apparent improvement in rail traffic in a mere four years in the benighted and backward tsarist land, the journey from Pyatigorsk back to the boundary between Russia and Germany took a much shorter time than it had when we came from Shklov to Pyatigorsk.

We arrived and for two weary weeks stayed in a border town. If ever a town fitted the description of such a place by Yudel Mark in his article on the *shtetl,* that was it. I can still almost see the mud in the streets on that cold, sleety November day.

Why did we have to stay in this forsaken hellhole of a town for two weeks? Our order of eviction was to leave Pyatigorsk and go back to the Pale where they said we belonged. So-called subjects of the Russian tsar were not permitted to leave without a governor's passport. This we could not procure because we were ordered to return to the Pale. The alternative means to leave Russia was to sneak across the border at night as they do now from East to West Germany, and then, as is happening now, risk having a potshot taken at us by the border guards.

To reduce the risk as much as possible and to increase the rapidity of movement, the leader of the fugitives, a paid individual living in the vicinity and well acquainted with the ground and the habits of the guards, advised the separation of large families, and so my sisters were placed in the charge of a childless couple.

As to the actual crossing of the border, I remember nothing, probably because it occurred in the wee hours of the morning. I may have fallen asleep and been carried by my father to our destination. At any rate, with the break of day, the weary, frightened plodders found themselves in a guest house in Memel, Germany [now Klaipeda, U.S.S.R.]. After a few days' rest, we bought tickets for Hamburg, our port of departure for America. It may be strange, but on further thought it is not. I remember riding in the train going across the city of Berlin. It seemed to my childish imagination that we were flying in fairyland. The twinkling lights of the street lamps appearing in all directions and my watching from the height of the elevated roof, for the railroads in Germany even at that early period were elevated over the city streets, left an impression on my youthful mind that even the prosaic explanations of later years could not eradicate or even minimize.

We arrived in Hamburg in due course and put up at a sort of immigrants' inn. Then started a wait of two or three weeks for fitting berths on a fitting boat to carry us the rest of the long journey to New York. Now by fitting I hardly mean *be*fitting or proper—I mean fitting the depleted state of Father's pocketbook. By that time his finances had become very low, and the poor man had to watch his step. Finally, after much running and figuring, he procured passage for all of us on a combination passenger, freight, and cattle steamer. The human cargo was treated not a whole lot better than the cattle.

A Far Happier World

After a long, stormy voyage of three weeks' duration, we arrived sick and exhausted at Castle Garden, where I

Castle Garden, New York City, before 1890

remember the Hebrew Immigrant Aid Society provided us with comforts that we had not seen since leaving Pyatigorsk. Castle Garden was the island in New York used before the Ellis Island era for an immigrant station in New York harbor. I can still remember the receiving portion of the building. The immensity of the room was astounding to me. I had never seen anything like it. Father passed the examination with flying colors. He produced enough cash to purchase railroad tickets for Philadelphia, our ultimate destination, and had the ten dollars over and above, thus complying with the law.

As I learned afterwards, Eliakim Zunser, representing the Immigrant Aid Society, took us to the railroad station, bound for Philadelphia. I mention particularly the name of Eliakim Zunser because he was the most famous Hebrew-Yiddish poet-folk singer of the nineteenth century and was widely read in Europe and America. When my father learned his name, he was delighted and honored to have such a prominent personage act as his counselor and guide. Zunser was a volunteer and was doing this work seven days of the week as a service to the great army of immigrants arriving at Castle Garden at that time.

We arrived at the Reading Station in Philadelphia very early that evening. We were hungry and tired, worn out simply by the excitement of finally arriving at a fixed place and hoping to meet friendly relatives and halt the seemingly endless journey. Fate, however, ruled against the early effectuation of such happy prospects for the travelers, at least not for two or three hours. At the time the Reading Railroad Station was located on Ninth Street between Green and Fairmount Avenue; the Stambler home was on Third Street between Fairmount Avenue and Brown Street, a distance between the two locations of about six city

From *Harper's Weekly;* courtesy of the Free Library of Philadelphia

Philadelphia and Reading Terminals in Philadelphia:
1. Broad and Lehigh 2. Columbia and Ninth 3. Broad and
Pennsylvania 4. Ninth and Spring Garden

blocks. I remember my father speaking on the train to a Jewish young man whose destination was Philadelphia. Father showed him the Stambler address and asked him to direct us there. The young man said that he was living in New York and knew little of Philadelphia, but he had an idea where that location was and he would direct us. As it proved subsequently, he had no idea whatsoever, and he took us by streetcar to the vicinity of South Street, then the heart of the Jewish section. Finally, to put an end to that nerve-racking circuitous trek through all of South Philadelphia Father had to hire a cab, quite a rarity in those happy days, and after a lapse of three hours we found ourselves in the Stambler household and with my sister Basha.

We did not stay very long with the Stamblers. Mother realized that staying longer than four or five days would place too big a burden on Aunt Pesha. She was the smallest of the six sisters and not too robust. Besides, the money problem was a most important factor in their home. Uncle Zussman had gone into business for himself. He had become a merchant of sorts. Yes, sorting was an essential part of his business. He had purchased a horse and wagon and made the rounds of the small clothing shops, purchased all the pieces left from the cutting process, brought his purchased wares home, sorted them for the different grades, and sold these assortments to woolen mills. I do not wish to be ungracious or unkind to the memory of a good, kindly man, but he really was a sorting merchant. Cousin Charlie, the oldest son who about two years later became my brother-in-law, was an apprentice clothing cutter. Morris became an apprentice barber, and Harry, the youngest, ten years old, was sent to school.

With this earning potential of the Stamblers in mind, Mother started looking for a suitable house for us. She succeeded in renting the dwelling portion of a house located on the corner of Second and Craven Streets. Despite the fact that the house was situated on a corner with an entire side open and exposed to the south, I heard remarks made by older and more discerning members of our family that it was dark, dingy, and musty.

Never backward in tackling a job, Mother, with the help of the three girls, had the place as clean and livable as it possibly could have been. After obtaining the absolute necessities for housekeeping, Father and the girls began the hunt for work. The girls had very little trouble in going to work in the shop where Basha had been working since the time of her arrival. Father, in the usual procedure of his craft or profession, reported to Rabbi Bernhard Louis Levinthal, who had just assumed the office of Philadelphia's chief Orthodox rabbi after the death of his father-in-law and predecessor, Rabbi Eleazer Kleinberg. Father presented his credentials to the rabbi, and they apparently were more than satisfactory. After being examined on the techniques, he was approved to act as a *shochet* in Philadelphia and its environs. From that time on the relationship between Rabbi Levinthal and Father was one of cordiality and mutual respect.

Three events that occurred within the first month of our arrival in America had a tremendous impact on my young mind. You must remember that these came almost simultaneously after a nerve- and body-racking voyage that had dragged on for almost three months. So when I witnessed these wondrous events, it appeared to me, a boy of seven, that now I was in a far happier world.

Second Street in those days was, next to South Street, the most important retail business street in Philadelphia, and two weeks before Christmas was the time when the shopkeepers did their best to emphasize the Christmas spirit in the display of their goods. Color, color everywhere, with red and green predominant. Tinsel, artificial snow suffused by plenty of light made each store a veritable fairyland. Above all, there were crowds everywhere. A week after Christmas, of course, came New Year's Day with Philadelphia's own Mummers' Parades. I am using the plural because in those days, unlike what we have now, there were many parades, as many as there were competing clubs, each marching on its own selected route, for prizes offered by merchants located on that particular route. Since Second Street merchants offered quite a number of prizes as was fitting to the importance of their section, we had clubs marching past our house from early morning till sundown. To me such a display—the fancy costumes and the antics of the funny-looking clowns—was a pleasant revelation. Moreover, I could watch all the parades from the comparative comfort of our second floor front room.

Now for the last but not the least reason for my youthful realization that we, all of us, had entered into another phase of our lives—Basha's wedding. You will recollect that Basha arrived in this country about three months before the rest of us. You will also understand that Basha was then between twenty-two and twenty-three years of age, an age traditionally beyond that when a girl should be married. Mother was very much concerned with the problem. In fact, it is my opinion now that it was one of the reasons Mother acted so hastily in sending Basha off with the Stamblers and hurrying off with the rest of us.

Basha, shortly after her arrival, went to work in a clothing shop and met a young man, Wolf Hersch Dissin. They fell in love and by the time we arrived were to all intents and purposes practically engaged. Wolf Hersch, subse-

From *Harper's Weekly*; courtesy of the Free Library of Philadelphia

Mummers' Parade

quently Americanized to William H., was a very likable chap and above all a hard worker. Mother, elated with the prospect of having solved at least one of her problems, arranged for a wedding within six weeks after our arrival. They lived with us for three or four months, then rented a small house on Vine Street below Second. They lived there for three or four years until about the time of Naomi's marriage to our cousin, Charles Stambler.

I think I had already stated that Wolf Hersch was a go-getter, a real hustler. Consequently, shortly after their wedding, perhaps six months later, my irrepressible new brother-in-law became dissatisfied with operating a sewing machine by foot power and decided to go into the business of subcontracting for a clothing contractor. He undertook to make buttonholes in cheap men's clothing and to do it from his own shop. The shop happened to be the parlor of his home—the largest room in the house. How he happened to procure three new buttonhole machines, innovations in the clothing-making business at the time, I do not know, except to presume that the installment business was already in full swing. After about six months, Wolf Hersch was able to rent a loft on Second Street and employ ten or twelve young immigrant boys and girls. This was his hustling spirit. He was always moving forward.

Bald as a Billiard Ball

Education was a cardinal rule on both sides of my family, and, of course, traditionally the males were the beneficiaries of this practice. Just before Basha's wedding and after the New Year celebration, schools reopened, and my parents decided that I should enter the public school.

The duty of acting as my guide and interpreter was

imposed on a nine- or ten-year-old boy, a cousin of my then future brother-in-law. That boy and his family had been in this country for about a year, and so he was, as the rest of his family judged, thoroughly Americanized. He escorted me to the principal, but because of my ignorance of the English language the principal turned me over to a German-speaking teacher. Strange as it seems, I remember her name—Miss Louise Stuckert. To test my intelligence, I presume, she placed a picture card before me—it happened to be a bird picture—and asked in German *"Was ist das?"* I thought it silly but immediately responded in my best Yiddish *"A feigle."* Miss Stuckert was impressed with my keen intelligent answer, and when she gave me a few examples of the simplest forms of addition and subtraction, thanks to my tutor Ivanka's teaching, I very readily wrote the results and was duly entered in the first grade of New Street School. This New Street School, I must state in passing, belied every phase of the meaning implied in the name of the street upon which it was situated. It was anything but new; in fact, I think it must have been built in the Jefferson administration.

The payoff was this ludicrous occurrence in the life of a young immigrant boy which came some months later when he realized that his name was not what it should have been. Instead of Harry Barroway, I was entered in school as Abram Bevitzky. As to Abram, I can account for that. The Dissin boy had an older brother whose Hebrew name was Arye, like mine, which was "translated" into the English Abram. At this point I think the boy used a minimal amount of judgment; but as to the Bevitzky part, I cannot for the life of me figure out by what process of reasoning the boy, or for that matter the teacher, came by such a meaningless and unusual name. It was not long before I realized that my school name was not Harry Barroway, but

Abram Bevitzky, and so despite my youthful years I think I used good judgment by not complaining at once to my parents, but waiting until a favorable opportunity presented itself to make the change myself and avoid a lot of useless and unnecessary excitement. The opportunity, however, was pretty long in coming. It took about two years and my eighth term to present my case to my teacher. I will describe the details of this momentous event later on in this story.

In the meantime, I was going to school very regularly and doing very well. Of course, I had a marked advantage over my classmates, either American or immigrant. To them school was new in every aspect, while I came in pretty well grounded in beginners' fundamentals. I soon realized that spelling in English, unlike Russian, was not at all phonetic and to write in that language one had to learn to spell by dint of memory. I had no trouble learning to spell.

My first-grade teacher, a Miss Ball, realized that I belonged to a higher class, and consequently before very long I found myself in the second grade and then in the third grade—all before the end of my first term in June 1892. You will remember that public school terms were really semesters or halves of school years. Promotions were made at the beginning of February and toward the end of June, so that I accomplished in half a year what it would normally take a child one and a half years.

I must tell you of a comedy scene in Miss Ball's classroom in which Miss Ball was the star. It was the kind of occurrence that could have been used by the writers of the early Mack Sennett movie comedies. Looking retrospectively at Miss Ball presiding over her little pupils, she appeared to have been at the time in her early sixties, tall, lean, and rawboned. She wore her hair combed straight back with a bun out of the braided hair resting on the nape of her neck. On this occasion she was standing at the blackboard with the pointer in her hand pointing to figures she had marked on the board and waving her wand rather nonchalantly when, by fate or mere accident, the moving pointer brushed past her head and was caught in a tangle of her hair. She let out a whoop that probably was heard out on New Street, and when the children looked up in horror, they saw Miss Ball grasping frantically at her head—her hairdo askew, the bun over one ear, and a shining bald pate on the opposite side. The immigrant children were unusually well behaved, but all the children seemed stunned by this calamity. Miss Ball ran out of the room to the teacher's toilet to straighten her coiffure, but the naked truth was revealed that Miss Ball was as bald as a billiard ball and wore a wig to conceal her partial nakedness.

New Street School not only was an old, ramshackle affair, but it was very small in terms of the modern school size. It had four grades and four schoolrooms, so the stay of even the average pupil was two years. I attended that school for one year.

Toward the end of that first year a number of what I would consider interesting events happened. Father had come to be recognized as one of the leading *shochetim* in Philadelphia. He was employed by the largest slaughterhouse in the city, the Philadelphia Dressed Beef Company, subsequently becoming the Consolidated Beef Company and located at Thirtieth and Market Street. He also did some slaughtering for the firm that succeeded Hammerschlag. My contemporaries, if still around, would recognize the name—especially in connection with the matzo-baking industry in Philadelphia and over the entire country. "Hammerschlag's matzos" was a Jewish household word when Manischewitz was only a name in the Brooklyn directory.

In connection with the slaughterhouse, Father worked with a man whom I remember well for his habit of drinking 180-proof raw and unadulterated alcohol right out of the bottle. At times when I was not attending school Mother used to take advantage of the opportunity to send me to Father with a noonday cooked meal. I would carry the food to Market Street and take a cable-car ride to Thirtieth Street. On the occasions when Father's co-worker saw me come in, his face would light up with keen anticipation and approaching me with a lovely compliment of "Ah, a *finer boychik*," he would hand me a thin dime and a small flask and in his finest English say: "Buy me for ten cents *mashka* [liquor]." My father used to turn his back to this scene, but I could almost see a broad smile on his face.

There was at that time a drugstore on the corner of Thirty-second and Market Streets. To that location I would wend my way, make my purchase (the druggist already having recognized the flask), and return to my waiting admirer. Then came the payoff. He would remove the stopper, tilt his head and beard up to the ceiling, and empty the contents in one draft. The only sound that followed was a long *"Ah"* of delight. That was the gentleman's noontime meal.

My Name Is Not Bevitzky

It was now the early fall days of 1892, and the city was agog with the presidential campaign—Benjamin Harrison against Grover Cleveland. If you will recollect your American history, you will recall that Harrison was the incumbent, having defeated the then incumbent Cleveland. The latter was running again in 1892, and it resulted in a knock-'em-down-drag-'em-out campaign. The heat of the battle did not fail to reach even the youngsters of my neighborhood. New Street, if I have not stated it up to now, was populated in the main by Russian-Jewish immigrants who were not yet entitled to vote, although there was a lot of talk afterwards of some illegal voting. But around the corner on Front Street and all through the wharf section was a thickly populated section of first-, second-, and even third-generation Irishmen; so the Sixth Ward, in which New Street was located, was predominantly Democratic and supported Cleveland. I can state parenthetically that the Sixth Ward was the only ward in Philadelphia that was strongly Democratic. The rest were all Republican.

I remember a story in connection with this election that almost proved to me that prudence sometimes is more useful than valor. I remember coming to school one nice bright autumn day when I was accosted by a gang from Front Street. The leader approached me and, grabbing me by the lapels of my coat, said: "Sheeny, who are you for?" Taken by surprise but wanting to be truthful I said: "Harrison"—whereupon the gang surrounded me, set upon me, and pounded me to a pulp. I never was truthful as to my politics in that ward after that.

Just about this time and before the High Holy Days of that year, my father gave me quite a treat. He took me to see Dr. Sabato Morais, the rabbi of Congregation Mikve Israel, the Spanish-Portuguese synagogue in Philadelphia, then located on Seventh Street just above Arch. This synagogue had been founded during the eighteenth century. The distance from our house was comparatively short. We arrived at the synagogue and were ushered into the rabbi's study. After the exchange of greetings, a difficulty of communication became quite evident. The rabbi, of Spanish descent, and born in Leghorn, Italy, where his family had lived for many centuries, spoke English and all the Romance languages; Father spoke Yiddish and a little Russian, but they found the common denominator: Hebrew. Of course, Father was an expert user of the Ashkenazic pronunciation, while the rabbi used only the Sephardic. Yet both being thorough in their respective accents and pronunciations, they were able to carry on a pleasant conversation.

I must point out that the spring of 1894 found me a pupil in the eighth term in the charge of a Miss Carr, but still bearing what to me in those days seemed a hateful misrepresentation, the name "Abram Bevitzky." So on that fine springtime afternoon session, I summoned up enough courage to force the issue and restore for myself the name to which I was rightfully entitled.

I remember Miss Carr's class in toto had gone out to take advantage of the balmy breezes in the schoolyard. The recess period of twenty minutes was in progress, but I remained behind offering some excuse, and as soon as the room was clear I approached Miss Carr's desk with the question: "Miss Carr, may I tell you something?" "Yes, Abe," she replied. "What is it?" If I had thrown a firecracker into the room, the surprised look would not have been more intense when I blurted out: "My name is not Abram Bevitzky." When she recovered a little from the shock of such a serious confession with all its implications, she asked me if I knew what my name really was. I told her and explained how it all had come about.

By that time the class commenced trooping in from the schoolyard, the bell having ended the recess period. When the class was seated and in order, Miss Carr made the terse but dramatic statement: "Boys and girls, Abram Bevitzky is no more; it is now Harry Barroway." The teasing and josh-ing of my classmates continued for some time after, but it was music to my ears. At long last I had rid myself of the terrible ignominy of bearing a false name.

Nothing of particular interest took place for about a year, when a family romance created quite a ruckus in the interfamily relationship of the Barroways and the Stam-blers. Of course, the leaders and main actors in the feud were the female heads—my mother and her sister, Pesha Stambler.

Mother, while not hidebound by all the traditions of the Pale, believed most religiously in the practice of getting an older daughter married off before the younger. And the pity of it all was that the two sisters, my mother, Sara Debo-rah, and Pesha, were closely attached to each other, and neither made any move, serious or less, without consulting the other. But this was an affair of the heart, and the reac-tion was very different.

You will recall that Charles Stambler was Pesha's old-est son and apparently, to my mother's way of thinking, was destined for marriage to Mother's older marriageable daughter. But unfortunately for Mother's peace of mind, Charlie preferred Naomi, the younger. Apparently no such tradition existed since the time of the Patriarchs, when Jacob had not hesitated to prefer Rachel over Leah [Genesis 29:16–18]. You cannot imagine the heat of the raging com-bat! At one time Mother even threatened not to arrange the wedding. However, she cooled down a bit, listened to rea-son, and Charlie Stambler married Naomi. They lived hap-pily together until 1938, when he died. They raised a family of eight children.

Necha, as the rejected bride, was soon consoled by meeting a very nice young man with plenty of good family background and a hustler in his own right. They left us and went to live in New York, where he died about the same time as Charlie Stambler.

Shortly after the marriages of the two girls, my father received word from his sister, Mrs. Hoffman, that she was in New York and that she would like to see him after a separation of some ten or twelve years. Remember that was his only sister and the only first-collateral blood relative. He had no brothers. Of course she received a fervent invitation to come on. The reunion was a happy event and cemented a close kinship between our two families for many years. I was the special beneficiary of the reunion because I formed a strong attachment for Willie, a boy three years older than I.

I will tell you quite a bit more about our strong friendship a bit later on in this story. After Mrs. Hoffman's visit to our home, Mother and I visited the Hoffmans, then living on the third floor of a walk-up tenement house on Cherry Street in the extreme Lower East Side of New York, and it proved to be one of the most enjoyable periods of my youthful days. The two older sons were employed in the fur business, at that time the most lucrative work for immigrants in New York, and they could entertain what could be considered lavishly in those days. They took Mother and me to see a Yiddish play at the Windsor Theater on East Broadway. Surprisingly, I remember the play—a dramatization of the story of Uriel Acosta, the Marrano Spanish-Dutch philosopher of Amsterdam. When we left for home I carried with me a small stem-winding and -setting watch, a going-away gift from the entire Hoffman family.

Willie Hoffman, the youngest child, was then a boy of fourteen, and I was eleven, but despite the disparity in our ages, a strong affection sprang up between the two of us that lasted for a couple of years after my marriage and then, like all good things, came to an end. We just unconsciously drifted apart.

I cannot explain it psychologically, but during those formative years I had a strong penchant for adopting, at different periods, one boon companion. This friend at the particular time was the keeper of my conscience and my father confessor. In him I reposed all my innermost thoughts and secrets, and invariably he returned the compliment. This kind of relationship began with my friendship with Willie. Now, do not get me wrong. I was not the lone wolf type of boy, and neither were any of the boys that were the counterpart in the relationship. I liked joining many in group activities. I loved to join others in games of baseball, football, and the like, but my preferences always tended toward the companion of the moment. I shall describe some of the more interesting details of these puerile attachments chronologically with the telling of my story.

I admit that my parents, especially my mother, pampered me scandalously. In the first place I was what is called in Hebrew a *ben yachid,* an only son, and then I came to them almost belatedly. Now my mother had passed the age of forty-five and had no illusions of bearing more children. My sisters were married off and had left the family hearth. I was left alone with a middle-aged couple to fuss over me.

That I amounted to anything in life is due more to dumb luck than my puny efforts to ward off the effects of too much maternal love. Where other boys were allowed, no, even encouraged, to go out in the street and sell newspapers, I was forbidden to do that because I might get hurt jumping on and off trolley cars. I rebelled against such pampering until one cold, miserable day I snuck out of the house and ran overcoatless to Twelfth and Chestnut Streets, where my cousin, Harry Stambler, was holding forth folding and dealing out the newspapers to his customers. When Harry saw me coatless and shivering in the cold, he unhesitatingly removed his own coat and threw it over my shoulder with a sharp command of "Put that on." I protested to him, but he said: "I have a sweater under my jacket, and am used to that." I remained with him the rest of the day, tending to customers on the opposite corner. I never saw a more selfless, kindly act the rest of my days, and I have never forgotten Dr. Harry Stambler. This was the extent of my experience in the newspaper business.

A Teierer Yingel

We have now reached the place on the calendar of 1897 where, if it had been fifty years later, there would have been much excitement in the Barroway ménage or in any other good Jewish home. In these days a momentous event is to take place, and this upsetting of the usual quiet routine of Jewish home life has continued for six months or more: Aryele or Jakele, or whoever the particular boy happens to be, is approaching the age of thirteen. The boy is being prepared for his bar mitzvah, and things are humming with the work and excitement of the preparations. Most importantly the boy has to learn to read and intone the *maftir*, the Prophetic portion, of the particular Sabbath. Starting from scratch, he must learn to recite the blessings when called to the Torah and perhaps memorize a five-minute speech written by the rabbi of the synagogue on the beautiful status of almost becoming a full-fledged mature Jew responsible for all his acts and omissions. All this to-do because the boy's Hebrew education lacks in every essential the elements of making him even a beginner in the complexities of Jewish life.

Fortunately for me, my Jewish training was such that Father just nonchalantly announced about a week before the appropriate Sabbath that he had arranged with the *gabbai* of our *minyan,* or prayer quorum, to call me up, not just to recite the blessings and read the *maftir,* but first to read most of the Pentateuchal portion of that week as well. That was all the preparation made necessary by the announcement, except that on the Friday preceding the Sabbath designated, Mother baked two large sponge and honey cakes. After the baking process she tucked the two confections beneath her shawl to take to *shul,* which was located on the third floor of a loft building on the corner of Second and Noble Streets, the first floor of which was occupied by an auction of secondhand furniture. On the way to the *shul,* she stopped at the Margolis Liquor Store at Second and Vine. Joe Margolis, the landlord of our first home rented at Second and Craven Streets, had advanced up the ladder of economic status. Formerly a grocer, he was now a liquor dealer. Mother bought two quarts of a white alcoholic concoction called "hooch" in Prohibition days, took the bottles with her, and left them in the *shul,* so that they could be used on the Sabbath without desecrating the sanctity of the Sabbath by carrying them in on that day itself.

Saturday morning services witnessed my advance into the covenant on assuming responsibility for my sins of omission or commission. Presumably I had become an adult Jew at the age of thirteen. I performed my part of the service creditably, and what is more important I understood, unlike the bar mitzvah heroes of today, what I read. After the conclusion of the services, each congregant, as he came over to the refreshment table, patted me on the yarmulke and said: *"Oy, a teierer yingel"* ("What a precious youngster!") and addressing Father, wished him the traditional *"Torah, chupah,* and *maasim tovim."* To give it a free translation, it meant a wish that the boy grow up to be a student of the Torah, get married, and be a doer of good deeds.

I hope that I will be forgiven for using the personal pronoun so frequently. All through my life I avoided to the utmost the sinful indulgence in bragging, and I do not intend to start now. Those who know me best will testify to this. I am bragging, but I am doing so truthfully and for the purpose of proving my point that the bringing up of a youth to be a Jew was more meaningful and cogent then than our efforts of the present day. It made me sick at heart recently on attending a bar mitzvah celebration to witness a display of wealth costing thousands of dollars and overemphasizing the importance of the occasion—the men in evening clothes and the ladies (God bless them!) wearing dresses that would be in good taste at a president's reception in the White House. True enough, our parents never possessed that kind of spending money, but it is equally true that they possessed a stronger sense of perspective and appreciated comparative values much better than people do today.

Spaghetti and Meat Sauce

The bar mitzvah was over and a milestone in my life was reached. June witnessed my promotion into the twelfth term and the final preparation for a course in the justly famous Central High School. The two events inaugurated a happy period in my life. I cannot tell at this moment whether the successful passing of the bar mitzvah period or the approach of the high school time had the greater impact, but I became more independent and more self-reliant. I, in a manner, had emancipated myself from Mamma's apron strings. I spent more time playing ball with the boys of the neighborhood, and when Father released me from Hebrew studying with him, I would go outdoors. During the vacation period between the eleventh and twelfth terms, I had, besides ballplaying, become quite a Phillies fan, and I admit I am still a staunch adherent of the modern version of the name.

There are more or less interesting occurrences during this vacation period that I simply must recount. I received regularly every Friday morning a large, lonely quarter as my allowance for the week to follow. It was my usual practice when the Phillies were playing at home to get out to the ball park at Broad and Huntington Streets. I use the words "get out," but in much more descriptive terms, we walked from the vicinity of Second and New Streets all the way to Broad and Huntington Streets, a conservative estimate of four miles. We left the house about 9:45 A.M. and reached the ball park at 11. That was the hour when the groundkeeper admitted the boys free to help tidy up the entire grounds. The games in those days, since night baseball was not even dreamed about, started at 4 to enable the working people to attend the game and lose only a couple of hours from their work. The modus operandi regarding funds was carefully planned in advance. A quarter for a whole week's spending could not go very far, even though carfare was only five cents and a cheese sandwich five cents. I, therefore, had to forgo riding and be satisfied with two sandwiches instead.

The summer passed, and back to school I went. The twelfth term, the culminating period for grammar school education, revealed a social situation rather startling in its harshness. The class, which in the eleventh term had consisted of about thirty-five, now appeared to have dwindled down to about twelve or thirteen pupils equally divided between the sexes. There were many reasons for this sudden shrinking of size of the class. First, compulsory education laws came in with the year 1897, and since this grammar school was situated in a poor neighborhood, the parents could not afford and did not wish to keep their children in school until they were sixteen. More importantly, the children themselves considered that they had had enough of school when they passed the eleventh term. The result was that the class that I found myself in was very small numerically but scholastically high. Almost all intended to go to high school and college.

I must mention two of the six boys especially because one figures quite largely in the story concerning my activities during this school year. They both were a little older than me; they were sixteen and came from outside. One, Joe Carlitz, was fatherless; his older brothers and mother operated a shoe store on Second Street. The other was Isadore Finkel, who came to Philadelphia from New York when his father, a noted Yiddish actor from Rumania, brought a very fine stock company from New York and leased the Arch Street Theater for the theater season of 1897–1898. The father rented a large house with a big side-yard garden adjoining. The property at one time must have been used by some prominent personage of old Philadelphia. It surely contained eighteen or twenty large, commodious rooms, and in such a home Mr. Finkel installed his family of five, consisting of himself, his newly acquired wife and new baby, a daughter of eighteen, and Izzie. Later I learned that Izzie's mother had been divorced from his father before he left with his children, and he had even turned over the theater which he had operated and owned to his wife, the mother of his two older children. She, it seems, was also an actress of sorts. Morris Finkel appeared to be a man in his early sixties; his new wife had barely reached twenty-one. The old adage "There is no fool like an old fool" applies very aptly in this case, as you will readily agree when I come to that part of Morris Finkel's story.

To come to the point, Izzie and I took to each other like spaghetti and meat sauce. We liked each other from the very beginning. I admired his physique and general good looks. He was at the time about 5 feet 6 inches and built like a weight lifter. For a lad of sixteen his muscular development was really something to conjure with, and his facial features were really handsome. What he saw in me I do not know. But one thing I do know—that Izzie was a lonesome boy. His home life was practically nil. His father, his stepmother, who was a sister to the famous Boris Thomashefsky, and his older sister were of the theater and lived in the fashion of the theater. They slept until noon, got up and went to the theater to attend rehearsal or the business of the theater, had dinner out, and returned for the evening show. Of course, at this particular time the stepmother had to remain at home with her three-month old baby, but a twenty-one-year-old stepmother was a poor substitute for a parent to a boy like Izzie. My home and I myself supplied him with what he lacked most.

I brought him to my home, and when Mother learned from me the situation at his house she in effect almost adopted him. He would come home with me after school and would have his evening meal with me. We would talk about our schoolwork, discuss our future in high school and college, and would wind up the day by going to the theater. After a comparatively short time I became acquainted with the entire troupe and theater workers and was known as Izzie's partner. So I became a part of the theater family. I saw all the plays and in some instances I could recite portions of the repeats from memory.

And so the school year of 1897–1898, a very happy period, passed on. I absorbed new material very readily and consequently was considered first in the class even though I received some stiff competition from Carlitz and Finkel. The result was that I received applause and adulation from teachers and schoolmates alike. Had I been a kid that waxed fat on flattery, I would have become a spoiled brat. But fortunately I exercised a disciplined equilibrium, always retaining a mental reservation that I did not do as well as I might have.

The Examination Was Over

All was excitement as the time for examinations to enter the four high schools approached for Carlitz, Finkel, and myself. I should call the three of us the "three musketeers," for we were inseparable, especially during school hours. Our principal, Dr. William McFarlane, and the class teacher, Miss Lawless, were having visions of Northeast Grammar, the smallest grammar school in Philadelphia at the time, establishing a record of having its only three entrants taking the examinations for Central High School and finishing within the first ten or twelve boys examined.

I must explain what Central High School meant to people at that time. Central High School was distinct and different from the present conception of what a high school means. It had more of the characteristics of a college than our present high schools do. It was—and according to my information still is—the only high school that grants degrees of A.B. and B.S. It had its faculty divided according to the subjects taught. Instead of a principal, they called the headmaster the president. It was not governed and controlled by the Board of Education directly, but instead was in the direct charge of what was called the Committee on Central High School. In fact, the Committee on the High School was a board of education in itself. There were three grades of instructors. They started their teaching at Central High School as instructors. From that stage they were advanced to assistant professorships, and from that post they rose to the rank of full professor and on occasion to heads of departments, a far cry from the positions that teachers hold in the present system of high schools. So you see, Central High was more like a small college than the present-day high school. Then, the curriculum of Central High was far beyond what they intend to teach present-day students. This is why there was so much ado and excitement attending the entrance of boys into Central High School.

But apparently the gods were not favorable to the hopes of Dr. McFarlane and Miss Lawless. Instead of the three of us finishing the exam within the first dozen, Carlitz and Finkel, for some reason that I could not fathom at the time, fell flat on their faces and finished within the first thirty-five. As for myself, I committed the most stupid blunder, which at that time I considered unforgivable. You should understand that Miss Lawless was very much concerned with the three of us finishing close to the top, and so she left no stone unturned to accomplish that end. The day before each examination she would hold a session with us advising us as to what actually should be done in the best interest of a successful examination. On that particular day, before we took the English exam she put us through a briefing, advising us in a manner not unlike that received by a contingent of the Air Force, at a much later date, about to go out on a mission against the enemy. She told us that we were to have so many questions in English, one of which would receive a credit of twenty points because of its importance. She therefore advised us that, as soon as we received the questions from the examiner, we were immediately to look down the list of questions and find the one relative to the writing of this composition. Because of its importance, we should get to work on this first before undertaking the other questions. She also advised that, when finished with the writing of the composition, we were to lay aside the composition in the bottom compartment of the desk. This is just the advice that I should not have taken.

In the excitement of the examination I finished the other questions, considered it a job well done—and forgot my composition in the bottom compartment of the desk. I handed in the questions, minus the composition, and went merrily on my way. I remember waiting a short time outside for my two pals, and after a confab about the examination, I left them and proceeded down Spring Garden Street to Ridge Avenue. As I turned the corner it was just like a bolt of lightning striking at my feet. The horrible thought came to me that I had forgotten to hand the composition in with my other answers! And in the words of a recent song, "I turned east and I turned west"—I didn't know where to go until I decided that I had to get back to that examination room, and so I ran full speed back to Broad and Green Streets. By the time I reached the school the examination was over. I met the monitor walking out of the room with the package of answers under his arm. He noticed my unusual excitement and in a kindly manner asked: "What's the trouble, sonny?" I composed myself as much as I could and related to him my terrible oversight. He had a wry smile and said: "Sorry, son, but I cannot help you and no one can help you. Monitors are sworn not to permit reentry of examination rooms during exams. Once you left the room, your examination time was over." I was so disgusted with myself I cursed the day I was born and, heartbroken, left for home.

The crux of the situation was this, that three subjects —arithmetic, English, and spelling—required a 70 grade regardless of what you received in the other subjects, and with the twenty points for the composition vanishing into thin air, I was afraid that I might not get the 70 in English. This would have been a tragedy. However, I did not reveal the matter to my parents. I figured it would not help matters, and there was no use in worrying them. When the grades were returned to the Northeast Grammar School, I found that my fears were greatly exaggerated.

The postexamination period was included in the vacation time; between the grades and high school time, the Great Healer set to work in my behalf, and by the time school reopened in September I appeared to have gotten over my disappointment in regard to the loss of a potential twenty points. In a great measure I recovered, and when school opened I was ready to work and recoup my self-esteem.

In the interim I had made the acquaintance, during the examination period, of a boy named Alexander Aron. He lived a few blocks from my home and was, as I usually found to be the case, two years older than me. His father was a tailor from Rumania. Despite his own lack of education, he wanted Alex and his younger brother to attain some degree of eminence, and as a matter of fact Alex graduated as a physician from the University of Pennsylvania, and his brother attained the office of Pennsylvania state senator. The same formula for making and keeping friends was adopted by me during this vacation period preceding the opening of high school, and we became firm and close friends. I elected the Classical Course, but Alex, who intended to become a doctor, chose the Latin-Scientific Course. That, in a great measure, separated our classes, but our friendship flourished just the same. My Classical Course included four years of Latin and four years of Greek. I reveled in these two classical languages, and as a result I built a solid foundation for the first two years. The following two years came very easy.

All this time there had been an irregular correspondence between Aunt Hoffman and my father. Shortly before I graduated from grammar school, we received the terrible news that Uncle Hoffman had passed away at the age of fifty-six. Of course he had not been very healthy, as I noticed when Mother and I visited them three years previously, but the blow was just as hard.

Shortly afterwards, Willie, at the age of sixteen, enlisted as a volunteer in the United States Army. I presume the loss of his father had contributed measurably to his determination to enlist. He fought all through the Spanish-American War in Cuba and was mustered out of the service after the end of the war. Willie did not long delay coming to our house to live, and then our strong kinship was renewed. He stayed with us from 1900 to 1905. In the meantime, in 1904, Saul Joffe arrived without formal leave-taking from the Russian army and also became a boarder at our house. And so 137 New Street, where we lived, became a lively and harmonious place to live. Both these boys had enormous sparkle. My mother used to remark that she now had a large family at home.

G. *George Fox*

THE END OF AN ERA

In 1905 other Americans of German-Jewish stock may not have seen it or wished to see it, but it was already obvious to Rabbi David Philipson, of Cincinnati: "The future of Judaism in America will lie in the hands of the descendants of Russian Jews." Philipson's perception would be substantiated by the career of a man like Russian-born Gresham George Fox (1884–1960).

Fox—Samuel Rosinger and Morris M. Feuerlicht are kindred examples—bears witness to the alchemy of turn-of-the-century America. Though he was brought here by his parents as a child, nothing of Russia persisted in the young scholar who earned a Ph.B. degree from the University of Chicago in 1904, was ordained at the Hebrew Union College in 1908, returned to Chicago for an M.A. degree in 1910, received his Ph.D. degree from Illinois Wesleyan University in 1911, and went on to become a notable member of the Reform rabbinate. Among his books in later years were An American Jew Speaks *and* The Religion of Abraham Lincoln.

"The End of an Era," written in 1953, tells a very Ameri-

can story. George Fox wanted to be, and he was, "representative
of the highest and best in Judaism and in Americanism." What
more could Philipson have asked?

❧

Some forty-five years ago, in 1908, I received the degree
of rabbi at the Hebrew Union College. I was the valedic-
torian of my class, and, as was customary with the men who
chose the profession of rabbi voluntarily, I was jubilant and
optimistic, and happy to be in the line of succession of the
four rabbis who had taught me before I went to the Hebrew
Union College—particularly Dr. Emil G. Hirsch, who had
induced me to study for the rabbinate, and Drs. Tobias
Schanfarber, Joseph Stolz, and Julius Rappaport. I had developed a tremendous admiration for the lovable Dr. Kaufmann Kohler, the president of the college, and I recalled
that when a prominent Chicago attorney once asked me
why I wanted to enter the rabbinate, I told him that I
wanted to make "bad Jews good and good Jews better." I
don't recall the comment of the lawyer.

On graduating I had the choice of three pulpits. One
of them paid a salary of fifteen hundred dollars, and the
others paid eighteen hundred dollars. I accepted Congregation Moses Montefiore in Bloomington, at the smaller salary, because of its proximity to Chicago, where I hoped to
pursue graduate work at the university. I came to Bloomington in the fall of 1908 and found that because the congregation was small I had a lot of time for study. One day
I met an umbrella-mender who asked me whether I knew
Talmud. I admitted that I was not an expert, and when he
told me that he had been for many years a *yeshivah bachur*
and offered to teach me Talmud, I grabbed the opportunity. I have never been able to repay him sufficiently for
his patience and help.

I loved my work and went happily about it, but received my first shock as rabbi in Bloomington. There was a nice young man in the town, a haberdasher from whom I occasionally bought items that I needed. One day I asked the president of my congregation if I could not propose the haberdasher for membership. His reply I have never forgotten. "Oh," said this man, who was reputed to be an outstandingly decent human being, "we don't want any kikes in our congregation." I was astounded and catapulted into a resolution to leave Bloomington at the first opportunity. That this vicious prejudice would extend to heads of congregations had never entered my mind. I had, of course, known of the terrific feeling of the German Jews against the East Europeans. I had seen it in high school and in the university and even in youth societies. I had learned early the meaning of *Aus Polen kommt nichts gutes* [No good comes out of Poland]. In my university days there was a sharp line between the "West Side Jews" and those of us who lived on the South Side. That attitude was exhibited even in my own fraternity. A "hinter-Berliner," a Jew of East European background, could not get into a certain Chicago club unless he was outstandingly wealthy. The Bloomington incident was just one of a pattern—and even rabbis were not strangers to the prejudice. I had even had the experience once of being told by one of my rabbinical teachers before I entered the Hebrew Union College: "If you are a Polack, don't come back." In the South, too, and in recent years, I have encountered this kind of narrowness. The distinction between Eastern and non-Eastern European Jews has thinned out, of course, but too many have not yet emancipated themselves from this vice. This is particularly true of some of the descendants of the "Forty-eighters." I am afraid that our early Reform coreligionists were largely responsible for the unfriendly attitude that used to exist and that they did little to eradicate it. Intermarriage between the decreasing number of German Jewish descendants and the larger number of Jews of Eastern stock will gradually eliminate all differences, and in this process, I hope, an expanding Reform Judaism will play an important role, as indeed it is doing already.

While serving the Bloomington congregation, I had been invited to teach courses in biblical history and the Prophets at Illinois Wesleyan University. I taught these courses with a good deal of enthusiasm, but in the fall semester of 1910 my courses were made electives and were scheduled for the same hours as a number of compulsory courses. This automatically suspended my connection with the university. The president of that Methodist institution had received a number of complaints that I was teaching "higher criticism of the Bible," especially in my course on Isaiah! I was learning the facts of life. There was also another complaint. A number of young men teaching at the school were good friends of mine and used to visit with me often. The landlady saw me smoke, and the other men also smoked. When we would leave the landlady would come in to clean and dust, and she complained that the room was so full of smoke that obviously all of us had been using the weed, not only I myself. It was against Methodist discipline for teachers in Methodist schools to smoke! Clearly I not only introduced skepticism into my classes but corrupted the faculty as well! Our good and pious landlady was greatly relieved when she heard that there were no registrations for my courses, and that two of the sinning young men had left the university—just before I left my Bloomington pulpit in the early part of 1910.

Rabbi George Zepin had met me at a rabbinical conference in New York in November 1909 and asked me whether I would like to come to Fort Worth, where he was serving the Beth El Congregation. He had been asked to become secretary of the Union of American Hebrew Congregations, and if I took the Fort Worth pulpit, he would be free to take the job with the union. I went to Texas on February 1, 1910, and he went to Cincinnati to the union. That is how I became a Texan, and that is how he became secretary of the Union of American Hebrew Congregations.

After I landed in Texas I decided to speak on Abraham Lincoln on the Friday night nearest his birthday, as was the custom among many rabbis in the North. The dailies carried notices of my subject: "Lincoln's Contribution to the Nation." All that week my phone was busy with people urging me not to give such a talk. Lincoln was all right up North, but this was Texas. Finally, on the morning of the Friday on which I was to deliver the Lincoln sermon, the president of my congregation called me. "Young man," he said, "this is Texas, not Illinois. Here Lincoln is not regarded as he is up North. I think that you ought to change your subject." I told him that I had no intention of doing so. I have never forgotten his answer: "Well, if you insist, I will not be responsible for what happens to you." I preached my sermon on Lincoln, but nothing happened. The next year I did the same; a northern Presbyterian minister joined me, and by the time I left Texas, no one hesitated to preach on the life of the great martyr.

I always had something of the missionary spirit and always felt that we Jews had made a great mistake in giving the field over to St. Paul. But if rabbis could not be missionaries to the Gentiles, they could at least try to reach unsynagogued Jews. I had heard of a town called Wichita Falls, a growing and prosperous community which had no Jewish congregation. I visited the place, and within a short time we had organized one. My main assistant, a Mr. Zundelowitz, then about seventy years of age, couldn't make up his mind whether he wanted an Orthodox or a Reform congregation. He decided to go along with me, and we started a Reform temple. I used to travel around the state in behalf of Dr. Joseph Krauskopf's farm school. One of these trips took me to Amarillo, where I found a number of Jews who were anxious to start a congregation but had no one to show them how. I organized the group, started a Sunday school, and went there once or twice a month until they got someone on a regular basis. I went to Gainsville too, until the Jewish population there melted away, and to Ardmore, Oklahoma, where I helped the Jews to buy a former church for use as a temple. After all these years, I still on occasion meet former members of my "missionary" congregations.

The Sixty-four Dollar Question

I was chairman of the Fort Worth Charity Commission, and because of the low level of social welfare work in Texas I helped to organize what is now the Texas Welfare Conference. I was its second president. Two other Jews of prominence, Rabbi Henry Cohen, of Galveston, and Mr. Jules Hexter, of Dallas, were also among the organizers. While head of the Fort Worth commission, I found myself mixed up in a drab affair. In those days, a bureau had been organized in New York—it was fathered by Jacob H. Schiff—which tried to divert Jewish immigration from the eastern seaboard to the South, the Southwest, and the West. Dr. Cohen, of Galveston, headed the Southwest office, because Galveston had become a point of distribution for the immigrants. But Galveston also became the distributing point for prostitutes from both the Old World and South America. Fort Worth was an important railroad center, so that in a comparatively short time we found a large number of Jewish prostitutes in the city. They were huddled together in a district called the "Levee." The notoriety of these women became so widespread that ranchmen were heard to make remarks in hotels and drugstores about the "Jew whores."

As rabbi I could not and would not escape the responsibility that was mine in this shameful business. I got permission from the mayor and the police commissioner to clean out the district. It was a heartbreaking job. We sent notices around to the houses of prostitution, notifying them that they would be closed on a certain date. But we told the police to inform the keepers that we were after only the Jewish girls and that I would see them privately if they came to my office. Only a few came. We got the names of the rest and had them arrested for disorderly conduct. Some of the Christian ministers asked me why I was concerned only with the Jews; I told them that they could join me and concern themselves with the non-Jewish girls.

I went to the jail and took along with me a man who could speak Yiddish. The stories we heard were tragic. They were in the sordid business because it was the only way they had of earning bread and butter. Some were supporting their children in what we now call foster homes. Some were supporting their parents, and one showed me a lavalier bearing a picture of her father, so she said: an old, bearded, Eastern coreligionist. We asked them to leave the city. We told them of the disgrace they had brought upon the community. There were varying responses from them. One asked me whether my rich, fat Jews would take her into their homes and give her a job. Another asked me what she could do, how she could live, if she wanted to stop. A third challenged us, in Yiddish, to give her a job in some store. Of course we were stymied. Our women's committee wouldn't even speak to them. Two of the lot married the men who were their pimps and went into legitimate business. They settled down to normal life and appeared to be happy. The rest left town, and whether we were right or not we breathed a little more easily. The job made me unhappy, though I could see no other way. But I was warned not to show myself on lower Main Street.

Dr. Cohen conceived the idea of settling some of the Jewish immigrants on empty land in Texas or Oklahoma. He asked me and Rabbi Isidor Warsaw, then of Waco, to see whether we could raise enough money to start a farm colony upon which to settle some of the immigrants who had been directed to Galveston by the New York immigrants' bureau. We made several contacts, but the plan had to be dropped for lack of support. I doubt whether any mention of this project has ever been made, but for the sake of the historical record of Texas Jewry I think it should be mentioned.

As everywhere else in the South, prejudice against Negroes was outspoken and rife in Texas. During the First World War everyone who could possibly help was enlisted in the Liberty Bond drive. After the drive was over the bond committee, of which I was a member, called in all its workers for a final report and luncheon. As I walked into the hotel where we were to eat, I noticed a group of

Negroes in a small side room, but when we sat down there were no colored people present. The chairman announced that after we finished the colored workers would be called in to make their report. When I asked why they were not with us, I was told that whites and Negroes did not eat together publicly. I arose and asked permission to put a question. Was the Liberty Bond drive an American enterprise for all Americans? Would there be any distinction in the money raised, based on color or race? Wasn't it true that all who worked on the drive had our country's interest at heart, and was it in the spirit of true Americanism to make any distinction among the workers so long as they were loyal to our country and worked for its welfare? I then told the group that, as far as I was concerned, I would not participate in the meeting if other Americans, even though black, were barred. There was a hush, some subdued excitement—then the Negroes were called in, and a real Liberty Bond celebration was held.

About the same time, the local alumni of the University of Chicago decided to organize a chapter. A few of us held a preliminary meeting to plan the organization. Among the alumni in the city was a fine young Negro physician whom I had known at the university as a student. He had worked his way through college by waiting on tables and after graduation had settled in Fort Worth. After the names of the prospective members of the alumni had been read, I asked why the name of this particular one was omitted. "That fellow is a nigger, isn't he?" asked the chairman. "Yes," I answered, "but does the university make any color distinctions among its alumni?" Someone spoke up and asked whether our association would be a social as well as a business organization. Of course it would. Then came the $64 question: "Would you let your wife dance with a nigger?'' The meeting broke up after that, and during my years in Fort Worth there was to be no branch of the University of Chicago Alumni Association.

That Was Too Orthodox

Fifty years ago, Texas was pretty much an unploughed territory so far as Jewish culture was concerned. Only San Antonio, Houston, Dallas, Galveston, Fort Worth, El Paso, and Waco had rabbis—and I believe there was one from time to time in Corsicana. I felt that a weekly was needed to spread information about matters of Jewish interest and to bring about closer cooperation among Texas Jews. Contrary to the advice of my business friends, I started *The Jewish Monitor.* It was unexpectedly successful from the beginning and became a real force in the South. Recently while visiting in Fort Worth, I spoke to one of the ladies who had met and married her husband through an exchange column in the *Monitor!* A few years later I started what was then the first B'nai B'rith luncheon club in the land, but both of these enterprises folded up after I left Fort Worth.

Shortly after America went into the First World War, I was requested by the late Adolf Kraus, B'nai B'rith president, to secure a leave of absence to take charge of the Chicago office of the Anti-Defamation League during the absence of the regular secretary, who had gone off to war. I did so, and a few months after I came to Chicago Kraus organized the B'nai B'rith Soldiers' and Sailors' Welfare League for war work. This was even before the National Jewish Welfare Board, sponsored by the American Jewish Committee, had been formed. For months after the Jewish Welfare Board was created, there was a heated rivalry between the two organizations. Kraus tried hard to maintain the Welfare League as the prime Jewish war agency, but the American Jewish Committee was stronger and wealthier and gradually ousted the B'nai B'rith's Welfare League from its place in the war economy.

My work often took me to Providence, Rhode Island, to see Col. Harry Cutler, the chairman of the Jewish Welfare Board, and to New York to consult with Felix M. Warburg, who was one of Cutler's main advisors. It was while I was on a trip to New York to meet with him that Warburg told me I ought to move to New York. I asked him why, and he said: "We want all the Jewish brains here in New York." It was a nice thing to say to me, and my bump of vanity was considerably enlarged. After a good deal of bickering the Welfare League became a part of the National Jewish Welfare Board, and peace came into the household of America. I went back to Fort Worth with the understanding that I would manage a number of southern cantonments, which I did until the end of the war. My experience in Chicago and New York had given me an insight into the problems and the jealousies which have not yet been eradicated from American Jewish life.

In the early summer of 1921 I was invited to meet with a committee from a large midwestern congregation with a view to becoming the associate of its rabbi. I met with the committee and the rabbi, and when I left the chairman of the committee said that he would see me again in that city on January 1. The rabbi of that congregation told me to begin packing my books when I got home to Fort Worth, but somehow or other I waited. One day I got the following note from my rabbi friend: "Dear George: The board met last Thursday night and elected so-and-so." What had happened? The young man elected in my stead had married the daughter of a prominent man in the community. He had been having trouble with his own congregation about this time, and so, despite our previous understanding, relatives of the young *rebbetsin* had seen to it that their man was elected. Congregational politics is not an invention of recent years!

Shortly after this, a friend of mine, the president of another midwestern congregation, wired that he had made arrangements for me to preach a trial sermon on a certain Friday night. I wired back refusing to preach a "trial sermon," and he wrote back saying: "Don't be a damn fool; if you don't, someone else will." Someone else did and got the position but didn't keep it long. I think now that the institution of trial sermons is not nearly as bad as I thought then. The congregation should have some opportunity of meeting a candidate, and I now see no sin in trial preaching, provided that it is done in a dignified manner.

By this time I had reached the conclusion that I was ripe for a larger field. I had always wanted to be in Chicago, to be near my dear ones and near the men who had inspired me to go into the ministry, particularly Emil G. Hirsch. Dr. Hirsch had, as a matter of fact, wanted me to take charge of what was then the North Shore branch of Sinai (later it became known as Temple Israel). I met with a committee one evening, and the meeting was historic in throwing light upon the religious attitudes of some of its members, most of whom have since gone to their reward. The head of the religious school was a dear friend of mine, an assistant professor in the Divinity School of the University of Chicago. He was a wonderful man and knew the Bible as it was taught at the university, but had no particular knowledge of Jewish traditions or of the inner pieties of our faith. He had asked to be relieved of his congregational post, and the opportunity for appointing a rabbi to replace him thus presented itself. So I met with the committee. We discussed the time of holding services. How about Friday night? No, that was too Orthodox, they insisted—even after I explained that it had been Isaac Mayer Wise himself who introduced the late Friday night service. Saturday was out, too. How about Sunday morning, like the practice at Sinai? There was one very serious objection: The people out on the North Shore had just organized the Northmoor Golf Club, and most of them were out on the links Sunday mornings. Suppose, said a member of the committee, services are held on Tuesday evenings—"There is nothing going on out here then." By that time, however, my temper got the best of me, and I suggested that what they wanted was not a rabbi, but a sublimated *shammas* [sexton]. I went back to Fort Worth, and a few years later the North Shore congregation changed its name, secured a rabbi, and went on to become one of the best in the Union of American Hebrew Congregations.

In 1922 Dr. Stephen S. Wise asked me to meet with a committee in New York to discuss the possibility of my becoming his assistant at the Free Synagogue. He was going to Europe and wanted the matter settled before he left. I had the greatest affection for him and admired his ability tremendously. I would have liked to serve with him, but, unlike Dr. Wise, I was a stubborn antinationalist and anti-Zionist. I had been asked by a very dear friend Judge Julian W. Mack to join the Zionist forces, as he himself had, but in truth to myself I could not change my position and so never met the Free Synagogue committee. Instead, I remained in Chicago for the summer.

One evening we met some friends who told us that a new part of Chicago, the South Shore district, was rapidly being settled by Jews. There was no Reform congregation there, though three attempts had been made to found one. The people who came out were young, and they just could not raise enough funds to pay a rabbi. Nowadays that is no problem; the Union of American Hebrew Congregations has subsidized I don't know how many new congregations —but in the 1920s, no funds, no rabbi. I had become thrilled by Stephen Wise's Free Synagogue principle. I have mentioned my missionary zeal above; here might be a missionary opportunity! I had saved some money in Fort Worth and told my hosts and their friends that if they started a congregation on the Free Synagogue principle, in which I so heartily believed, and if there were prospects for a congregation of any size, I would ask my Fort Worth congregation for a release, though I had just been reelected for a five-year term. I told them also that I would come to the South Shore without salary for a reasonable time. I would, of course, first have to consult with my wife, who had heard me make the offer.

My hosts suggested that I speak to a somewhat larger group, and this was arranged. I think that there were some there who couldn't quite understand why a sane man would make such a proposition, but they came along. We met a larger group, organized the South Shore Temple without any stipulation as to the rabbi's salary, and my wife and I began to make preparations to go back to Fort Worth. In the meantime Mrs. Fox met with a group of women and organized a sisterhood. On the train I asked her again whether she would be satisfied to come to Chicago without any definite salary in view. Remarkable woman that she is, she said that she was willing to do this, if I thought it best! That is how the South Shore Temple started a synagogue based upon freewill dues, which members were to pay in accordance with God's material blessings. Now, after thirty years, the congregation still maintains its freewill ideal. Membership is denied no one who sincerely wants to belong, even if he can't afford the amount that it costs to maintain his membership. I fear that many of the younger members of our rabbinic craft are not as sure as Dr. Wise was, and as I still am, of the wisdom or the success of the Free Synagogue idea. But I hope that the South Shore Temple will never close its doors to respectable Jews who are sincerely religious, even if they cannot afford to pay regular membership dues.

I did not believe that the new South Shore Temple would need me in less than a year. If information to be supplied by its officers indicated slow growth, I would not have to be in a hurry to tell my Fort Worth folks about the matter. A few days after Rosh Hashanah, however, I received a letter from the South Shore president that the news about the organization of a congregation was spreading like wildfire and that membership was growing fast. After Yom Kippur I saw a notice in *The Sentinel* of Chicago, in which its editor, Dr. Rudolph I. Coffee, congratulated the South Shore Temple "upon its selection of Dr. George Fox as its rabbi." I was surprised that the matter had been made public so soon and immediately showed the article to the president of my Fort Worth congregation. I assured him that I had no intention of leaving unless the congregation permitted it, and at that I would not leave before the end of the summer. He took the paper, threw it down on his desk, and shouted: "If you ever expect to leave, you might just as well do it now!"

I came home to find a telegram from the president of the South Shore Temple. The membership had now reached 150, and if I could not come, I was to designate someone to act for me. I knew of no one who would take the position without salary. Something had to be done. The next Friday I informed my congregation of the state of affairs and told them that I had the president's permission to leave now, and that I would avail myself of that permission. I was hit by a storm of protest. Members stopped talking to us, and for a while things were very unpleasant. Strangely enough, my non-Jewish friends came to our rescue. The Chamber of Commerce arranged a farewell banquet, at which the Texas head of the Ku Klux Klan presided, and a check was given me as a going-away present, with which I was to buy a new car when we got to Chicago. Then the Jewish community began to honor us, and our last days in Fort Worth have never been forgotten. Some months ago the congregation invited us to celebrate its fiftieth anniversary with it, and we had a glorious time.

We arrived in Chicago after Sukkot and found that a house had been acquired and remodeled for services. The Sunday school had already started with an enrollment of one hundred pupils. Membership increased, but not enough to pay all expenses. I served several months without salary, and when I received my first salary check, it was one-third of what it cost us to live. But we were thrilled at the thought that, for a time at least, we had served the cause of our faith without making the Torah a spade with which to dig! Little did we think then that thirty years later the South Shore Temple would have a membership of nearly seven hundred, a school of almost six hundred, and a plant worth more than three-quarters of a million dollars.

In the spring of 1923 I called in two non-Jewish friends of mine—ministers—and we organized the South Shore Ministers' Association, the first of its kind in Chicago and, I have been told, the second in the country. The Roman

Catholic priesthood was the only ministry not represented. Under the inspiration of the association, an annual Thanksgiving Day service and an annual good will dinner during the week of Washington's birthday were inaugurated. There was later to be a Women's Good Will Auxiliary to the Minister's Association, and the South Shore community good will spirit would become proverbial among those interested in interfaith and community good will work. One of the sidelights of the friendly feeling in the South Shore is the fact that in the 1950s two Jews served on the governing board of the local Y.M.C.A.; one of them was myself and the other was my brother. I wonder how many rabbis have ever sat on the boards of directors of Y.M.C.A.'s!

The Test of Time

One day I received a letter from a priest who was the Roman Catholic chaplain at the penitentiary in Joliet. In a kindly spirit he ridiculed the Jewish community of Illinois for not providing some kind of religious service to Jewish convicts there. I became interested, made a trip to the prison, and found that Rabbi Abraham Cronbach had visited the men there on a few occasions under the auspices of the Union of American Hebrew Congregations. No one had been there recently, however, and I arranged for the late Rabbi David Rosenbaum to go there from time to time. An organized effort had to be made to have regular services there, and I asked for the appointment of a chaplaincy committee by the Chicago Rabbinical Association. I was made chairman, took the matter of rabbinical services up with the lamented Governor Henry Horner, and in a short time we had arranged regular visits for the inmates not only in Illinois prisons but in state hospitals as well.

The latter project was a heartrending one. There were

in the 1920s many hundreds of Jewish patients in state institutions. Some of them, particularly ambulatory patients, could attend services if any were held, but the great Jewish community of Chicago was too poor to pay for such services. The Director of Public Welfare of Illinois was sympathetic to the inauguration of weekly services in the larger institutions and of occasional services in the smaller ones. For this, officiating rabbis were paid nominal sums. At the present time, in the 1950s, there are approximately two thousand Jewish inmates in the mental hospitals of the state. Services are now held in the hospitals, and as an outgrowth of our chaplaincy efforts a regular weekly service is conducted in the state penitentiary, while religious instruction is offered in the two industrial schools. After a great deal of effort, finally the Jewish Federation began maintaining chaplains in the city of Chicago, and recently I persuaded the state welfare director to give us a full-time chaplain for the three largest mental hospitals in the state. I believe that Illinois now has what is, next to New York, the best organized state chaplaincy.

Hopefully, the Chicago Jewish Federation can be persuaded to give us an appropriation to extend the work. The Jews in Illinois ought to be ashamed of themselves for the criminal neglect of mentally sick Jewish men, women, and children. Years ago our Jewish welfare officers used to tell us that it was foolish to try to serve mentally sick patients. Now, when the experienced psychiatrists who head state mental institutions tell us that religious therapy is an important element in restoring mental patients to normality, our *balabatim* [communal leaders] listen with less impatience and more respect.

There are satisfactions in the ministry. For me one of them was my participation in the founding of the Chicago branch of what is now the National Conference of Christians and Jews. The first sermon under the auspices of that organization in Chicago was preached in my temple. With the late Rev. Theodore C. Hume and Judge John McGoorty, and the assistance of the late Clifford Barnes, of the Chicago Sunday Evening Club, we held the first brotherhood meeting in the city. The Rev. Joseph R. Sizoo, subsequently of New Jersey, was the preacher of the evening. All these interfaith matters are now common occurrences, but thirty years ago one had to fight for every bit of progress. I shall not forget the first time I asked a noted Protestant minister to occupy my pulpit. One of my leading congregants said to me: "What's the matter, couldn't you get a rabbi to preach for you? Did you have to have a *goy* [non-Jew]?"

Soon after I came back to Chicago a former rabbi, now gone, who was an active member of one of the foremost Reform congregations in the city, suggested that we might introduce a little more sentiment into our worship. I agreed with him. I had veered away from the Einhorn-Kohler-Hirsch attitude of an antiritual Reform and I had begun to realize that we needed more ritualism in our services. He could achieve nothing with his congregation because of its long-established worship traditions, but mine was a new organization, and I could introduce new things. At his suggestion I worked out modernized Friday night bar mitzvah and bat mitzvah rituals and introduced them into the South Shore Temple without consulting the board. Mine was the second bat mitzvah ceremony conducted in Chicago, the first on a Friday night. The ceremony as I arranged it symbolized the handing down of the Torah by the congregation to the father, who then handed it on to the son or to the daughter. Where a grandfather participated, the head of the congregation handed him the Torah, he gave it to the father, and the father passed it on to the child.

In this way, the continuity of Jewish tradition from ancient days was to be maintained. The Torah scroll was taken from the ark by the head of the congregation; it was replaced in the ark by the child. The child, whether boy or girl, not only said the blessings over the Torah, but actually read from the Torah verses in the *parashah* [Pentateuchal portion] nearest its birthday. Bat mitzvah, a modern concept, placed girls on the same level as boys—also a concept of Reform Judaism. The innovation was accepted by many, though members of my own family objected. The opposition grew louder when I started a two-day-a-week Hebrew school to prepare boys and girls for these coming-of-age rituals. Then I introduced the *kiddush* ceremony [sanctification of the Sabbath by means of a cup of wine], then Friday evening candlelighting, and on Yom Kippur the wearing by the rabbi of a white gown (I had used a black one for the services held on Friday nights). I was accused of "going Orthodox," even after I offered numerous explanations that Reform had never banned these ceremonials and that every single innovation could be harmonized with present-day Reform belief. My "reforms" have stood the test of time, and very few in the congregation would now think of giving them up. In order to spread the Sabbath spirit, I introduced a social hour after services—now practically universal in Chicago synagogues. I felt that I had gone far enough, and I still believe this— despite the rush to traditionalism of some of my younger colleagues.

Money in the Treasury

In 1932 I became an honorary member of a fraternity which called itself the Tau Delta Phi. After meeting with them a few times, I persuaded them that they really did not form a Jewish fraternity but rather a fraternity of Jews, and

that they ought to start learning something about their religion. We began to have weekly lectures, and other fraternity men were invited to come. I asked the aid of professors,
and soon we had interested a fine group of students and a
number of University [of Chicago] officials, including
President Robert M. Hutchins. One of the most consistent
helpers was Dr. Charles Gilkey, dean of the Rockefeller
Chapel, who welcomed all religious activities on the campus. Now that the group was getting larger, I began to think
of turning it into a foundation. As a matter of fact, two
deans had told me that something should be done to influence "Jewish students, about whose honesty and integrity
some instructors were beginning to have doubts." I was
alarmed. In all the years that I had been around the university—and I got three of my degrees there—I had never seen
a Jewish society flourish. But to quote one of the deans:
"The Jewish students needed shepherding," and the fraternity was willing to help. I went to the wealthiest Jew of the
city at the time and asked him to finance the organization
of a Jewish student body. I knew him very well and was
certain that he would help because of his interest in Jewish
affairs and in the university. He put him arms lovingly about
my shoulders and came forth with this advice: "I don't think
the Jewish students really need an organization. If they need
any advice they can go to Dr. So-and-So, who is a member
of the faculty, and I am sure he would help them. I wouldn't
waste my time if I were you." It turned out that his Dr.
So-and-So also opposed the organization of a Jewish student
body.

I went to the Chicago Rabbinical Association and explained the whole situation. I was given an appropriation of
fifty dollars and was asked to be the director. My own
temple clubs and those of a few other congregations gave

me donations. I went to Dean Gilkey and told him what I had done. He was delighted and with Mrs. Gilkey offered us his home for a reception to Jewish students on the campus. The hosts were Mrs. Fox, myself, and Dr. and Mrs. Gilkey. We had enough money to pay for a decent affair and counted upon welcoming possibly fifty students at the utmost. The affair was advertised as a "tea for Jewish students and others who may want to come." At 3:30 students began to come by, and by 6:30 some 136 men and women had signed the visitors' register. The Gilkeys felt with us that it was a glorious afternoon, and the students went away enthusiastic, for we had told them that the tea might become a regular feature of Jewish student life. At a subsequent meeting, the Jewish Student Foundation of the University of Chicago was organized, and I was named director. Lectures were instituted, as were Friday night fireside sessions, which were addressed by some of the outstanding men of the university. I instituted an annual Maccabean festival at Hanukkah, and this festival has become one of the outstanding religious events on the campus. The foundation prospered so that by the fall of 1939 my physician told me that I would have to give up either the foundation or my pulpit, but that I couldn't hold on to both. I turned the Jewish Student Foundation over to the B'nai B'rith Hillel Foundation—and there was even some money in the treasury to go along with it!

In 1942 the University of Chicago, through its alumni association, awarded me a "Citation for Public Service." It was the first time that the university gave such an honor to one of its former students. Two other Jews were similarly honored at the same time—Jacob Billikopf, the social worker, and Alfred K. Stern, the son-in-law of the late Julius Rosenwald.

Some years ago the pastor of a Swedish Covenant church came to me and told me that his church had been sold to Negroes and that he needed a place for worship until his congregation could find new quarters. The only building in the vicinity that could accommodate his group was a large undertaking parlor, and his members objected to gathering there. Could we let his congregation meet in our temple? We did, but it took longer to find a place than he had expected, and soon the autumn was approaching with nothing in sight. He had a wife and two children, and his church would disband unless something was found. The man was desperate. After some planning we managed to let him have our gymnasium for Sunday mornings, while we used the auditorium upstairs. When people came to services the ushers were instructed to ask those who seemed to be strangers whether they had come for Jewish or for Christian worship and to direct them properly. Once I was standing at the door when a non-Jewish lady came in, and I directed her to the Christian services. Someone got a laugh out of a statement that was made about the rabbi of the South Shore Temple directing people to the Christian services. Where else but in our country could such a thing happen? The payoff came a few years later, when the president of the Swedish seminary, addressing a meeting of the Chicago Biblical Research Society, referred to the "brotherly action of one of our members, who with his congregation saved one of our churches by giving it a home when it needed it —our friend Dr. Fox." The seminary later reciprocated by offering its premises to a new Jewish congregation in the neighborhood.

The South Shore Temple has housed not only the church referred to. When the Y.M.C.A. was started on the South Shore, it met under our roof until a home was found for it. The Roman Catholic church across the street from us, lacking a gymnasium of its own, had its athletic teams use ours. We were the headquarters of the South Shore Church Baseball and Basketball league, even though once in awhile there would be a flare-up of anti-Semitism. Old gentile settlers in the South Shore district often commented on the neighborly feeling created by the temple, something which they had not known in the earlier days of the district. I have often thought it a pity that we Jews nearly always have to make the advances in the matter of interfaith activities, but I assume that that is part of our mission—or is it our desire to contribute to the peace of our land?

I have been a longtime advocate of adult Jewish education and in Fort Worth and again in Chicago held two "revivals." Each lasted a week, and both were eminently successful. The one in Chicago was held in conjunction with what Dr. Maurice N. Eisendrath, president of the Union of American Hebrew Congregations, called "the Cavalcade." I had the cooperation in this enterprise of my then associate, Rabbi Selwyn D. Ruslander, and of Dr. Jacob Singer, who assisted me with the music. Our temple was crowded from Monday night to Friday night, when Dr. Eisendrath gave the sermon. I regret that such revival weeks have since been eliminated by the union. I have the feeling that so much adverse criticism was leveled against the term "revival" that the president of the union dropped the matter. I think it was a mistake. I am certain that Chicago alone could hold revivals which would literally shake the community. But Chicago Jewry—certainly its Reform element—is not as wide-awake as it might be. I pioneered downtown services during the "Solemn Days" [the Rosh Hashanah–Yom Kippur period] for a number of years. The Federation of Jewish Synagogues—the local Reform congregational organization—

took up the work later, but ultimately voted to discontinue these services because an average attendance of two hundred was thought not large enough to warrant spending some seven hundred dollars. Here we have a fine example of the battle between spiritual values and dollar costs!

Not Profession but Practice

When I was still a young rabbi Dr. Joseph Stolz, one of my revered teachers and the rabbi of my parents' temple, invited me to be present at a conversion. The convert, a young nurse, had learned the *Shema* ["Hear, O Israel": Deuteronomy 6:4] and some of the ritual blessings, and Dr. Stolz asked her to recite these and an additional Hebrew passage which she had been instructed to prepare. With perspiration on her brow and a very definite effort, she recited and translated the Hebrew. It was a hard and tedious task. When she finished I asked her fiancé whether he could do as well. He looked at me, shrugged his shoulders, shook his head, and laughed. "I don't know anything about that," he said in what seemed to me to be a scornful tone. He had had no Jewish education to speak of, though his family, one of the most prominent in Chicago, belonged to an old congregation whose Sunday school he had attended —irregularly. The incident set me to thinking. Here was a splendid girl, a graduate nurse, of good family, forced to learn a number of things that meant nothing at all to the man she was to marry. She had expended effort, energy, and thought for something quite unimportant to her Jewish fiancé. He had the advantage, he was born of Jewish parents; she was not, so she was at a disadvantage.

What this meant to me was that because he was of "Jewish blood," he was not compelled to trouble himself about a knowledge of Judaism. She, because she was not of "Jewish blood," had to pay a penalty, as it were, by learning what she recited for Dr. Stolz, though it was of no consequence to her future husband. I felt that this was a grave injustice and that there must be another way for decent people who, for one reason or another, want to enter the Jewish household. I felt then and I feel now that the whole attitude of the "conversionist" is closely related to the "blood and race" theory that so outraged the world during the Hitler barbarities. I decided then and believe now that a non-Jew who wants to enter the Household of Israel need not be subjected to formal conversion or the kind of test that I witnessed that evening. I think it proper to demand that, when a mixed couple comes to me to be married, both parties assert their belief in God. Neither may believe in the divinity of Jesus; and both must promise to rear their children as Jews. Both must promise also to join a congregation and to make an effort to study the principles and precepts of Judaism. If it seems to me that these promises have been made in good faith, I will perform the marriage; I am on Jewish ground here. I do not demand formal conversion, however, because I have no more faith in its permanency than I have in an honest declaration of belief. I will convert anyone who requests formal conversion, but I have found that many who come to me have some sort of revulsion against a formal conversion ceremony.

I am disturbed by the increase in intermarriage. My own experience is that it occurs much more often among the children of Orthodox parents than among those of Reform antecedents. My experience on the University of Chicago campus for some seven years taught me the ineffectiveness of rearing children under the stresses and strains of traditional customs without explaining to them what these meant. I found innumerable students not only ignorant of the meaning of the customs and practices of their parents, but actually hostile to them. I discovered that the great majority of these students, particularly the girls, had had no education whatever, either in Hebrew schools or in Sunday schools. Then, too, I came across male students who though they had a smattering of *cheder* training had completely forgotten even the little they had been taught. I don't mean to imply that the children of Reform parents were models in their religious attitudes, but at least many of them remembered the teaching, minimal though it was, that they had gotten in Sunday school.

I don't know how well I have realized my boyish ambition to be a constructive force in the lives of my coreligionists. I suspect that to some degree I have. I have seldom regretted becoming a rabbi. Moments of doubt come to all people who think, and I have at times been disappointed with my abilities. I have come to believe that with the exception of a very few colleagues who have been endowed by the Almighty with extraordinary ability, most of us can be divided into three classes or categories. The first is that of those who belong to the classical tradition of the rabbi —*lamdan* [scholar], student, thinker, and saint. His role in life is to seek knowledge and to impart it—because *chochmah,* wisdom, is the very heart of our religion. The world may pass him by, but he cares little. In his daily life he is not part of the secular world. Then there is the second kind of rabbi, the one who achieves fame through his organizational activities: he assumes the presidency of various organizations, until his name becomes synonymous with the various activities of the community. He flits about from one presidency to another and is overwhelmed with administrative duties, but attains renown through wide publicity and his reputation for expertise in public relations. He is not necessarily an *am ha-aretz,* an ignoramus, but he is not the classic student or the creative scholar. The third kind, as I have figured it out, is the consecrated and humble servant, who applies to his daily conduct the principle of Rabbi Shimon ben Gamaliel: *"lo ha-midrash ikkar, ela ha-maaseh"* —not profession but practice is the principal thing [Abot 1:17]. For him *torah,* learning, and *abodah,* service, are synonymous, and he strives to make of himself a *shittuf bivriat ha-olam*—a partner with God in the creation of the world. He may be something of an administrator, he may be studious, but he is not, generally, a creative scholar. He can be a good public relations representative, an ambassador to the Gentiles, but he qualifies best as a good servant of God who tries to bring into the lives of those whom he serves the commandments that will sanctify their lives and glorify their Creator. He is a teacher, a pastor, a shepherd, an advisor, and at all times a friend, sharing the joys and sorrows of those whom he serves.

Although I had begun to prepare myself for the first classification, circumstances threw me into the last. I have had moments of regret that I permitted various activities and temptations to pull me away from the classical rabbinic ideal, but I believe that despite occasional regrets my ministry has been a fairly successful one from the point of view of that kind of service which is expected from an ordinary rabbi. I think that I made my influence felt in the religious field, both Jewish and Christian; in the civic area; and in the political field, when moral issues were involved. I have tried to defend that ideal of American Jewish life which is based upon the democracy of our basic organic national documents. I have tried so to live that the word rabbi, applied to me, maintains its historic symbolism as representative of the highest and best both in Judaism and in Americanism. When I went into the ministry it was against my father's wishes. I had been carried away by the enthusiasm and the promises of Emil G. Hirsch. This was my "call." It may not be a call in the Christian sense of the term, but my feeling was akin to that which a Christian feels when he speaks of a call. I have been told that today when a young man enters the Hebrew Union College and tells members of the faculty that he feels he has a call to the rabbinate, they smile. I hope that this is not so, particularly when a young man becomes enthusiastic over the possibilities of the American rabbinate.

His Father Wore a Yarmulke

I became almost fanatical in my belief in Reform Judaism as I had learned it in my home life and as it was practiced in Chicago. I helped in my day to fight for it. As I grew older I came to disagree somewhat with my first teacher, Dr. Hirsch, and to follow more closely the traditions of Rabbis Rappaport and Schanfarber, and also Rabbi Stolz, to whose congregation my parents belonged. Still, I have never gotten away from what I call "Western" Reform, in contradistinction to what has been called "Atlantic Coast" Reform and to the present "liberal Judaism" of the newer Reform regime. My more than forty-five years in the ministry have persuaded me that "classical" Reform was a more meaningful Judaism for America than the namby-pamby mixture that we are getting now from a number of our younger men, who, I think, have failed to grasp the meaning of progressive adjustment to the customs and mores of American society.

I did not like the reversion to nationalism in our newly

revised *Union Prayer Book,* and I am still an unregenerate antinationalist. I mean that I am opposed to making Judaism a national religion, as I am opposed to making any religion a national religion. Even in the realm of politics, I am not happy at the narrow nationalism that appears to be inundating our land. I don't believe that the world will ever again see a religion ruling the state, despite the ambition of the Catholic Church. I do not believe that we Jews are a nation in the accepted political sense of the word. I am, however, a firm supporter of the State of Israel. When I became emeritus at the South Shore Temple in 1950, the congregation sent my wife and me on a visit to Israel. It had been some twenty-five years since our first visit to Palestine, and we were thrilled by the progress made there and by the promise of new religious, political, and social contributions by the Jewish people. Even aside from the fact that Israel has given asylum to hundreds of thousands, we felt that the state was an achievement on which every Jew who had a whit of Jewish loyalty left should look with pride. We found many Israelis who did not want to be called Jews and did not want their state to be called a Jewish state. They wanted to be called Israelis. Despite this desire of the secular-minded people there, however, the contributions of the Israelis will have their roots in the Bible and will be called Jewish. I regard the State of Israel as a political entity, with the majority of whose citizens we have a religious and cultural, as well as a historical, bond, just as the Catholics of various countries or the Moslems of various lands have historical, cultural, and religious bonds. I have not changed my basic Reform philosophy by this attitude.

I am restudying Dr. Mordecai M. Kaplan's Reconstructionism. It seems to have gotten into the blood of many of our younger and a few of our older alumni. Thus far I haven't found it necessary to change my opposition to Reconstructionism. When I delivered the Founder's Day address at the Hebrew Union College some years ago, I said that Kaplan was a thoroughgoing Reform Jew and ought to admit it. His kind of Reform may not be mine, but leaders of Reform Judaism have never agreed on all details or even on all theological views. All I ask is that Kaplan admit that he has utilized Reform principles of change and adjustment, the fundamental governing factors of Reform belief and practice. But apparently he has been conditioned to hate Reform—and probably Reformers. That is the implication that I get from his constant use of the word "Reformist," and from his attitude toward Reform itself. He admits that he has departed from Orthodox tradition—but this divergence is not Reform, according to him. I have no objection if he insists on naming his particular kind of Reform *Reconstructionism,* but what sense does it make to belittle the principle of Reform Judaism while utilizing its approach? The chasing of many of our colleagues after Kaplanism roils me, for what they apparently want can just as well be accomplished by remaining within the orbit of that type of Reform which has been evolving in the last twenty-five years or so.

I have been an ardent missionary of Reform Judaism because I believe that it best fits into the matrix of American mores and customs. It comes nearest because of its fundamental relationship to the eternal verities of our faith and to the democratic ideals of our land. We are living in a Western land and can assimilate Western social amenities and habits without injury to Prophetic teachings. When I go into a house of worship I don't care to be reminded of the customs of the Arabs. When we visited the mosques in Palestine, some of those with us thought they were entering an Orthodox *shul.* I want my fellow Jews to have a clear and thought-out conception of their religion, particularly in the West, where religion becomes the most important element in our individual lives as Jews. But I don't want Jewish differences to be so marked that we may be mistaken for foreigners, especially in religious spheres that do not interfere with our ethical ideals.

Once in recent years I was asked to take the pulpit of a small town, in a presumably modern Reform congregation. We got along splendidly until I noticed that a certain group of people among the "best payers" were not attending services. I saw one of the most consistent absentees, and he asked me to take lunch with him. I did—I had a cheese sandwich; he asked for ham. He told me that the reason he and some of his friends were not attending services was my failure to wear a yarmulke [skullcap]. To him, he frankly admitted, it meant that the service was *goyish.* The only thing he knew about Judaism, he said, was that his father had worn a yarmulke when he attended services! A minister who wore no yarmulke could not be a Jewish rabbi! It was my last battle with the yarmulke; I asked to be relieved of my duties and left the position. I cannot tolerate a Judaism whose most important symbol is a head covering; nor can I tolerate a Judaism which insists that its adherents wear yarmulkes and maintain kosher kitchens at home and synagogue, though they feed their stomachs with rich *trefa* [nonkosher] foods at their clubs and lodges. I just don't like that kind of Judaism, seemingly enjoyed by people who have kosher mouths and *trefa* stomachs!

Half-Baked Reform

Whether for good judgment or bad, I have always taken the role of an American Reform rabbi, but as a standpat Reformer of the classical school, I feel that we are at the

end of an era. I am not one of those who see "an amalgamation of Conservative and Reform (liberal) Judaism just
around the corner." I would like such an amalgamation if
the Conservatives become Reformers, but that doesn't
seem to me to be a matter of the near future. On the other
hand, I am convinced that if such an amalgamation does
come, some of the reforms that we hold dear will be sac-
rificed, not because they are bad, but because they do not
fit into the conditioning of the traditional ceremonial mind.
I believe that in time my radical or classical Reform will
outlive its usefulness, just as I believe that Orthodoxy will
pass. Conservatism will hold the fort for a while, but Western life will in the end dominate the social customs of
Judaism, and the result will be a Reform Judaism. We shall
have to stop giving in to Orthodoxy-Conservatism, as we
often do, and we shall have to demand equal recognition
for Reform from those who now appear to belittle it. I do
not look with inner satisfaction upon the U.A.H.C.'s current practice of starting new "Reform" congregations and
asking them to use the *Union Prayer Book,* while they are still
half baked, unacquainted with the philosophy of Reform
and inclined to utilize Orthodox-Conservative ceremonials
without having the slightest idea of their meaning. I am not
convinced of the value of such proceedings. I don't believe
in mass production in the area of religious life. I would
rather have a smaller Union of American Hebrew Congregations that is definitely Reform in conviction and in practice than a great big one composed of synagogues which are
neither Orthodox, Conservative, nor Reform, but an inde-
scribable potpourri of all three. At this time, I can still tell
when I step into a temple whether it is Reform or whether
it is Conservative or Orthodox. I fear it won't be long,
however, before Reform congregations under the guard-
ianship of certain "liberal" leaders come dangerously near

to losing their Reform identity, if indeed that has not already been lost.

Too many of our younger men appear to me to be turning backward. Perhaps it is their early conditioning, the fact that so many of the younger Reform rabbis have come from deeply Orthodox homes, or perhaps it is a feeling of despair because Reform has not accomplished as much as we had hoped. But when I hear my young colleagues prate about Reconstructionism; when I hear them advocate traditionalist usages like the *chuppah* [canopy], the breaking of the glass, and the seven blessings at weddings; when I hear them defend the *mikveh* [ritual immersion], the wearing of the yarmulke, the inclusion of *kashruth* wherever possible, and the Orthodox circumcision; when I hear them saying that the *Union Haggadah* has outlived its usefulness and that Hebrew must be the major element in our religious school instruction; when I hear their pleas to orient the Jewish child toward a definite nationalistic Israeli conception and their calls for Jewish parochial schools; when I find them introducing the celebration of *Tu-Bishvat,* Israeli Arbor Day (they don't seem to know that there is also an American Arbor Day); when I see the National Federation of Temple Youth issue a songbook in which twenty-seven of the thirty-six responses, parodies, and hymns are in Hebrew; when I see our religious schools loaded with young teachers who in their hearts have little or no use for Reform, know little or nothing about it, and are almost completely Israel-oriented—when I hear and see all this, I can't help being pessimistic about the future of Reform Judaism as my generation understood it.

That older Reform cannot be so bad. I came to Fort Worth to conduct worship in a $6,000 edifice. When I left, the congregation had built a $200,000 temple. I came to Chicago and started my new congregation without a cent in its treasury, but in the 1950s a band of men devoted to Reform Judaism were to complete a $400,000 structure, as part of a $750,000 plant. One simply can't accomplish these things with a religion that is uninspiring and unserviceable! Other rabbis of my generation have accomplished even more. Reform Judaism has to my mind saved the Jews of the last three generations.

What I am about to say may sound terrible to some people, but I am sincere in believing it. If the American Council for Judaism were not so unjustly inimical to the State of Israel, a state which to me seems a miraculous godsend to our overseas brethren, if the council were not so barbarously callous to the consideration of our historical kinship with the Israelis, if the council were not so completely wrong in its interpretation of the Prophets of Judaism and their role in the world, I would be greatly tempted to join it. I have a feeling that the council will remain within the limits of what some now call "classical Reform." There is, of course, the great danger that its present-day direction will lead the council to extremes, which will finally put an end to it as a Jewish movement.

I stand where most of my generation of rabbis stood, within the framework fashioned by Isaac M. Wise and the other giants of Reform. Wise and his Reform colleagues objected to customs and rituals which had lost their meaning, to any catering to ignorance and superstition, to kosher-feeling-but-*trefa*-eating Jews, to an unreasoning nostalgia for the past. Wise in particular objected because of his dedication to the belief that American Judaism had to adjust itself, its customs and its practices, to the new Western life while always holding fast to its eternal truths—the spiritual truths of Judaism.

I stand at the end of an era, but I have faith that Reform will in the end conquer. If it be God's will that the kind of

Reform that I have lived and preached shall pass, I would bemoan it, but I should want to become reconciled to its end. After all, Judaism is larger than any of its parts, and I believe it will exist as long as there is evil in this world, in order to bring about the day when "the Lord shall be One, and His Name shall be One."

Florence Reichert Greenberg

FATHER WAS
A RABBI

What was it like to grow up in an American rabbinical household around the turn of the century? For a girl named Florence Reichert and for her brothers and sisters, it was fun. That is Florence's testimony in a memoir which she wrote in 1944. By then she had become Mrs. Abe Greenberg, of Tallahassee, Florida. Mrs. Greenberg offers us as vivid and as high-spirited an account of rabbinical family life as we could hope to find anywhere.

Rabbi Isidor Reichert (1870–1922) and his helpmate Miriam Pakas Reichert (1870–1944) did not find it easy to raise their ebullient brood, but in tribute to the elder Reicherts let it be said that their two sons were undiscouraged by the vicissitudes of the rabbinate. They attended the Hebrew Union College and became rabbis themselves. Mrs. Greenberg's pride in her brothers is as just as it is vast: brother Irving F. (1895–1968) was for a generation a leading member of the West Coast rabbinate; brother Victor E. retired in 1962, at the age of sixty-five, from three and a half decades in the pulpit of Cincinnati's venerable Bene Israel Congregation (Rockdale Temple).

I was born in 1898 in Greenpoint, Brooklyn, to a very respectable rabbi and his fine, upright, wonderful wife. My mother told me that I was received with open arms and a particularly hearty welcome—not, she hastened to assure me, that all her children weren't welcome, but I came at a time when my father received a handsome salary—all of four hundred dollars a year, which I believe he supplemented by selling insurance on the side. Five years after my appearance on the scene, we moved from Brooklyn to Johnstown, Pennsylvania, and after a year there to Uniontown. I recall Mother's saying that when my father "received the call" to come to Temple Israel in Uniontown, Pennsylvania, he wrote to the president of the congregation that, as he had a big family—two boys and three girls (another little sister had come along after me)—he would require a large house. That, it seems, was a difficult assignment. However, finally one was secured at 70 Nutt Avenue. We arrived, and, Mother went on to say: "The shades of the houses on both sides of ours were drawn to the very sills." But my father's charm, distinguished appearance, and air of culture plus my dear mother's wonderful cleanliness, sweetness, and wholesomeness proved too strong a magnet, and slowly, inch by inch, the shades were pulled higher, and the Browns and McCrumbs began calling. They had evidently expected a rabbi to have horns as well as a beard and to speak in broken, unidiomatic phrases, with a slovenly wife and a household of dirty, snotty kids. In all these matters, they were happily disappointed.

Helen Wants to Play

I dimly remember the evenings spent in Uniontown before a roaring fire, while father read to us. He read well

—he did all things well—and we listened intently. That I am interested in poetry today is because of the manner in which beautiful phrases rolled from my father's tongue. The winters were rather severe, and it was such a safe, happy feeling to sit around the fire watching Mother's busy hands always engaged in some task, mending, knitting, crocheting, while we contentedly munched apples or nuts. And if one drowsed, it was only to awaken the next morning in bed wondering how one ever got there. One night my brother Victor fell sound asleep. Father read; Mother sewed; we all listened. Suddenly Victor stood up, motioned with his hand as though turning a doorknob, and—to the huge delight of us kids—employed the fireplace as though it were the bathroom. His task completed, he sat down, still asleep. Poor boy—what a ribbing we gave him the next morning, and for many mornings to come! He was all of six at the time.

And then I recall a holiday morning. We were having company for dinner, and Mother was busy in the kitchen with Hulda, our little Polish maid-of-all-work, who received, I think, the munificent sum of eight dollars a month —the only bill Father paid without grumbling. We loved Hulda, and she loved us. She would kiss us and spank us, enjoying the one emotion as much as the other.

The job of bathing my little sister Helen [she would become Mrs. Abram Weiss] was assigned that morning to big sister Natalie [who would become Mrs. Abraham Sprung], with the admonition to "wash our hair as well, and good and clean behind the ears." Natalie, the eldest, had a new pair of roller skates, and several of her girl friends were waiting for her, but with the meanness of kids we refused to be hurried. She pleaded—she threatened—she cajoled. Finally we agreed that if she would make snowmen out of us, we would let her finish in a hurry. "Making snowmen" meant completely enveloping us in soapsuds from head to foot. No sooner said than done. She took a bar of soap and a glass of water, made a thick, soapy solution, and poured it over our naked bodies. We helped along, lathering the solution until only our eyes remained free of soap. "Well," she said, "now you're snowmen, so let me rinse you off quickly and dress you." I was agreeable, but Helen was adamant. She was about two years old and the darling of our hearts. "No, no!" she said. "Helen wants to play more." Once more Natalie pleaded and coaxed, all to no avail. Finally she threatened, "If you don't let me rinse you off, I'll—-I'll throw you out the window." Helen gurgled with delight. "Throw me out—throw me out!" And Natalie, exasperated beyond sanity, picked up the soapy child, opened the window, and—found the little one slipping out of her grasp! Our bathroom was on the second floor of the house. The window faced the front lawn. Father was one of those ministers who scorned reading his sermons, but used to memorize them word by word. He would pace up and down the lawn, the notes in his hand, and commit the words to memory one by one. Fortunately, at that moment, he was doing just that. When Natalie realized that the baby was slipping out of her grasp, she screamed for help with all her might. Father looked up. Somehow he controlled himself sufficiently to beg her to hold tight, and he would be right up—and then he ran up the steps as fast as human legs could travel—only to find the bathroom door locked.

How he got me to unlock the door with my soapy little hands and how he managed to pull that other slippery body back through the window—and how he refrained from killing Natalie on the spot—still remains a mystery. For my father truly had an ungovernable temper. Perhaps it was the look on Natalie's face, for the baby was, if anything, dearer to her than to the rest of us, or it may have been her begging him to "beat me, Father! Kill me—do anything you will because I almost killed my darling, precious Helen!" He wiped the sweat from his brow, looked for a long moment at Natalie, and then handed the now thoroughly frightened little Helen back to her. "No, I won't whip you," he said. "I think you've been punished enough."

Straight from Heaven

A terribly ignorant woman once had the effrontery to say to Mother: "Mrs. Reichert, I know your charming daughters, but do you have any sons?" For one moment the air was pregnant with Mother's shock at the question, and then, drawing up all three of her chins, Mother said: "Have I got *sons!*" in a manner which left the answer fully covered.

My two brothers, Irving and Victor, are about as different as any two human beings could possibly be. Irving is brilliant, quick-witted, with a keen sense of humor, and a born leader. Victor, the younger, is a poet, a dreamer with his head in the clouds or buried in a book, yet with a strong practical sense. The night before any exam it was Irving who sat up with a pot of strong black coffee and "crammed" until the first rays of the morning sun. Victor spent the evening studying carefully as he always did and went to bed no later than usual, secure in the knowledge he had so painstakingly acquired. That Irving passed invariably the highest in his class was also true, but question him a week later: pertinent dates and facts were "gone with the wind." Wake Victor in the middle of the night and in his sleep he would answer slowly and carefully whatever questions were put to him.

Irving led. Victor followed—blindly, devotedly, unquestioningly. What comrades they were—what friends! Irving could no more keep out of mischief than a monkey could. My father, believing firmly that to "spare the rod" was to "spoil the child," kept a cat-o'-nine-tails. Irving felt it often and keenly. Under his trousers, as part of his daily wearing apparel, he kept a square board to soften the blows. Father must have known, but he respected the keen mind which believed in preparedness.

In the winter the boys in our neighborhood used to take their sleds and cut and hammer and work until they had made long bobsleds out of several smaller sleds. On top of the sleds they would nail strips of carpeting. I have ridden in everything from a roller coaster to an airplane, but never have I experienced the same thrill as that long icy ride down Nutt Avenue to the railroad tracks. We'd pile on, eight or ten of us on one bobsled, and off we'd go, our pigtails and mufflers flying in the wind, rosy cheeked and starry eyed, shrieking in delirious excitement. It was a long ride—and such a glorious one. Sometimes—not too often —the boys would let some of the girls sit on the sled and ride back. Helen, the baby, always got to ride back. She was very cunning, and few could resist her.

One particularly cold winter's day Mrs. Brown, our neighbor, came out to call Clay in for supper. The gang was just starting out, and Clay pleaded for "just one more go-round, Maw." For a moment Mrs. Brown wavered in the door, and then, *sans* hat and *sans* coat, she jumped on the sled and away they went. I'm sure she got as big a kick out of it as did the kids, and if she ever suffered from her experience, I don't think I heard of it.

Christmas, too, was a happy time. The local theater threw its doors wide open, and every child in the town was invited to come and see the show, and get a gift and candy to take home. No second invitation was necessary. All five of the rabbi's children were among those present. There always was a good show—a clown, usually animal acts as well, and rapture on rapture; at the finish a big, fat Santa Claus came flying down a wire—right straight from heaven.

Somehow or other the gifts were always mixed up. The boys would get dolls, the girls, guns or soldiers; and then, of course, a lot of swapping took place. Irving started with one but invariably ended up with a dozen gifts—which he always shared generously. He just was smart and could no more forgo taking advantage of a situation than he could breathing—but to accomplish the thing was enough. Once he had outsmarted the other fellow, he'd bend over backwards trying to help him. And then, too, on Christmas Eve, Mother, who always remained a child at heart, would fix five little plates with all manner of goodies, but never with Father's knowledge—or here, too, is it possible that he was blind in order really not to see?

Friday and Fish

Spring was beautiful in Uniontown. Even today I can smell the lovely violets, white and blue, and the bleeding hearts which carpeted the path to school. And after spring came summer, with all the happy, carefree hours of childhood.

The ugly face of anti-Semitism had not yet shown itself in Uniontown, save for the one little gesture on the part of our neighbors when we first arrived. We played with Christian boys and girls. Our neighbors on all sides were Christians, and Mother's dearest friends. Father Lloyd, the dear, sweet priest of the little Catholic church, was a staunch admirer of my father, and a regular guest at our home on Friday nights. To this day, Friday and fish are synonymous terms to me.

The Jewish community was a close-knit, warm, kindly one. They took us all to their hearts and utterly spoiled us. Mother was especially loved. Notwithstanding the busy household ours was and the fact that we rarely sat down to the table without an extra guest, she still found time for kindly deeds—carrying broth to someone sick or saying just the right word to some aching heart. And Mother had plenty to do. Father's worn pants were repaired, washed, and pressed; in due time they appeared on the person of one of the boys. Every stitch of clothing we girls wore was made by Mother's own hands—frills, ruffles, and dainty embroidery. How many times, though her back was breaking, she would sit up until the wee hours fashioning doll clothes to delight the heart of a little one! Cooking, cleaning, mending, she was on the go from the earliest dawn until late at night, but never too tired to smile tenderly at her little ones, to pat a head, or to administer a well-deserved slap. Yet when occasion demanded it she would discard her house dress and appear resplendent before the delighted eyes of her family in evening clothes, ready to accompany her husband.

The boys were a bit luckier than we girls in the matter of clothing. One of father's admirers had a clothing store on Main Street. Twice a year—before the [High] Holidays in the fall and the Passover in the spring—he would call up and say: "Rabbi Reichert, I want to see those boys of yours in my store after school this afternoon." He always pretended that he wanted to scold them for some misdemeanor, but what he actually did was to outfit both of them from head to foot—including twenty-five cents in cash for "candy and soda pop" on the way home. When Father thanked him, he was the more embarrassed of the two: "Oh, shucks, just some old stuff I couldn't sell," the darling old liar would say.

The little congregation grew. Father was the type of orator who needed no artifices or special acoustics. He would start in a soft, low tone, gradually increasing in tempo until he made the very rafters ring. We thought he was wonderful. His gestures were so dramatic, the fine phrases rolled so easily from his tongue, and his climaxes were—climaxes! None of your namby-pamby conversational speeches for our father! Preaching was something to be performed with gusto. He put so much of himself into his sermons that you could wring him out when he was finished.

On one occasion when my brother Irving was a mere babe, certainly not more than three, Father paused at one point to make his words more effective. Irving, who had been in the room while Father was rehearsing his sermon, thought he had forgotten and prompted him, to the amazement and delight not only of the congregation, but, secretly, of his mother, who knew then what a genius he was. This was one story of Mother's that I listened to with my tongue in my cheek, but Mother swore it was true. She also swore that Irving had sung "Daisy, Daisy, I'm half crazy all for the love of you"—at the age of nine months.

Uniontown Was Too Small

The years passed. The people in the nearby towns began coming regularly to services. Father's reputation as an organizer and preacher spread. There seldom were empty benches in the little hall where services were held, and finally plans were formulated for the building of a temple. Such excitement! Committees on floor plans; committees on decorations; committees on subscriptions—all were carefully appointed, with Father supervising all of them. Our gentile friends, too, were most generous and insisted on contributing to the new temple. The rejoicing when the cornerstone was laid was great. Father was doing a fine job.

Strict discipline was enforced to the fullest degree when I first started school. Modern methods, especially those employed by the progressive schools, would have been looked at askance by the pedagogues of old. You obeyed the teacher or rued the moment when the impulse hit you to disobey him. Each teacher had a paddle—a slab of wood shaped like a table tennis racquet—and employed it often and *con brio.* One day I did something. Exactly what the offense was I cannot recall, but I remember that my teacher called me to the front of the class, made me turn over a chair, and proceeded to beat me. I was stubborn and refused to yell. Fortunately my brother Victor happened to pass the door (on his way to the "john," most likely) and saw my predicament. He rushed to my defense and with his little fists started beating the teacher and crying : "You big bully—you leave my sister alone!" The teacher grabbed hold of Victor, and what happened to him you can well imagine. Both Victor and I had to stay in after school.

When we came home late, Father questioned us, and when he saw the welts not alone on my backside but on my arms and legs as well, I thought he would burst a blood vessel. Mother finally calmed him down, but the next day Father started a crusade against that sort of punishment in school which resulted in its being finally abolished. That was Father. He rarely, if ever, started something he couldn't finish, but once the job was done he looked for other worlds to conquer.

So it was with the congregation in Uniontown. Father had taken a handful of people, organized them into a community, and created interest in the hearts and minds of the folks in the surrounding little towns. Then when the temple was completed he became restless. Once more he wanted to be on the move. Uniontown was too small; the children were growing and needed more adequate schools. His reasons were varied and numerous, and Mother at last consented. The congregation reluctantly parted with their rabbi, and words describing the depth of their emotion and sincere regret at his departure were beautifully embossed on a handsome parchment scroll. The scroll, a purse of five hundred dollars, and a lovely brooch pin for Mother were all formally presented to them at a dinner given in their honor.

Thus in the winter of 1908, when I was ten years old, we left Uniontown. The sexton of the temple went to the station to see us off, and I remember him so fondly because as he kissed us good-bye, he slipped a quarter and a package of gum into each little hand.

Was It an Omen?

On to New York. After the many feverish days of packing, and disposing of those articles Mother felt it would be foolish to take along—her prize chickens, for instance— here we were, actually on the train. Does one ever really forget the first train ride? I doubt it. Then, in the cold gray morning, Mother routed her little brood. Grimy hands and faces were washed, hair combed slick with water, all the little bundles and books and crayons gathered together, and finally the porter called: "Next stop New York," and we were there.

It was that period of New York when the streetcars were drawn by horses. I still feel shivers all along my spine at the memory of the long, cold ride to Brooklyn, where Uncle Victor Pakas, Mother's only brother, lived. The ride took hours. The horse plodded along; it was dark and cold outside, but it was adventure. Tired and cold though we were, our eyes were shiny and our hearts joyous. This was New York—the city where Papa would become famous!

At last we found our way to South Ninth Street, where Uncle Victor lived. We walked up the steps, rang the doorbell, and waited as the door was opened. Uncle Victor stood there. He took one look at Father and Mother, and then slowly his large, protuberant eyes scanned each and every face. His mouth opened but the words stuck in his throat. Finally, wringing his hands in despair, he offered the heartwarming greeting: "My dear sister," he said, "I can't give you anything."

My father replied with contempt in his voice: "Who asked you for anything?"—and with that Father turned and would have marched away with all of us, but Mother, always making allowances for this only brother of hers, gently kissed him and said: "Victor dear, no one wants anything from you. We've just arrived and thought you would want to see us. Don't worry, we shan't cost you a cent." Without further words she entered the house.

Father fumed and fretted—he really was madder than a wet hen—but, of course, we all knew what a weakling Uncle Victor was, and no one ever really paid much attention to him. That my mother, who was such a determined

Horse–drawn cars in Times Square, New York City

person, so generous and fine, could have had such a brother seemed incredible. Mother always found excuses for Uncle Victor. "It really isn't his fault," she would say, "because he was born after Grandma had lost several babies, and if she could have breathed for him, she would have. When the boys would fight with him and she was nearby, she would run to him, wrap him inside her great skirt, and cry: 'Don't fight my boy! Fight me instead!' So," Mother continued, "whatever spark of manhood was in him died a-borning."

Mother had gone inside the house, and we children followed. Timidly Uncle Victor placed a placating hand on my still seething father: "I'm sorry, Isidor—I really didn't mean it—come in, please, come in. It's only that business is bad; I have such trouble with my tailors." Uncle Victor always had "trouble" with his tailors, probably because he didn't pay them enough. "I thought . . ." he went on, and here his voice faltered. "You thought," said Father, contemptuously, "you thought that I would park my family on you. Well, you can just take another thought. I wouldn't eat a crumb from your table." Just then the tantalizing aroma of fresh-made coffee came through the door—and Father said: "I'll just come in for a minute and warm up. But only for a minute, mind you." Uncle Victor heaved a sigh, shrugged his shoulders, and entered the house.

The house on South Ninth Street was a large duplex affair. The room we entered was large and dark. I remember especially a cuckoo clock—I suppose the bird fascinated me, and it stands before me vividly now, for as we came into the room the clock struck, the little door opened, and ten times the bird called out, "Cuckoo, cuckoo." Was it an omen?

During all the commotion no one had paid much attention to Aunt Carrie, but she more than made up for whatever her husband lacked in cordiality. She emerged now from the kitchen, warm and rosy and friendly; and what a furor she made over all of us! She kissed Mother and Father and each of us in turn, keeping up a running fire of sarcastic remarks directed at her husband. She commented on how we had grown and what lovely children we were and how hungry we must be. Somehow or other she had coffee made and the table set, and soon we were eating.

Uncle Victor and Aunt Carrie were a perfect example of marriage in its worst form. They were never completely happy unless they were nagging each other. He was stingy; she was generous. He loved to stay home, eat a great, heavy meal, and then sit down, book in hand, until his full belly forced his eyelids closed and sleep enveloped him. Aunt Carrie, however, though a marvelous housekeeper, loved to go. She adored eating out and wearing pretty clothes. Uncle Victor would complain to Mother and tell her of things that Aunt Carrie was supposed to have said about her, and then he would go to his wife with words, supposedly from Mother's lips, to be interpreted by Aunt Carrie as she saw fit. My mother was too big a person to listen to such petty gossip, and the most Uncle Victor got for his trouble was a scolding from Mother and the advice—which he never followed—not to be a *shlemiel,* but to try and be a man.

Grandpa Taught Hebrew

My parents located a house on Marcy Avenue, three or four blocks from South Ninth Street. It was a four-story affair—a large kitchen and dining room on the street floor, a parlor and back parlor (used by Father as a study) on the second floor, and the upper two floors consisted of bedrooms. Mother, practical as ever, decided to rent out a few rooms until Father secured another position. We were all placed in school—I believe that we were put back a grade, as the schools in Pennsylvania did not measure up to those in New York—and life went on.

Those were worrisome days. Even then it was costly to feed, clothe, and house eight people, five of them growing youngsters with keen appetites. There couldn't have been much reserve in the bank, and though Mother was the soul of economy, the money was slowly beginning to dissipate. Father was more difficult than ever, but Mother was, as always, cheerful and optimistic. When he regretted the impulse which had prompted him to leave the security of Uniontown, she would assure him that he had acted wisely. *"Naar hoyisi, gam zokanti,"* she would say. "I have been young and am grown old, but never have I seen the righteous forsaken or his seed begging for bread" [Psalms 37:-25]—and she would kiss him and give him a reassuring pat.

Mother would see to it that Father's linen was as immaculate as ever, his suits pressed, and in every detail his appearance all that it should be. Though her own clothes began to show at the seams, and the ribbon on her hat was turned until the color was completely faded, Father always looked as though he had just stepped out of a bandbox. Poor Mother—how she toiled to make the dollars stretch! Every once in awhile Father would perform a wedding ceremony or a funeral, or prepare a boy for bar mitzvah, and was rewarded well or niggardly, depending on the financial condition of his clients. Even then, when money was so desperately needed, he was as proud as ever. If a young man after a wedding ceremony offered a sum which Father felt niggardly, he would return it, saying "If that's all you can afford, you keep it—I'm sure you need it more than I do, but if that's really all you can afford, you have no business getting married!"

Children really live in a world all their own, and though we knew that our parents were worried—Father's worries especially were always being aired, since he wasn't the sort to suffer in silence—we went happily along from day to day. One of our greatest joys was to walk across the bridge to 43 Avenue B, where Grandpa [Fishel Pakas] and Grandma [Jennie Rotholz Pakas] lived. They were my mother's parents, and we children adored them. There was a couple! Grandfather was a saint, if ever one lived. I can see him now, though more than thirty years have passed since he died. He was a little more than average height. He wore a small beard, and it tickled when he kissed us. He never was without a book. From earliest morning until late at night he would ponder over the great works of the sages and scholars of old. When absorbed in his books he would push his glasses, his *Brillen,* way up on his forehead, and then as his eyes watered from the strain of trying to read without them he would start looking for them: *"Wo sind meine Brillen?"* he would say, as he frantically searched for them. We kids knew, of course, where they were but wouldn't tell him until he had been looking for quite awhile —or perhaps until Mother came into the room. And how she scolded us for teasing Grandpa! But he never really was annoyed.

For a living Grandpa taught Hebrew, and though in all other respects he was the calmest, gentlest, sweetest soul that ever lived, he would become fairly livid with rage and would shake from head to foot when his beloved Hebrew was mispronounced or carelessly spoken by his pupils. The money that he earned he treated with contempt. Many times unless it was actually put in his pocket he would never think of it, and had it not been for Grandma, who was as practical as Grandfather was impractical, it would have gone ill with him. But though she loved him dearly and respected his mind, she kept him tied to her apron strings when his soul would have reached to the stars.

Grandma took all Grandpa earned and allowed him just so much for each day. And even that small amount he would give to the first poor beggar who whined at him. One winter his properous brother had given him a fine warm overcoat. Grandpa started out from home to visit his children in Brooklyn. Walking toward the streetcar, he was asked for help by a beggar who knew him. It was bitterly cold. The snow was piled high on the ground, the wind blew, and the beggar shivered in his rags. "Have you no coat?" said my Grandpa. "Coat? Certainly not," answered the beggar. "Wouldn't I be wearing it if I had? But you— look what a fine garment you have on." Without a word, Grandfather took off his coat and handed it to the beggar. In the pocket was all the money he had. So on that raw, wintry day my dear grandfather walked the length of the Brooklyn (or was it the Williamsburg?) Bridge, and at last stumbled, half frozen, into the house on South Ninth Street.

Was Fuer Eine Schoene Grossmama

You never gave Grandfather even a piece of candy that he didn't thank God for before eating. Mother was the apple of his eye, and she in turn loved him devotedly. Grandfather was Orthodox in his thinking. He believed firmly in the Law as it had been written in the Torah and the Talmud. My father, though a religious liberal, a Reform

Jew, respected Grandfather for his convictions. And yet in his own way my grandfather was a liberal also. In his own home the dietary laws were strictly adhered to, but when he came to our house, although he knew that my mother served butter with meat, he blessed God for the food before him and ate what she gave him. "If there is a separate hell for you because of this, then I want to go there too," he would say. He loved Mother, too, because she was smart. No matter how he tried to teach Uncle Victor, it was useless. He simply could not learn. But Mother was as quick as a flash and as a little girl had sat at his knee and absorbed all he could teach her.

Now, Grandmother was the antithesis of Grandfather. Short and round, she must have been a very pretty girl in her youth. And what a housekeeper she was! Everything shone in her cosy little apartment. Her linen was snowy and white; her silver goblets and candelabra sparkled. Grandma loved to wear aprons in the house. She had great, deep pockets in them, and what treasures these pockets held: a piece of chocolate, raisins and nuts, a handful of marbles— oh, the wonderful, wonderful treasures in my grandmother's pocket!

She was so proud of herself and carried her head high. Though she could speak English, she almost invariably spoke to us in German. I remember when I visited her one time she took me to the window and pointed to a neighbor, an old, dusty-looking woman who wore a wig: *"Siehst du, mein Kind, was fuer eine schoene Grossmama du hast?"* ("Do you see, my child, what a beautiful Grandma you have?") —and then in English she continued: "How would you like an old witch like that for a grandma?"

There were so many angles to Grandma. One never knew when one was going to be kissed or scolded. She gave me a penny on one visit, and I flew downstairs and bought a bag of polly seeds. Munching contentedly, I came back upstairs, only to find that Aunt Carrie had arrived in my absence with Freddie, the baby. "Well," said Grandma, "what did you buy for your penny?" When I showed her the polly seeds, her wrath knew no bounds. "You foolish child," she said, "why didn't you buy a piece of chocolate like I told you to? Then the baby could have some." She really hadn't told me to buy chocolate. I guess she just felt bad to think that she had to spend another penny for Freddie. A penny was a lot in those days, and she had to make hers go far.

There Wasn't a Milquetoast among Us

The months passed and the bank balance began to reach a new low. Father was really worried. He began to answer advertisements for a rabbi, which appeared in the various Jewish publications. His handwriting was beautiful, each and every letter carefully and painstakingly written. Typical of his letters was this one:

Dear Sir:
I have seen your advertisement in the *Hebrew Standard* and would beg to apply for the position of minister of your congregation.
I consider myself well fitted for the position, having officiated as rabbi, reader, and also having conducted a Sunday school. While I have had more occasion to preach and perform marriage ceremonies in the German language, still, if required, I would use the English language. While I feel confident that I should give satisfaction, I would desire to be assured the payment of at least half the expense of coming to your town. Should you deem this application worthy

of consideration, I would state that I will be unable to present myself until about the 29th of this month.

Kindly answer at your earliest convenience.

Yours respectfully,

Isidor Reichert

(References sent on demand)

Evidently one of his letters met with the approval of a congregation, and he was invited to preach a trial sermon at Temple Hand in Hand, on 145th Street in the Bronx. That's all Father ever needed. Once he had preached, the pulpit was his. Once more we packed and enthusiastically moved to the Bronx.

It was impossible to locate a house immediately, and so we moved into a large apartment. That wasn't for very long. Even our landlord was on the lookout for a house for us—not that we were a particularly noisy bunch of kids, but we were five, sturdy, independent souls, and there wasn't a Mr. Milquetoast among us! Finally a house at 462 East 140th Street was vacant, and we moved into it. It too was a four-story, brownstone building with the same sort of setup that the house in Williamsburg had.

New York is supposed to be a cold city, one where you can live in a house and never get to know your next-door neighbor. That may be true of some sections of New York, but it definitely was not true of 140th Street. We came to know everyone on the block. Mother scarcely had time to get straightened out before our neighbors all started to call. It was the sort of block where, the day's work done, families would gather on the front stoops and exchange greetings with the folks next door. The children would roller-skate. Down the street, a piano would be heard, and young voices singing "ragtime." We started school again. Natalie was in high school. Irv went to P. S. 9, Victor and I went to P. S.

37, and Helen went to a school nearby.

Helen was a delicate child and had to be handled gently. Father used to carry her upstairs at night and would favor her in many ways. It might have been her cunning mannerisms and pretty face that accounted for the special spoiling. To all of us, Father was a strict disciplinarian; but Helen had only to crawl into his lap, curl his hair around her fingers, and he would melt. Whenever the rest of us wanted anything, we would have Helen petition for us: "Oh, Papa, you're so handsome"—and he was putty in her hands.

I wonder if I was jealous of Helen. I know that when people looked at her—at her shiny black curls, big eyes, and little rosebud mouth—and then at me with my long pigtails, sort of square and dumpy, and said with surprise: "You're sisters!" I quivered within. But I loved her dearly and took such pride in her. I loved all my family. I thought my father the handsomest man I ever knew. When, as the months passed and he became acquainted in the neighborhood, he was asked to speak in my school by the principal, Elijah D. Clark, my pride knew no bounds. I guess the principal knew that too, for it was my pride that brought me the greatest heartache I'd ever known up to that time of my life.

I had acquired a "best friend" soon after moving to the Bronx. Ruth Winderman was her name, and I thought she was simply wonderful. She had very pretty clothes and was "terrifically rich." At lunch every day we were given our choice of a penny or a piece of fruit, but Ruth not only had the fruit, but five cents spending money each and every day. We were together for two terms, and then assigned to different homerooms, though we had the same teachers for the same subjects. What prompted us to do what we did at exam time I really can't say, for we were both good students and on the honor roll at all times. However, before the exams we made a pact. She was going to have her history exam before me, and at the same time I was going to have a geography exam. We decided that I could write down the questions to my exam on a piece of paper—she would do likewise with hers, and as we passed each other in the hall, we would swap questions.

The only mistake I made was that I wrote my questions down on the reverse side of the paper on which we had written the arrangement and then left the paper in my desk. It was discovered—and so was I. Ruth wasn't punished much, but I had to bring my father to school. It was an unhappy experience for me—one I shall never forget. Not only did I have to hear Mr. Clark say in shocked tones: "That *you* of all people should cheat, the daughter of a rabbi"—but I had to bear my brother Irving's contempt. "It's bad enough to cheat," he said, "but to think that my sister would be caught! That is inexcusable!"

France v. Poland

Shortly after we moved to 140th Street, we got a *shiksa,* a Polish girl, husky, rawboned and usually very good-natured. Annie never ate much when you watched her, but she used to steal bread and carry it around in her pockets. Her round, rosy face with its halo of braids is clear in my memory. At that time also we had a French maid— not that we were so affluent; it was just a question of expediency. A man named Taube used to visit our home. He was an interpreter for one of the lesser known steamship companies. One evening he came, very much excited, and asked to speak to Father privately on an important matter. It seemed, we found out later, that his daughter, who had been attending some orphanage in France, was about to graduate, and he wanted to bring her to New York. The immigration authorities refused to permit her entrance to this country unless some responsible party vouched for her and would take care of her. He pleaded with my father to do this, and after consultation with Mother, Father gave his consent. Shortly thereafter Hélène came to our home. She was very petite and rather plump. I believe she was about eighteen at the time. Her curly brown hair framed an oval face with a nice, regular set of features. She would blush easily and had the florid, peasant look which was thought typical of foreigners at that time.

Hélène and our Polish servant Annie were archenemies from the very beginning, and we kids loved it. We would make up stories and tell "Frenchy" what "the Polack" had said and vice versa, and then the fur would really fly. Hélène, all fingernails and fists would scratch and pummel Annie, and she in turn would give Hélène a clout to send her reeling. Our maid was almost a six-footer, and Hélène may possibly have been five feet—certainly no taller. *"Psiakrew!"* [best left untranslated] Annie would screech—and *"Allez au diable!"* ["Go to the devil"] Hélène would reply hysterically. It was too good a show to waste, and once more Irv's talents were exploited. One Saturday night when we knew that Father and Mother would be away we printed tickets:

SEE THE BIG FIGHT
FRANCE V. POLAND
THE REICHERT'S KITCHEN
ADMISSION—ONE PENNY OR TEN PINS
SATURDAY NITE

It was a complete sellout. The contestants were in utter ignorance of what was scheduled to take place, but we knew that Irving was capable of handling that detail. Our confidence in him was unlimited. Saturday night came—Mother and Father, resplendent in evening clothes, left the house. Victor was stationed at the basement door to collect the tickets, and all was in readiness. Irv went up to Annie's room and evidently incited her to a wrath which knew no bounds. Hélène, in the meantime, unaware of what was in store for her, was calmly shelling peas in the kitchen. When our audience began filing in, she wasn't particularly concerned, for the Reichert kitchen always was a gathering place.

Soon the two washtubs (the stationary kind with tops on) were packed with kids, all the chairs were occupied, and children were seated on boxes which we had thoughtfully provided. Victor whistled, and that was the signal for Irv to let Annie down. And did she tear down those stairs! "That d——Frenchie! I'll kill her—just let me get my hands on her! I'll tear her apart!" She flew into the kitchen, grabbed hold of poor Hélène, innocently occupied with her household task, and then the fun began. It was a rough, knock-down, drag-out battle, with plenty of heckling on the side. The audience rose to the occasion superbly—they clapped, they yelled, they shrieked. No holds were barred —hitting was any place a fist could land. It was magnificent. In the midst of this pandemonium, Father and Mother returned—Father had forgotten something. Shall I draw a curtain over the scene that followed? We've had many a good laugh over it since, but I do know that for over a week Victor and Irving ate from the mantelpiece—literally. Father could be terrible when aroused.

The Lord and Master Sat

I guess all the worry and care of raising a family and trying to keep up with the rather keen competition in the ministry in those days began to take its toll. I should interpose at this point a brief description of Father's background. He was born in Konin, Poland, the youngest son of quite elderly parents and, as is so often the case, was a very brilliant person. Later he went to Germany. Although Hitler was not to come into power for many years, Germany even then had a quota for Jewish students, and it was therefore quite an achievement for a Polish Jewish youth to be admitted to a university. My father made a splendid showing at the University of Berlin and, in consequence, received a fine education. Not only did he speak German fluently, but his English bore not even a trace of an accent —or whatever accent he may possibly have had he had lost long before I was born. I recall Mother saying that when they were first married they were on a streetcar, and the usual advertisements were printed on the sides. One of them read: "Take cake for breakfast." Father, anxious to impress Mother, pointed to the sign and said: "May, shall I read that for you?" "Of course," said Mother; so Father proudly read: "Taaka caaka for brea-ak-fast." It probably didn't sound right even to him, and he worked diligently at pronunciation. He had a beautiful vocabulary and was, of course, thoroughly versed in Hebrew.

When Father first came to America, my mother's uncles, very successful, wealthy businessmen, tried to discourage him from continuing in the rabbinate. "You'll never get rich being a rabbi," they told him, "but we'll set you up in business, and then you'll be somebody." Father may have weakened, but Mother refused to listen. "I married a rabbi and a scholar," she said, "and that he'll be, even though I scrub floors to help him." Mother loved my father's beautifully kept, carefully manicured hands and intended them to stay that way, no matter how hard the struggle. And it was a terrible struggle all the way through.

My father brooked neither interference nor criticism. He definitely was not a tolerant man, but he was competent and a perfectionist. Looking over many of his old sermons and speeches, I found each word meticulously written. I also found pages and pages of synonyms written and rewritten. He never spared himself, but toiled until the wee hours. Noisy as our household was, we knew better than to make too much of a racket in the morning, for that was when Father slept. At ten or ten-thirty he would awaken and dress leisurely, but so meticulously. Bathing, shaving, polishing his nails and shoes were all daily scheduled affairs. You never saw my father that he didn't look absolutely immaculate. Even on his deathbed he deplored the fact that his nails hadn't been manicured that week.

The fact that he didn't hold a diploma from the Hebrew Union College gave him much concern, and I guess it made him work twice as hard to overcome what he felt was a handicap. And so with the strain of all these things his health began to suffer, and he had the first of those "spells" which ultimately resulted in his very early demise. He would get a "spell" after a fit of anger, and as his temper was easily aroused the spells became quite frequent. It really was the beginning of high blood pressure. The pressure would make him nervous and easily angered, and the anger would bring up the pressure—a sort of vicious circle. Not that Father went around with a chip on his shoulder; it was just that he was so many-sided.

All the Reicherts are extremists. Father was either singing—his head thrown back, his voice beautiful—or he was in the depths of despair. The world was either a paradise or a hell—he never walked on an even keel. I guess he was so ambitious that he felt a sense of frustration. Still, for all his shouting and blustering, Father could be gentler than a woman. No one could be as tender as Father, no hand as soft as his. In the presence of illness he was the soul of sympathy; in the presence of sorrow he was so comforting. He loved his wife devotedly and was terribly proud of his children. I have in my possession a family portrait: Father resembled Teddy Roosevelt to a marked degree, and in this picture he is seated, head proudly thrown back, chest out, one hand holding the baby's, who is seated at his knee. Mother stands right behind Father; all the rest of us are grouped on both sides. In those days a woman always stood while her lord and master sat.

Finger to Nose

It was always very important for Father to have his vacation in the summertime; and "going to the mountains," or perhaps to Saratoga Springs to drink the water, was most essential and a definite part of the year's schedule. Sometimes Father went alone. Occasionally, when the bank balance warranted it, Mother accompanied him. In the summer of 1909—I must have been about eleven years old —Mother, Father, and Helen, the baby, went off for a month to the Catskills. Before she left, Mother arranged to order staples—meat, fish, and groceries—on credit, but she gave me one dollar a day for incidentals. Natalie was also away at the time. We were maidless, and I was to be in full charge. The morning of their departure the boys and I went into a huddle. We decided that we would be most economical and at the end of the week divide whatever cash we had left. The week passed, and though I strove with might and main not to spend my daily allotment I succeeded in saving only one dollar. To make it look and sound like more, I had the dollar bill changed to pennies.

Saturday night we gathered around the table: "One for me—one for you." The odd penny, the boys decided, belonged to me because after all I was the cook and manager. The division made, we looked at our little piles of pennies—I gloatingly, for money was always scarce in our household; Vic, complacently; Irv, definitely dissatisfied. Finally Irving broke the silence: "This," he said, "is silly. None of us has anything worthwhile. What's thirty-three cents? Nothing—absolutely nothing! I'll tell you what—let's match for it. Then at least one of us will have a dollar."

Victor and I were rather hesitant, but when Irving decided to do something no one could oppose him. We matched—and I won. Gleefully I raked in all the pennies. One whole dollar! I couldn't remember when I had such a fortune! The world was my oyster. It was a thrilling moment. But, alas, it wasn't to last long. My brother Irving stood up, folded his arms, and assumed an expression of such contempt, such scorn, such utter disgust that I could slowly feel my blood chill within my veins. For a long moment he regarded me thus. And then in the voice which was years later to bring thousands to their feet in acclaim, he said: "To think that my sister Florence would stoop so low as to gamble! My sister—reared in this home, steeped in the tradition of scholars and sages—to do such a despicable thing!" He went on: "The words die in my mouth—I am put to shame—my head is bowed in the dust! The minute Father's back is turned—it is too much, I can't bear it!"

And heaving a deep sigh, he turned as though to leave the room.

At first I thought: What a sore loser you are! But as he continued, his eloquent voice, fraught with emotion, overpowered me, and sobbing I gathered all the pennies together and begged him to take them. "Oh, Irving darling," I cried. "Please, please, take the money! I don't know how I could have done such a thing—oh, Irving, please!" He continued to stare at me reproachfully; then, as my sobs grew in violence, he put out his hands and took the pennies. He walked as far as the door and then finger to nose gave me the "Bronx cheer"—"Ha, ha! What a sucker you are!" —and with a whoop was out of the house. My chagrin was great, but my respect for his eloquence even greater. In less than ten minutes he was back in the house with candy and soda pop, and all was forgiven. It didn't surprise me years later, when he was making a plea for the refugees of Europe, to see women actually pull the earrings from their ears and the rings from their fingers. When Irving wanted to, he *could* get blood from a turnip.

The Cantor Carved

Father always delivered two sermons each week. Friday night he spoke in English, Saturday morning in German. It was a strenuous task, and finally the services of a cantor or assistant were procured for him. The young man was a foreigner, a young German with a very pleasing voice —and an obnoxious personality. He used to stand in front of the mirror and say: "I like myself—I am very pretty"— but he was one of the people (and there was quite a long list) whom Mother insisted we had to be nice to.

With this admonition in mind I consulted the boys

during our parents' absence, and we decided to invite the cantor to dinner on Saturday after services. Friday morning I called the butcher and told him to send the usual order, forgetting to mention that Mother was away. My Mother liked to "draw" her own chickens, so the butcher sent one with all its innards—only the feathers had been removed.

Irving was in the house when the chicken was delivered. Together we gazed at it. What a fine bird! The feet were still on and so was the head. "I can cook it, I'm sure," I said. "I've watched Mother often enough, but what am I supposed to do with the head and feet?" "Oh," Irving replied, "there's nothing to that!"—and he took the hatchet and quickly removed the offending appendages. "All right, now go ahead and cook it." I took the chicken to the sink, carefully washed it, picked off the few little pin feathers, and feeling very proud of myself placed the bird in the soup kettle, added celery, onions, and carrots, as I'd seen Mother do, filled the pot with water, and went about my other household tasks. Soon the delicious aroma of chicken broth filled the air. It whetted our appetites and made us all conscious of the approaching Sabbath. Hours later, the chicken tender, I removed it from the broth and put it in the oven, from which it emerged brown, crisp, and tender. I strained the broth, and all was in readiness for the morrow.

Saturday dawned, and three little Reicherts went to temple. I had gotten up very early to set the table, so that when we returned from services, dinner could be served almost immediately. Services over, I ran home ahead of the others. Victor and Irv followed with our guest. All was ready. We sat down to the table, and I brought in the steaming soup, to which noodles had been added.

"What a smart little girl you are, Florence!" the cantor

beamed at me approvingly. "You'll make some man a fine wife some day," and he leaned over and playfully pinched me on the arm, leaving a mark which turned black and blue later in the day. "Yeah," said Victor, "it is pretty good soup at that." Irving, too, seemed to approve, and I ate every drop.

"And now the chicken—ah, I suppose you have chicken," the cantor observed hopefully. "Of course there's chicken," I replied, "and I'm going to ask you to carve it for me." "A pleasure, a pleasure," he beamed, rubbing his hands together in anticipation.

I went to the kitchen and brought back the chicken. What a fine bird it was, to be sure! Never had I been so proud of myself. My brothers, too, beamed in approval; the cantor licked his lips and then, knife in hand, began to carve. A quick slash down the breast, a peculiar plop like exploding gas—and a stench that slowly filled the air. I had forgotten to "draw" the chicken and cooked it with all its entrails. For a sickening moment the cantor regarded the fowl in front of him. Then turning green, beads of perspiration forming on his forehead, he made a beeline for the bathroom.

Victor, Irving, and I looked at the chicken, then at one another—and then had hysterics at the table. We laughed until we cried, and then we laughed all over again. Had we planned it, it could not have been more perfect. Fortunately, the three of us had eaten the soup also, or I'm sure the cantor would have thought that we'd planned to poison him. It would be many months before he ate in our home again.

Joseph Hyman

ANCHORS AWEIGH

Theodore Roosevelt's Great White Fleet was long gone. Even Wood-row Wilson's eagerness to make the world safe for democracy be-longed to the past. It was February 24, 1920, and young Joseph Hyman (1896–1966) had been in the United States Navy for twenty-two months when he began the brief memoir—actually, more a diary than a memoir—presented in the following pages.

Chief Petty Officer Hyman had come to Newport, Kentucky, from his native province of Grodno in 1907 as a youngster of not quite eleven. His account might suggest that he was rooted in a Calvinist ethic. In fact, he had grown up in a home dominated by a kindred puritanism, exemplified by his father, the rebbe-shammos *of Newport's Hebrew Congregation. The Navy as Hy-man experienced it in the years 1918 to 1920 did not share his sober values, and before long he left the service to study physics and chemistry at the Ohio State University, from which he was gradua-ted in 1926. Uncle Joe (he was my wife's uncle) married Dora Kuller a year later and went on to follow what he called "the long but narrow path of life." That path led him to an undramatic, land-bound, and very solid career as a realtor and builder in Cincinnati.*

🌿

I was examined at the Naval Recruiting Station at Cincinnati, Ohio, on March 5, 1918, preliminary to being enlisted in the navy for service, but was turned down on account of shortage in weight. The standard was 130 pounds while I weighed only 121 pounds. On May 6, 1918, I again appeared for physical examination and requested a waiver on weight. The second examination showed that I had gained two pounds since the first examination and Lt. Brooks, the recruiting officer, wired BUNAV [the Bureau of Navigation, which administered personnel matters] and received authority to enroll me. Took the oath on May 13, and at the same time took out ten thousand dollars of war risk insurance. I was told to return home and await further orders.

Orders to report to Great Lakes Naval Training Station for duty came on June 12, and I reported in Camp Farragut on June 16. Stayed in this camp two days and was transferred to Camp Boone, otherwise known as Old Detention Camp. In this camp I was given my first outfit of clothing, which not only used up the sixty dollar government allowance but put me in debt to the extent that I received no pay for three months.

Everything but Agreeable

During the detention period I got my fill of the navy. In fact would have had purchase discharge proceedings started the second day I was at Great Lakes, but I knew it would be of no avail. After twenty-three days of detention or quarantine the company which I was in (Co. 297) was disbanded, and the men were distributed according to their trades or rating. I was sent to the Yeoman School and detailed as a mess cook pending the organization of a new class. I served as messman for one meal in Room G of mess hall of Camp Perry. This was the hardest work I had for some time. The MAA [master-at-arms] made the messmen go on the double, and after every man was served, we had to clean up and scrub the deck, tables, and chairs for two hours. I was pretty tired when I left the mess hall at 3 P.M. with orders to return at 4 P.M. to do the same work again.

When I arrived at the barracks Roy C. Holbert, whose acquaintance I had formed at Cincinnati before leaving for Great Lakes, had told me that he had volunteered for foreign service and also put my name on the foreign draft. When I was asked if I would volunteer, I replied in the affirmative and immediately started to pack my bag and hammock to go to the New Aviation Camp, which was then the outgoing camp for the training station. After one day's waiting there, got started on the run to Philadelphia. Two trains were provided to take the draft. The trip was quite novel and was very comfortable, as we had Pullman chairs.

Before reaching Philadelphia, orders were changed and we proceeded to New York and at 12 P.M. (I forget the date) arrived at Ellis Island. That night we slept on benches, hard cement deck, and some even went on the roof to rest their weary bodies. But few got rested at that place as every few minutes during the whole night MAA's would come around and kick the men, wake them up, while he was looking for a certain man on an immediate draft. If they couldn't find a man within a reasonable time, they would have Quarters and all hands would have to get up and dressed any time of the night and go to the yard for muster. This was very regular and was interrupted when a theatrical performance was being staged.

On the morning of July 19 the *Harrisburg* draft was announced, which included me, and we were all checked up and put on a tug and went up the North River to Dock 62 where the ship in question lay, and we boarded her for work. Here I got my first taste of life on a ship, which was everything but agreeable. However, the fellows took it all in philosophically and acquiesced.

The Trip Was Fatal

July 22, Monday morning, shoved off, destined to Liverpool, England. I was given a station on the bridge as lookout. Six men were on the bridge watching the seas and reporting everything in sight, be it wood, grass, weeds, fish, submarines. Once just after I got on watch the general alarm was given and General Quarters was held. This was 12:05 A.M. and was quite an excitement as it was believed that a German sub was in the vicinity.

Two days before arriving in Liverpool one of the transports sighted a sub, and our escort which consisted of British destroyers (about ten) left the convoy, and it seemed that a general battle ensued with the invisible enemy. After forty or more depth charges were fired, the escort returned and nothing official was reported.

When we arrived in Liverpool the foreign draft got off and [gave] thanks to the Y.M.C.A., who gave us cakes and coffee to revive us from the awful trip. The mess was unpalatable and the ship overcrowded, necessitating the draft to sleep on the main deck which was usually occupied by soldiers who found it too hot below decks. Also the trip was fatal [*sic*] as most of the draft suffered from the mal de mer one time or another during the trip. I was mighty glad that I was in for land duty.

That same afternoon the draft was assembled and got in train for Southampton, arriving there at midnight. We proceeded from the depot to the rest camp, zigzagging thru the pitch-dark streets for fully an hour before we arrived at our destination. There the officer in charge disappeared and no one was apparently left in charge of draft. While waiting in the camp we witnessed a division of British return from the port of embarkation, due to the presence of German subs in the channel and the sinking of a Red Cross ship and drowning of many female nurses and sick disabled soldiers. We spent the night on the ground floor of the Y.M.C.A. tent under British horse blankets that savored very strongly of some cootie disinfectant and itched mercilessly.

Bright and early the next morning we were aroused and although tuned to a very keen appetite found breakfast was not to be had. The draft wandered around the camp aimlessly for the entire morning. Those with money were able to buy some corn cakes and tea. About 11 A.M. an ensign I later learned was Ensign Westbrook arrived in camp and attempted to take hand of the draft, but as most of [the] members were scattered far and wide [he] was unable to master the situation before the day was over. In time we were assigned to quarters in barracks where we remained for about six days.

We used a mess hall after the English had finished their meals, and as we were without mess gear and none were furnished us we were quite unable to partake of the coffee or tea or in fact anything except bread and marmalade, of which none of us boasted of ever getting an overabundance. The more shrewd fellows found empty tin cans and used them for their tea or coffee.

After six days we were taken to the U.S. Naval Aviation Repair Base at Eastleigh, England, and introduced to our new home. The next morning I was assigned to duty in the executive office, my friend Roy C. Holbert to the commanding officer. There I began learning about the navy and have not relaxed yet. Nothing of interest occurred. One day followed another, the daily routine consuming most of the day. Liberty was granted to half the crew from 6 P.M. to 11 P.M. Roy C. Holbert and I stuck to each other better than sanguine brothers, always going on liberty together, coming back together, sleeping alongside each other, eating together; in fact, one was never out of sight of the other.

As Far as We Liked

On September 1, 1918, Roy was rated Y2C [yeoman second class]. Later in the month I was rated Y3C, having been recommended by young Ensign Smith, a reserve officer, the son of a wealthy family, and approved by Lt. J. F. Dunn, executive officer. A chief yeoman [petty officer] with a hash mark [service stripe] was about the first of September assigned to the executive office and took charge. On returning from two days [off for] Rosh Hashanah I found the chief did not appear friendly to my inclinations, and I immediately lost all interest in my work and was transferred to the Supply Department, where my duties were almost nihil. Spent the time reading newspapers, discussing the progress of the war.

About November 1, 1918, was recommended for yeoman second class and was transferred to the C.O.'s office for court-martial duty. Lt. (jg) J. Allen Haines, N.R.F., was impressed with my work and put me up again for yeoman second class. I wrote all of this officer's personal letters and for my good work he recommended me for yeoman first class. Was rated November 1 yeoman second class and December 1, 1918, yeoman first class.

The Armistice was signed November 11, 1918, news having reached us at noon and the officer of the day told us to go as far as we liked. A promiscuous potato fight, a motley parade to Eastleigh, and later unrestricted and unlimited liberty to Southampton, where all people turned out with song, wine, and contributing each in his own way to the joyous celebration of peace.

Immediately a draft for the states was created and on December 2, 1918, a draft of 1,600 men, including Roy Holbert, left the station on their way to Liverpool to the United States via the great ship *Leviathan*. Later in January [I was left] in charge as captain's writer. On January 1, 1919, was rated chief [petty officer] due to my own request and aggressiveness in seeing it go through. After the draft of 1,600 left, the men remaining were allowed five days to see London, and I spent five days in that big city, most of the time in Eagle Hut, a Y.M.C.A. on the Strand.

About February 1, 1919, nucleus crews for German ships to be taken over by the United States were beginning to be formed. Eastleigh had to cut out sending men to the U.S., but retain them for these crews. Five crews were formed at this base. The latter part of March and first of April the German ships came in at Southampton, and when the crews were being transferred to these ships I experienced the hardest work of my time there. I had to make out orders for each officer and all the reports to F.C. [force commander] and BUNAV and was kept busy all the time.

During first of May was transferred to London, England, in draft of ten yeomen. In London we lived at Eagle Hut and ate there on tickets furnished us by London H.Q.

There I requested twenty-five days' leave and was granted [it]. Got a free travel warrant to Boulogne, France, from London and return. I started out in the morning from Victoria Station and proceeded to Folkestone, got a cross-channel boat to Boulogne, and there got in a first-class car to Paris. Failed to get fare but presented to conductor the leave papers, who, thinking that the paper represented the railroad fare, punched it and handed it back to me. Was in Paris a week. Went on Y.M.C.A. hikes and on a truck ride through the city. At Versailles went through the palaces built by Louis XIV—the Hall of Mirrors, the beautiful gardens and architecture, sculpture, paintings. Then went to Rheims, back to Paris, then to Toul, Nancy, Metz, Luxembourg, Treves, and Coblenz, the towns on the Rhine, and back to Paris, Boulogne, Folkestone, and London, where on reporting from my leave was given orders to the *Black Hawk* for duty via Base Inverness. I spent at Inverness exactly one week and proceeded to *B.H.* on the minesweeper *Turkey.*

Stayed on *B.H.* one week and was shanghaied to the minesweeper *Oriole.* There I got all kinds of experience in sweeping mines, getting hit, coming close to the end of nowhere many times. Many men were lost in [the] minefields. On July 5, 1919, was transferred to *Wm. Johnson,* a very small boat rigged for minesweeping. The first time they experimented, on July 12, a mine went off hitting the *Richard Bulkeley,* in which accident seven enlisted men and one officer were drowned. I was the stenographer at the board of inquest that followed. I was also stenographer when a mine went off under the stern of the *Bobolink* and killed the captain of that ship. I was then transferred to the *Panther* on July 29 and was assigned the duties of ship's writer.

Fifty-eight Pages in a Day and a Half

My many attempts at getting out of the outfit were in vain. My first request was made while on the *B.H.,* second on the *Oriole,* third on the *Wm. Johnson,* and last on the *Panther.* Here I worked with little or no interest until the bureau authorized the transfer of reserves into the regular navy. On August 10, 1919, I changed over to the regular navy at Kirkwall, Orkney Islands, Scotland.

About the middle of August moved to Lerwick, Shetland Islands, and returned to Kirkwall and started on our long trip back to the states. Made Devonport, England, where I made many liberties to Devonport and Plymouth, at which latter place spent five days' leave. From Devonport, Plymouth, and the Hoe proceeded to Brest, where the liberty was so skimpy limited I only made one liberty there. From Brest we went to Lisbon, Portugal, and remained there one week and went on about five liberties and enjoyed some excellent beer there. Azores was our next stop, where we coaled but didn't get any shore liberty. At Bermuda, our next stop, went on liberty one evening and drank plentifully at the English canteen. We had swimming call several times and erected a diving board. Leaving Bermuda we set our faces toward New York and arrived there at 8 P.M. on November 19, 1919.

Stayed there over Thanksgiving, when we had a turkey dinner at Astor Hotel where Secretary [of the Navy Josephus] Daniels spoke to the men of the minesweeping detachment and disbanded the "suicide squad" as some of the newspapers styled us. On the ensuing day left New York for Philadelphia, where we laid up for repairs.

At this time a board of investigation convened on board [the *Panther*] for the purpose of inquiring into the contentment or discontentment of the crew. I was one of the witnesses [and] was also the stenographer. It [the report] filled fifty-eight pages which I and a chief yeoman off the *Minnesota* wrote up in a day and a half.

On December 10, 1919, went on a twenty days' leave and found brother Harry home. About a week later sister Lillie got married, at which wedding all of the family were present. Even [sister] Blanche from Chicago was at the affair. She came without notice and disappeared the same night. I returned to the ship January 1, 1920, and found about ten men were on it. Didn't like Philadelphia much and made only two liberties there. On February 6, 1920, left Philadelphia and the U.S.A. for the Azores en route for European waters for duty. In port at Ponta Delgada, [Azores,] 18 February and layed [*sic*] in harbor until 21 February, when we got under way for Brest in accordance with orders from the force commander in London.

February 23 [*1920*]. Celebrated Geo. Washington's [birth]-day. Had turkey for dinner.

February 25. Excellent day; had emergency fire and collision drills in morning, aired bedding; and [in] afternoon captain inspected hammocks and bedding. Expect to be in Brest by 6 P.M. tomorrow.

February 26. Held abandon ship drill. The day was nice, a little windy. [For] dinner we had chicken. Late in the afternoon we sighted land and sailed through the breakwater in the harbor of Brest at 6:30 and moved to Buoy No. 2 at 6:40 P.M. No liberty for the crew.

It took thirteen days to the Azores and twenty-one days to make the entire trip. Crew is glad to come to anchor, this being the first trip, and most of them have been affected by the mal de mer on the way across. Turned in early and indulged in studying a French phrase book to pick up a smattering of the country's dialect.

February 27. Started on liberty and visited Brest second time. Found quite dirty and filthy; people are considerably lax in morals as may be expected in a seaport. Due to Brest having been a port of entry and exit for Americans, many storekeepers understand English, and it is very easy for an American to get along in Brest. Buildings are almost entirely of stone, very old and dirty, streets very narrow, although not quite like those in Ponta Delgada, Azores.

March 2. Got five new desks—typewriter desks—in office, mine a double desk.

March 3. Liberty from 6–12. Mail for first time, fifteen bags.

March 4. Collision drill. Kate, the ship's mascot, gave birth to seven pups. She has been on *Panther* since she left in July 1917 from Charleston, S.C., having served during the war in foreign waters and earned two war service chevrons pinned to her collar. Kate picked the wardroom to give her offspring a dignified start in life. Lt. Henifin is godfather. Chaplain J. A. McCarthy, Lt. (jg) (CHC [Chaplains Corps]) USN, present and full of good cheer as well as all of the wardroom officers. The ship's doctor was on the job and ministered professionally.

Some Never Draw a Sober Breath

Did not go ashore tonight. Have had enough Brest already. The only places of attraction are saloons and bawdy houses, and I won't stoop to enter either of these. Clothes are very cheap and sell for at least half [the] price in the U.S.

From *Harper's Weekly*; courtesy of the Free Library of Philadelphia

United States seamen

To complete the history of our stay in Brest, the subject of dissipation by the officers and men so tawdry and glaring, flagrant and without [*sic*] ignominy, must not be lost sight of. Liberty parties, in a body, go to the bawdy houses, cafes, and other houses of ill fame, expose themselves to the lowest wretches of humanity, risk their health, drink to such an excess that their lower limbs refuse to hold up their burden and have to be carried back to the ship, where the offense of intoxication is overlooked and [a] man is put to sleep anywhere at all on the ship. Almost 90 percent of the men spend their money on spiritous drinks. The older men, or petty officers, set the pace and the younger men, from sixteen to twenty-two, serving their first two years, soon learn to ossify and saturate their bodies with the vile venom. The practice is encouraged by the immunity against punishment. Lack of officer material on board ship is the only cause for this condition.

The enlisted men get drunk periodically, every other day [on] liberty or, if [they are] C.P.O.'s [chief petty officers] every night. Cognac is introduced on board ship by returning men from liberty, and some men never draw a sober breath for days. I know one who has been under the weather since we arrived in Ponta Delgada and is at present time under the influence of liquor. All this exists in the face of the stand the [Navy] Department takes that petty officers who periodically get drunk are worse than useless for the service.

The Department ruled: Every naval officer, and especially a medical officer, whose use of intoxicants is carried to such an extent that . . . [he is] convicted of drunkenness on duty should be dismissed from the navy. They are worthless members of their profession and should in every case be forced off the list of officers of the navy. Out of twenty-one officers, I know of only two who do not indulge in this dissipation.

John Paul Jones said: He [an officer] should be, as well, a gentleman of liberal education, refined manner, punctilious courtesy and the nicest sense of personal honor. He should be the soul of tact, patience, justice, firmness, and charity. The Articles for the Government of the Navy require officers to show in themselves a good example of virtue, honor, patriotism, and subordination . . . to guard against and suppress all dissolute and immoral practices and to correct . . . all persons guilty of them. Any commander who offends against this article shall be punished as a court-martial may direct.

All this is empty, meaningless, weak, and so flexible that it all appears a lot of mockery and a possible defense against accusations from the outside world. The patrol officers from this ship are never seen after they leave the dock until 12 P.M., when it is time to return to ship.

Most of the men are in the navy as a consequence of some domestic troubles, while a small percent are in it for the adventure. Those who remain and make the navy their lifework are those who want a home without responsibilities; [they] go out, get drunk, lose all their money, and go back to ship as well off as they could be. At the same time he is protected by the U.S.A. Then there are some who remain after one enlistment by reason of contraction of sexual diseases. It is no place for one who desires to follow the long but narrow path of life. I maintain that if the mothers of the youths in the navy could see their youngsters carry on while on liberty in a foreign port, not one would not condemn the organization and demand the release of their boys.

The most vulgar, foulest language under the sun is

used by the men-of-war's men, and the talk is so rank at times and surroundings so cussedly wicked, I wish I could be released and never see a ship again the rest of my life.

March 5. Fire and rescue drill in morning. At 1 P.M. got underway for Rosyth, Scotland. Just prior to sailing it was discovered that five men were still over leave and the C.O. and a party of chiefs went ashore on a hunt for the missing men-of-war's men. Four returned, and five are now stragglers, left in Brest.

March 6. Quarters was held at 11 A.M., followed by inspection of the crew and main deck and boat deck, after which the A.G.N. [Articles for the Government of the Navy] were read by the executive officer. As the wind was bow on and the reader was facing the taffrail as he spoke, very little was heard.

Always Blame the Yeomen

In the afternoon two SCM's [summary courts-martial] were held. In the latter one I lost my head (almost) and began to find fault with things, not, however, [saying anything] to the officers, but the seaman witness felt my disgust at having to sit and jot down all the foolishness and pusillanimous questions put to the witness. Worked until 10 P.M. on the transcription of the "not guilty" case, which involved a S2C [seaman second class] alleged to have assaulted a lieutenant of the U.S. Navy of this ship. The accused was at the time of assault under the influence of intoxicating liquor. The court consisted of a medical officer and two young officers just out of the [U.S. Naval] Academy, and it seemed that one was trying to show the other one how many questions he could formulate to puzzle the poor deckhand with about five months' experience with the navy.

March 7. Uniform changed to blue hats this morning. Steaming along the English coast in English Channel en route to Rosyth. Expect to reach our destination by noon tomorrow. Had chicken for dinner, and one of the cook shipmates brought me over a large platter of chicken and half a mince pie. Worked several hours on the not-guilty S.C.M., which is now finished in the rough.

The weekly hull report from the various officers which is due Saturday noon is not yet turned in. These officers do not seem to have the slightest sense of responsibility. However, whenever they are reminded of their shortcomings, they always blame the yeomen—the clerical men who have no one to turn to to pass the buck. An enlisted man was disrated by S.C.M. for a lack of a sense of responsibility, yet these division officers commit unnumbered mistakes in writing up the log, in their inspections, fail to submit reports required, partake of intoxicants, indulge in profanity and vulgarity to a provoking degree, and are none the worse off for their conduct. These men sit at court and pass sentences upon enlisted men for the same offenses they themselves commit at the same time and place, in company with each other.

In spite of a few freaks, the navy has some splendid officers without whom the navy wouldn't last ten minutes. Such men are more than an encouragement to the enlisted men in the navy; they are the backbone of the service. Were it not for such as these, I believe half of the ship's company, instead of five men, would have left the ship with intentions of never returning.

The sea grew rough tonight and a number of the crew are suffering from the malady, so well known to seafaring men, known as the mal de mer, which experts now claim they have overcome by the introduction of the gyroscope in ships. Travel de luxe will be very popular on the high seas if the gyroscope becomes a widely recognized installation, especially in passenger liners. I suppose the *Panther* will be sold for junk when sea travel will be done exclusively by gyroscopically equipped vessels.

March 8. Rough sea running. Quarters in morning as usual, but contemplated General Quarters drill not held due to inclement weather. Ship rolled about twenty degrees and took on a heavy sea many times over the forecastle and several heavy seas over the stern. I didn't turn to for actual work the entire day; however, got an extension of one hour for lights from 8 to 9 P.M. on pretense of work, during which time several boys in the office passed the time away in pleasant conversation dotted with juicy coffee prepared by the mess cook.

March 9. Arrived in Port Edgar near Rosyth, Scotland, at 11 A.M. On way to our berth we passed the Edinburgh Bridge, said to be one of the largest in the world. Also noted anchored in the harbor about six of the scuttled German torpedo boats now raised from Scapa Flow, and rumor has it [they] are allotted to the U.S. as her share of the booty of the surrendered German fleet. It is supposed that the *Panther* will be required to repair these ships and prepare them for return to the U.S. Liberty is from 4:30 P.M. to 8 A.M., the best and most liberal we have had so far.

March 13. Crew was inspected, but not so closely as on former occasions. Forty-eight hour liberty was granted to the crew. Went to the beach and returned at 12 P.M. Stopped in a store (proprietor Jewish) and found that woolen cloth was selling at approximately $1.50 per yard. Bought a necktie for 3/6 which is about 60¢ in American money.

March 14. Slept until 11 A.M.

Jacob Maurice Chyet

FROM ROVNO
TO DORCHESTER

My father never fancied himself a man of literary graces. On occasion, to be sure, he did see his writings in print—invariably they dealt with the telegraphic mysteries from which he gained a livelihood. When he died at the age of sixty in December 1962, he left behind no memoirs as such—only scattered notes, dating from the late 1950s. I have taken it upon myself to shape them into a narrative: a matter of reorganizing rather than rewriting. The style, the expression, the diction—these are his own.

Literature was at most of peripheral concern to my father. I believe it would have surprised (and embarrassed—and pleased) him to hear that his nontelegraphic efforts might be worthy of publication. If he was remote from belles lettres, however, he was no stranger to books. He read as widely as his spare time permitted, often the texts I was assigned at college, and he pondered the meaning of the world around him. It is a pity that he never found time to set down his thoughts on, for instance, the Nazi gezerah, *which he felt deeply, or the Zionist promise, which he took very seriously, or wartime Washington, which he saw when his employ-*

ers sent him there soon after Pearl Harbor to help train others as
telegraphers. He spoke often of these things, and spoke of them with
a sensitivity and an astuteness which bore witness to an agile mind
and a superior character. And withal he was a loving man, a man
it is good to have had for a father.

❧

I was born at No. 23 Shkolnaya Ulitza (School Street) in the
Ukrainian city of Rovno on July 25, 1902, and given the
Hebrew name Yaakov Moshe ben Aryeh Laib Halevi. I was
named after my maternal grandfather. My ancestors were
law-abiding subjects of the Russian tsar and typical religious
members of the East European Jewish community. My father, Aryeh Laib (he was called Louis in the United States),
his father, and his grandfather had all been born in Rovno,
a city of about forty thousand at the turn of the century.
They had all been tailors—which accounts for the surname
Chyet (or Chait and Chayet, as some of my cousins spell it),
an anglicized version of the Hebrew *hayyat* for "tailor."

No ancestral birth records were kept, but as nearly as
I can figure out, my father was born in the year 1876. He
was conscripted into the Russian army at the age of twenty-
one in 1897. That same year he married my mother. The
army sent him to Port Arthur, close to the Chinese border,
and just prior to the end of his military service there the
Boxer Rebellion broke out. To combat the Chinese, Russia
allied herself with a number of foreign powers, including
England, Germany, France, and the United States. My father was sent to Peking, where the Allies were constantly
under gunfire till 1901, and he was fortunate to come away
unscathed. I remember his telling us how cunning the Box-
ers had been in the use of gunpowder and land mines, as
we call them today. He also told us about the wall around
Peking; the wall had been built in 500 B. C. E.

On his being mustered out of the army and returning to Rovno, I was conceived. My parents saved up as many rubles as they could for migration to the United States, where two of my father's brothers, Max and Joseph, and a sister, Baileh Steinberg, had already settled. I was only two months old when my father set forth for the Land of Freedom. By the early part of 1904, he had landed in Boston. My mother and I arrived in Boston in April 1904, on the steamship *Cedric.* Uncle Hillel, my father's oldest brother, remained behind in Rovno, where, I am told, he enjoyed comparative prosperity and had in his employ five tailors who sewed by hand all the clothing and uniforms of the tsar's representatives in the city.

I have spoken of my father and his family; I want to say something about my mother and her family. She was born in the year 1879 in Klevan, a small town five miles or so outside of Rovno. Her given name was Malka Leah bat Yaakov Moshe—in America, she was known as Mollie. Yaakov Moshe Feldman, her father, had also been a tailor, but he died when she was only seven years old. My grandmother Rivka was left to support five small children, Yshia (Isaiah), Essa, Malka, Chaim, and Yosef. She earned a livelihood as a cateress and became known as Rivka di Sarverin ("the Cateress Rebecca"). That no doubt is how Rivka's daughter Malka, my mother, acquired the skill of cooking *maacholim* [special delicacies] for which she was later noted.

Non-Jews, Too, Have a Spiritual Point of View

When my mother and I joined my father in Boston in the spring of 1904, my parents immediately set themselves up in housekeeping on Parkman Street in the West End of Boston. They were young, and it did not take them too long to intermingle with their new neighbors. The old West End was a melting pot of Jews, Irish, Negroes, Italians, and Poles, all of whom lived together in peace—with the usual exception of the few fanatics of all nationalities who cherished their jealousies, misunderstandings of unfamiliar customs, and ignorance. My father, I remember, never thought ill of his non-Jewish neighbors or held them inferior. *"Zey hobn eychet a geistliche anshaung,"* he would say—they, too, have a spiritual point of view.

My parents and relatives all considered themselves Orthodox Jews, and later, when we moved to the suburb of Dorchester, my father was a charter member of the little Orthodox *shul* known as Congregation Beth Jacob Anshe Sfard, on Norfolk Street. I, however, consider my parents to have been more Conservative than Orthodox. They were really assimilated (in the best sense), modern Jews who believed in giving their children a good Jewish background, but never poured it on so that Jewish religiosity would become burdensome or distasteful. On arriving in the United States, both my parents took advantage of the night school sessions available to them and learned to read the English-language newspapers and to keep up with what was going on in the world in general. My father and his brothers all became members of the Knights of Pythias, the Brith Abraham, and the Free Sons of Israel. Many years later, in 1937, I was chancellor commander of the Revere lodge of the Knights of Pythias and eventually joined the Masons, too.

In addition to me, my mother bore my father five children, all of them in this country—Myer, who died at the age of three, Rose [Mrs. David Kawadler], Irving, Hyman, and Fagie (Frances) [Mrs. Henry Gossman]. We lived in comparative comfort, as my father was a hardworking and sincere family man. As the family grew, we moved to larger quarters on Lowell Street and then to Beacon Hill. In 1919 we moved out to the countryside, as it was then—to Dorchester, where my folks purchased a brand-new, modern, three-family building, a "three-decker," at 387 Norfolk Street [which would remain in Chyet family hands until 1967]. They were still living there when my father passed away on May 30, 1937; my mother lived there until she went to her eternal resting place on November 15, 1944.

We Chyets, as I have said, were all law-abiding citizens, whether in Russia or here in the United States. In fact, I am the only one with a "criminal record." Let me explain how that came about. It happened in 1920 on a Sunday evening at 387 Norfolk Street. A number of us, including myself, my mother, and some of the neighbors, were playing penny ante when the doorbell rang. My father, who never cared about cards, opened the door to find a young police officer there. Father invited him in, and what did that miserable cur of a policeman do but announce to us: "You are gambling on the Lord's Day, so I will ask the males to come down to the station house"—Station 19, just around the corner on Morton Street. He took the cards and fourteen pennies in the pot as evidence. It may seem funny now, but we actually had to be bailed out by my father, and it cost each of us a ten-dollar fine the following day. That was no joke at the time. Incidentally, the same policeman was later fired from the force for taking bribes!

McLaughlin Had a Heart of Gold

I commenced my schooling in the kindergarten of the Washington School in the West End of Boston, and I graduated from the Wendell Phillips Grammar School in 1915.

In 1919 I graduated from Boston's English High School (my son did not follow in my footsteps, since he went to English High's "rival" school, Boston Latin, from which he was graduated in 1948). While attending English High School, I worked after school hours as a messenger for the Western Union Telegraph Company. I always look back to those days when I worked as a messenger after school. The company assigned me to a branch office in the South End, which was a "Skid Row" even then. I think the sights I saw there in those years were of such educational value to me that later, as an adult, I took care not to throw myself to the lions. In the South End I saw filth and poverty. I saw bums, opium smokers, and the like all go down, down, down. That was a lesson I will never forget. I was too young to see service in the First World War, but youth did not keep my cousin Matthew Woodrow Chait, my Uncle Joseph's son, from the war. He ran away from home at the age of sixteen and served with the American Expeditionary Force in France. Later, during the Second World War, he held the rank of captain, was provost marshal in Frankfurt, Germany, after the war, and took part in the Korean conflict, too. Another cousin, Jacob Chayet, my Uncle Max's son, became a physician and also served as a captain in World War II; he was stationed in the Pacific Theater. Jack's brother Ely, who became a judge, was, like me, not of an age to serve in either war.

The Western Union gave me a chance to acquire a knowledge of the Morse Code, and eventually I became a proficient telegrapher. On my graduation from high school, I was assigned a day tour as a Western Union telegrapher and attended the Bentley School of Accounting and Finance in the evening for three years. Around this time, in the natural course of events, I became interested in girls and dating. In 1923 I met Beatrice Lillian Miller, of Revere Beach, the lovely queen who became my wife on December 16, 1924. My Litvak father-in-law, I might add, was not too enthusiastic about his daughter's choosing for her husband the son of a Ukrainian *shnayder,* but Bea and I have had and, thank God, still have a splendid, happy, and joyful wedded life. The two children we brought into the world, Stanley Franklin in 1931 and Roberta Elaine [Mrs. Melvin Charney] in 1936, and later their mates and children have been the center of our happiness and attention.

By 1918 I had already become a member of the Telegraphers' Union, and in 1919, when a strike was called against the old Postal Telegraph Company, I walked the picket line. I was seventeen at the time. The union was weak and fell apart when the strike was lost. It was not until 1937 that the union movement became reactivated among Western Union and Postal Telegraph employees. At that time I was working for the Postal Telegraph Company, whose telegraphers chose the Congress of Industrial Organizations (C.I.O.) as their union representatives. I was a charter member and executive secretary of our union local, and in 1939 was elected grievance representative for the entire eastern division, extending from Washington, D. C., to the Canadian border and from Pittsburgh and Buffalo to the Atlantic Coast. Trade unionism was of course, just in the process of reviving, and the C.I.O. was brand new, so that my office as grievance representative did not carry a full-time salary. I still worked for the Postal Telegraph, but whenever a grievance within the boundaries of the eastern division could not be settled locally, I would receive the union appeal. My management counterpart was Robert G. McLaughlin, general manager of the Postal Telegraph's eastern division.

McLaughlin and I would arrange to meet together in Buffalo, Syracuse, Washington, Philadelphia, Boston, or wherever the most grievances had occurred. Of course, I had to travel within the limits of the small union treasury —which meant traveling by bus, with a two-dollar per diem allowance for meals and $2.50 for a hotel room. McLaughlin was quite a character: here was a $15,000-a-year company official (and $15,000 was big money in those days) meeting with a puny $2,500-a-year wire chief. When we first began meeting, I found this Irishman rough, tough, and ready to fight, but when I proved to him that my only defense was sincerity, fairness, and truthfulness, he became one of my closest business friends. Actually, McLaughlin had a heart of gold. He respected my stand and agreed to many requests I made on behalf of the workers, even though these requests were not in the contract, because he thought that they were fair and that I was telling the truth.

In 1943 came a change. Western Union and Postal Telegraph merged, and the A. F. of L., the American Federation of Labor, which was then battling the C.I.O. for labor supremacy, won the election held among the Western Union employees. All former Postal Telegraph employees, especially C. I. O. officers, were now in the doghouse. I became and remained just a dues-paying union member until 1952, when Western Union employees struck for seven weeks. The following year I was elected an officer of the A. F. of L. union local which had originally fought me. I carried on as vice president of this union for five years and attended the conventions in San Antonio, Texas, and in Buffalo, New York, during my tenure in office. After five years, I felt I had given enough time as an officer to the union, and I declined to be elected again.

It had been a wonderful experience for me, one which

money cannot buy and books do not teach. During the years I held vice presidential office in the union, I also earned the respect of the company officials with whom I had to deal—and this was true even though, in numerous cases with McLaughlin or with the Western Union, labor and management representatives did not always agree. The differences of opinion between us were honest interpretations of the contract and carried no personal animosities when one or the other party was overruled.

A Sincere Man Is a Good Man

There is one important thing I want to point out. I was the first Jew to be employed as night chief operator by the Postal Telegraph Company. Later, after Postal Telegraph had been absorbed by Western Union, I was elected executive union head of a department, the Plant and Engineering Department, composed of approximately three hundred employees in Boston. The percentage of Jews in this department was only about 3 percent; yet I was reelected annually.

When I chaired a reception for one of my associates, a Roman Catholic, I invited his pastor to deliver the main address. I was the master of ceremonies and in introducing the priest to the five hundred people in attendance did not hesitate to let the priest and his audience know what my own faith was—as if they would have suspected anything else by looking at me. Believe me, they liked what I said, but that is not why I did it. I did it because I think, as my father thought, that a sincere man is a good man, regardless of his nationality, creed, or color. If my children think the same, it is a belief they have obtained from me.

INDEX

Sentinel (Chicago), 288
Shad (musician), 66
Shakespeare, William, 58
Shallenberger, Ashton C., 111
Sharp (stage manager), 58
Sharp, Andy, 51
Shevlin (family), 229–33; Aaron, 232; Aryeh, 231–32
Shimon ben Gamaliel, 301
Shklov, Byelorussia, 227, 229, 234–37, 240–41, 243
Shulchan Aruch, 142–43
Sierras, 61
Silverburg, Adolph, 203–5
Simmonds (of Cincinnati), 42, 44, 47
Singer, Jacob, 297
Singer, Marion, 74–75
Sizoo, Joseph R., 292
Smith (navy ensign), 347
Smith, Fred, 105
Smith, Mrs. W. H., 89
Smithsonian Institution, Washington, D. C., 102
Socrates, 124–25
Soldiers' Home, Danville, Ill., 85
Solomon, Levi, 54–55, 57
Sothern, E. H., 49
South America, 280
South Bend, Ind., 54–55
South Carolina *see* Charleston
South End, Boston, 365
South Shore, Chicago, 286–87, 290, 296–97; Church Baseball and Basketball League, 297; Ministers' Association, 289–90; Women's Good Will Auxiliary, 290
South Shore Temple, Chicago, 287–89, 292, 296, 303
South Side, Chicago, 57, 276
Southampton, England, 346, 348

Spain, 37, 67, 190
Spanish-American War, 272
Spanish-Portuguese Synagogue, Philadelphia, *see* Mikve Israel
Springfield, Ill., 94–96, 100–101, 104, 108
Sprung, Mrs. Abraham (née Natalie Reichert), 312
Stambler (family), 246, 248, 250, 259; Charles (Charlie), 241, 248, 252, 259–60; Harry A., 242, 248, 262; Morris, 242, 248; Pesha, 241, 248, 259; Zussman, 241, 248
State Board: of Charities (State Welfare Board), Indiana, 166, 206, 208; of Charities and Correction, Indiana, 196, 205, 207
State Conference of Social Welfare, Indiana, 166
Statue of Liberty, New York City, 124
Stefani (opera singer), 47
Stein, Ludwig, 123
Steinberg, Baileh, 362
Stephenson, David C., 197, 199, 207–8
Stern, Alfred K., 295
Stolz, Joseph, 190, 275, 298–99, 302
Stone, William J., 111
Strakosch, Maurice, 47
Stubbs, George W., 165
Stuckert, Louise, 253
Supreme Court: Illinois, 98; United States, 106–7
Susini (bass opera singer), 44, 47
Swift, Jonathan, 204
Switzerland, 123
Syracuse, N. Y., 367